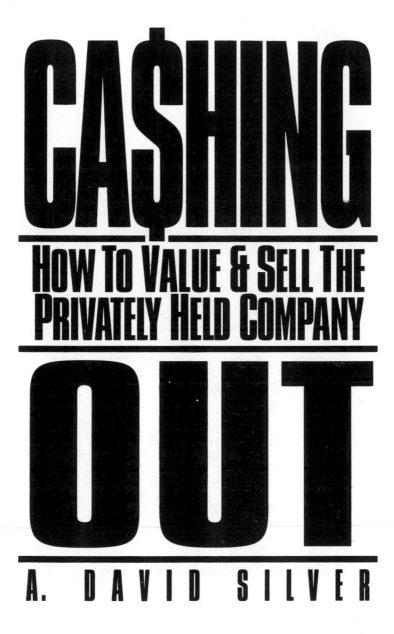

CA$HING

HOW TO VALUE & SELL THE PRIVATELY HELD COMPANY

OUT

A. DAVID SILVER

Enterprise · Dearborn
a division of Dearborn Publishing Group, Inc.

While a great deal of care has been taken to provide accurate and current information, the ideas, suggestions, general principles and conclusions presented in this text are subject to local, state and federal laws and regulations, court cases and any revisions of same. The reader is thus urged to consult legal counsel regarding any points of law—this publication should not be used as a substitute for competent legal advice.

Publisher: Kathleen A. Welton
Associate Editor: Karen A. Christensen
Interior Design: Professional Resources & Communications, Inc.
Cover Design: Salvatore Concialdi

© 1993 by A. David Silver

Published by Enterprise • Dearborn
a division of Dearborn Publishing Group, Inc.

Printed in the United States of America

93 94 95 10 9 8 7 6 5 4 3 2 1

Library of Congress Cataloging-in-Publication Data

Silver, A. David (Aaron David), 1941–
    Cashing out : how to value and sell the privately held company/A. David Silver
    p. cm.
    Includes index.
    ISBN 0-79310-469-6
    1. Close corporations—Valuation. 2. Consolidation and merger of corporations. I. Title.
  HG4028.V3S55 1993   93-2629
  658.1'6—dc20   CIP

Dedication

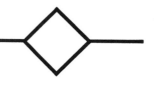

Jane Timm and Matthew Silver

Acknowledgments

"You should never start a business that you cannot someday sell," the wise old investment banker at Kuhn, Loeb and Company advised me as I left the firm in 1970 to venture out on my own. He was absolutely right. But what he did not tell me, and what I had to learn for myself, was how to sell my company, indeed, how to sell *any* company profitably.

Anyone can get liquidation value for his or her company if it has assets. But what is the value of a person's business over and above the price it will bring at auction? What is the value of its customer list, supplier relations, market niche, technical know-how and that marvelous intangible—its *franchise*? Once you have learned to measure these add-on values, how do you convince others to pay a premium for them? That is the key to selling a company at a handsome profit. I believe that is a subject worthy of a book, and my editor, Kathy Welton, at Dearborn Financial Publishing, Inc. agrees with me.

The book would be incomplete without a directory of buyers of nongeneric companies and important advisers and helpers—appraisers and deal lawyers. To assemble the directories I relied on the skills and tenacity of Harrison Jacaman, Benjamin Thom and Mara Dalton. Special thanks go to the impresario of the word processor, Dorothy E. Moore.

A. David Silver
Santa Fe, New Mexico

Books by A. David Silver

- Corporate Venture Capital Investing
- The Radical New Road to Wealth
- Upfront Financing, Revised Edition
- The Entrepreneurial Life
- Who's Who in Venture Capital, 3 Editions
- Entrepreneurial Megabucks
- The Silver Prescription
- Successful Entrepreneurship
- Venture Capital
- When the Bottom Drops
- The Business Bible of Survival
- Your First Book of Wealth
- The Inside Raider
- The Middle Market Leveraged Financing Directory
- The Middle Market Business Acquisition Directory
- The Bankruptcy, Workout and Turnaround Market
- Close Any Deal
- The Turnaround Survival Guide: Strategies for the Company in Crisis
- Strategic Partnering
- Cashing Out: How To Value and Sell the Privately Held Company

Contents

Introduction

Profitable Exit Strategies

To most owners of privately owned companies, selecting when, how, to whom and at what price to sell their companies—known in merger and acquisition parlance as the *best exit strategy*—is a difficult and gut-wrenching experience. This is a profoundly complex time in a person's life because it places a value on the measure of that person's contribution, the tracks he or she has left in the sands of time.

When the poet Walt Whitman was asked how he wished to be remembered, he said, "In estimating my volumes, the world's current times and deeds, and their spirit, must be first profoundly estimated. A time of optimism about one's market will produce a greater measure of value than a time of heavy concerns about the future. But many other variables come into play besides the spirit of the times."

These other variables include the size of the owner's ego; his or her financial goals; his or her age and health; the number and kind of company shareholders whose desires must be considered; the existence or lack of in-place, competent middle management; whether or not the company would make an attractive publicly traded company; and whether or not the company would make an interesting strategic fit with a large, public or private company in the same industry. These factors will determine which exit strategy the owners select among the options available to them:

- ◆ Sell the company to existing management.
- ◆ Take the company public.
- ◆ Shut it down and liquidate its assets.
- ◆ Sell the company to a strategic buyer.
- ◆ Sell the company to a financial buyer.
- ◆ Sell the company to an acquisition fund.

Frequently, owners are unable to choose the best exit strategy and hold onto the company well beyond its optimum time for selling. In one instance a mannequin and apparel display manufacturing company, owned 50/50 by two quarreling families whose brothers started it in the 1940s, was left to decline in value from sales of approximately $5 million per year (and profits of $750,000) to $3.2 million per year. In the company's state of decline and neglect, a daughter of one of the founding partners tried to save it when her father left the company's presidency. The family who did not operate the company insisted that the company was worth more than the incoming offers to buy it and would not approve any sale below their inflated idea of the right price. The legal fees paid by the company to both families' attorneys soon outweighed the company's profits. Finally, no profits were left at all.

When the company was thriving at sales of $5 million per year and supporting two families, it had *franchise* value. That is, customers knew the name; thought of the company when they needed a display or mannequin; knew they could call to get prompt service and quality merchandise at a fair price; and relied on the company to keep their businesses running smoothly. Then one of the partners died, and his wife and children knew nothing about the business. Their opinion of its worth always exceeded reality, and their advisers fed into that opinion because doing so profited them. The quarreling between families—time spent in board meetings, payments to lawyers and accountants, expensive valuations paid to business appraisers and an unwillingness to slash the fees and rents paid to outside family members as their negotiated share of the company's rapidly dwindling cash flow—drained the company of its resources. As customer calls dwindled, the sales staff fled to other jobs and could not be replaced.

When orders dry up, purchases from suppliers become smaller, rumors fly in the trade and soon the franchise dies. There was a point in time in which the company could have been sold for its *opportunity* value—that is, the discounted present value of future cash flows generated by an energetic and talented new owner. But offers from these buyers were rejected as too low. Thus, the company was finally sold for the liquidation value of its remaining assets—what the inventory and fixtures would bring as scrap, or by the pound or at a bankruptcy auction—less the company's liabilities. Clearly, this example portrays an unprofitable exit strategy.

The Timeliness Story of Acquisitions

Since the beginning of recorded time, in fact since Isaac transferred his property to his son Jacob and bypassed Esau, the measure of value of one's property has been the subject of considerable debate and discussion. The Bible tells many stories of profitable exit strategies, and not just *Exodus*.

In biblical times, a man's property included his land, animals, slaves, wife and daughters. Selling these assets occasionally required the advice of rabbis. One section of the *Talmud*, or Jewish book of laws, instructs us that a man can acquire a wife from her father either personally or through an agent. Yet in another section of the *Talmud*, Rabbi Yehuda argues that acquiring a wife through an agent is preferable so that he may hear a report of her dowry and beauty. The rabbi writes, "One is prohibited to be betrothed to a woman before he has seen her, for upon seeing her he may find something repugnant in her and she may be detestable to him."[1] The rabbis of old make a strong case today for using the services of a broker to handle the sale of one's business; yet this point of view remains the subject of debate, which is discussed in Chapter 2.

Some business owners regard a merger and acquisition broker as a hybrid creature, a combination of the biblical Paul and Strato, Brutus's faithful servant in Shakespeare's *Julius Caesar* who holds Brutus's sword as Brutus runs upon it to kill himself. They see the merger and acquisition broker as an android who shuffles between a file of bottom fishers and a word processor and who fills the air with fatuous import and opinion, fully bereft of substance. And some fit this description well.

The debate concerning the transfer of property, with or without the assistance of a broker, is as old as the concept of property itself. You will see that when a seller accepts cash or assets that can be immediately converted to cash in exchange for his or her business, the value cannot be challenged later on. But when there is a *back-end payment* (which can take one of four forms: a note; a royalty based on sales; an *earn-out*—a percentage of the company's earnings paid to the seller; or a *noncompete agreement*) disputes are common. Just as the *Talmud* contains conflicting points of view concerning selling a person's assets, there are differences of opinion thousands of years later on the same subject.

The "Theatre" of the Sale

In primitive societies the acquisition of property took on a new meaning. Among the overriding values of primitive society, according to anthropologist Claude Levi-Strauss, was a sense of community obligation. Work was done by small bands of *hunter-collectors*, homogeneity was achieved through mutual usefulness and celebrations and feasts to honor society's traditions became important. The *financial buyer*, modern society's equivalent of the hunter-collector, has brought "theatre" to the sale of a private company. If an owner sells the company to a financial buyer (not recommended as a first choice), the drama enfolds from the financial buyer's pitch to his or her request that the seller finance the purchase.

Hunter-collectors in primitive society lived in small roving bands, "each person a generalist except for the traders who exchange the bands' booty for more flint axes."[2] Hunter-collectors knew that to achieve greater rank "... and greater weight in the councils of the tribe and greater renown among the whole people," they must "... distribute more and more property at each subsequent festival."[3] The financial buyer seeks to become wealthy by acquiring many companies and with their cash flow, give gifts to the community to shape his or her image from businessperson to philanthropist.

Gift-giving is common in primitive societies. Among the Malekula tribe in the New Hebrides, "Entrance to a grade necessitates payments, often on a *large* scale, by the aspirant to those who are already members of it ... these are made in pigs ... one pig for ... a carved wooden image."[4] Valuable objects are owned temporarily in primitive society rather than possessed. Some are too large to wear and too valuable to hang in the tent. "Yet owners get from them a special kind of value pleasure by the mere fact of being entitled to them."[5]

"Possession of wealth is considered honorable and it is the endeavor of each Indian to acquire a fortune. But it is not as much the possession of wealth as the ability to give great festivals which makes wealth a desirable object of the Indian."[6] The society pages of local newspapers, fashion newspapers and chic magazines portray the happy faces of the country's financial buyers enjoying festive balls in honor of their gifts to the local art museum, paid for with the cash flows of companies whose owners sold out "on the cheap."

The hunter-collectors of primitive society are the financial buyers of today. They acquire companies to create personal wealth, not because the companies they acquire are strategic fits with their businesses. And with their personal wealth they give great festivals for important charities and achieve great renown in their communities. The possession of companies to the financial buyer is a stepping stone to achieving rank in society, crossing the line from nouveau riche to a gift-giver to the community.

If you are planning the sale of your company, you will likely meet the modern version of the hunter-collector who will attempt to lure you into his or her web with the lullaby of *leverage*. But these are just words. Read David Mamet's 1984 Pulitzer Prize-winning play, *Glengarry Glen Ross* and listen to Ricky Roma hypnotize a moneyed person with perfectly targeted gibberish:

> A guy comes up to you, you make a call, you send in a brochure, it doesn't matter.
> 'There're these *properties* I'd like for you to see.' What does it mean? What you want it to mean.
> Money?
> If that's what it signifies to you.
> Security?
> Comfort?
> All it is is THINGS THAT HAPPEN to you.
> That's all it is. How are they different?
> All it is, it's a carnival. What's special . . . what *draws* us?
> We're not the same.

Stirrups

With the invention of the stirrup in the 15th century, ownership of private property and the attendant issues of selling it became a paramount catalyst in shaping social organization. The stirrup enabled men to wear armor on horseback. Men who could afford armor became formidable; they subdued men who fought on foot. The small farmer, who could not afford armor, became either a serf or a craftsman who made armor for the lord who captured his land. The discovery of the stirrup changed the landholding pattern and the control of wealth for centuries to come. More blood has been spilled over property disputes in the subsequent 600 years than as a result of any other single causal factor.

The American Civil War was fought over the principal of self-determination: the right of residents of the southern states to own slaves and the right of slave owners to take their slaves into the new territories that were being granted statehood. From 1861 to 1865 more than 400,000 people, 15 percent of the population of the country, gave their lives to resolve that argument. More than 50,000 men and boys gave their lives at Gettysburg alone. Southerners clutched to their bosoms the arguments of their eloquent leader Jefferson Davis, who argued that slavery was a blessing for the African, "bringing him out of ignorance and degradation to a land of Christian enlightenment where the slave 'entered the temple of civilization.' "[7]

When Davis spoke in Congress in 1850 on the issue of extending slavery into the territories, he said: "It is enough for me that [slavery] was established by decree of Almighty God, that it is sanctioned in the Bible, in both Testaments, from Genesis to Revelation."[8] He warned that if war came, the north would suffer more than the south because the south had "King Cotton" (he did not say picked and processed by slaves). He also predicted that an independent south "would flourish as the world beat on its doors for 'the great staple,' while the industrial North, like Venice, Carthage and Tyre in earlier times, would perish as all commercial states had perished. 'Grass will grow on the pavements now worn by the constant thread of the human throng which waits upon commerce.' "[9]

What does the Civil War have to do with the sale of your company? Nothing, in a direct sense. But this clash of arms that arose from property disputes is similar in *form* to the clash of values as seen by the seller and the buyer, and the dichotomy between the seller's craving to play with society's newly anointed and revered hunter-collectors and their poverty of billfold and richness in the insight of instinct. You are not selling your company because you need therapy. A financial buyer can persuade you that it is a privilege given only to you to finance his or her purchase of your business. Your inexperienced lawyer may endorse the sale, and boom, your pocket has been picked. Think it cannot happen to you? What then was the brouhaha over Michael Milken all about (see Chapter 3)? If you are planning to sell your company, you are going into battle. Arm yourself appropriately.

The Financial Buyer's Stirrup

The transfer of ownership of valuable assets has become significantly less sanguine and more fluid with the development in the early 1970s of the *leveraged buyout* (LBO). The new stirrup is leverage, borrowed money. With it, people without property can borrow on the assets of the company they seek to acquire by paying the owner up-front cash plus a back-end payment and repay their borrowings from the acquired company's cash flow. Management teams can buy the companies they have worked for but never owned, and ambitious young men and women who have served in large corporations can join the Association of Parents of Trust Fund Children by buying profitable companies using the modern stirrup—the LBO.

This creates more opportunities for owners of privately held companies to find eager buyers willing to pay the price they seek; indeed, sometimes in the owner's opinion more than the true worth of the business. But beware financial buyers. They will in most cases offer you less and tie you up more than *strategic buyers* and cause you more worry about the back-end payment. *The most profitable exit strategy is an all-cash sale to a strategic buyer.*

The Measure of Value

There is no simple rule or formula for valuing a privately held company, but owners can use certain strategies to maximize their selling price. To "learn you all my experiences" in the merger and acquisition business, as Yogi Berra described what Bill Dickey taught him about catching, you must first regard the sale of your business as an *intellectual game*, or if you are more systems-oriented, as a *process*. Games have winners and losers. The reason I wrote this book is to help you become a winner in exiting, or cashing out of, your company. I have been an agent of change in more than 200 transactions over the last 20 years, and I believe I can set forth the rules, fundamentals and tactics for selling your company for the highest price and on the most favorable terms in a clear and concise manner.

Here are six rules to keep in mind about the sale of your company.

1. *Do not listen to free advice.* A community of experts toils daily in the merger and acquisition marketplace—brokers, attorneys, accountants and appraisers—and provides advice that is worth far more than any tips you pick up from your stockbroker, company or personal attorney, tax accountant or country club know-it-all who just sold his or her company for *millions* but hasn't picked up the tab for lunch since his or her hole-in-one in 1976.

2. *Do not discuss your plans with relatives.* The sale of a business is a strategic process like a military battle; the watchword is *secrecy.* From beginning to end, everyone involved in helping you sell your business must promise to be bound by an oath of confidentiality. Relatives may not appreciate the need for secrecy. However, since they probably cannot contribute much constructive advice, why tell them anything!

3. *Do not develop an inflated idea of your company's worth.* At the very least, your company is worth its *liquidation value*: the price that its tangible assets would bring at auction. This value can be quickly obtained by hiring an equipment appraiser, and if you own land and buildings, a property appraiser. These appraisals, net of the company's liabilities, will provide you with the bottom—that is, the lowest all-cash price that you should consider from a buyer. To that, you can add the intrinsic values of the company as a going concern: its cash flow to a new owner; franchise; customer list; intellectual properties—trademarks, patents, copyrights, tooling and blueprints; and trained, experienced managers, department heads and employees. What are they worth? That is one of the answers I intend to provide.

4. *Look for a strategic buyer before you sell to a financial buyer.* A strategic buyer is a company in your industry or a related industry that seeks to acquire your company for strategic purposes. These purposes might include extending product line, expanding vertically toward the consumer or toward a source of supply, or finding a new marketing channel for its products. Cable television carriers are acquiring telecommunications hardware and software companies to carry new services into homes. Low-growth, giant cereal companies acquire other food processors linked to wellness because cereals carry the burden

of a high-sugar content, which lacks the growth prospects of health foods.

On the other hand, a financial buyer will pay an amount equal to the amount it can leverage on your company's assets plus a back-end payment. The financial buyer will offer you less than the strategic buyer and should be considered only when your company cannot attract a strategic buyer. The problems of selling to a strategic buyer are, of course, finding a merger and acquisition broker who can locate a buyer and maintaining confidentiality when disclosing your financial records and private information.

5. *No one ever lost money selling too soon*. This axiom ties into the tendency of owners of private companies to overvalue the worth of their businesses. Although an early offer may seem too little, it may be the only one you receive. If you reject it out of hand, you may never sell your company, and your heirs may not be able to carry on without you.

6. *Consider selling to an acquisition fund*. If the strategic buyers are dawdling over your company and the financial buyers are trying to structure the back-end payment with frankincense and myrrh, consider selling to an *acquisition fund*. These are professionally managed pools of capital that seek to acquire companies that they can fatten up, put experienced managers in to run and take public at higher prices in three to five years. In Appendix III you will find the largest directory of acquisition funds ever assembled.

Cadence

This book is divided into four parts that match the cadence of the selling process: *Preparation, Show and Tell, Negotiating with the Buyer* and *The Closing*. As you know from negotiating contracts and financings, every deal tends to have its own rhythm and form. If it moves along at a reasonable pace, you can almost hear the cadence of the deal. The same applies to selling your company. There is a preparation period in which you review your personal objectives and attempt to have them dovetail with the kind of buyer you wish to attract. You locate, interview and hire the best agents that you can find amidst a cacophony of their dubious claims of delivering higher than expected riches in a shorter-than-expected time. The more you invest in preparing the company for sale, selecting the most qualified merger and acquisition broker and qualifying the most likely buyers, the greater the probability that you will sell your company to a qualified buyer, receive the price and terms that you want and accomplish this in the shortest possible time.

Part 1 covers preparing the financial statements for presentation to buyers; cleaning up areas of risk and concern such as litigation; codifying deals that have been awaiting definitive action; locating, interviewing and hiring the best business broker, appraiser and *deal lawyer*; pinning down your objectives; and asking the all-important question: *Is this the best time for me to exit?*

Due Diligence

When you sell your business, you will have to learn about 25 new words and phrases. One of them is *due diligence*, which is essentially the kindergarten game of *show and tell*. It is the title of Part 2, which discusses visits to your company by prospective buyers and everything that can go wrong or go well during that visit. There are two kinds of buyers of privately owned companies: *strategic* and *financial*. A strategic buyer covets your product for its marketing channels either to keep its third shift busy and profitable or to snuff out your company's existence. A financial buyer covets your company for one of five reasons:

1. It is affordable using LBO financing techniques.
2. To generate strong cash flow to pay himself or herself a handsome management fee.
3. To turn it around and make it more profitable.
4. To rapidly grow and *flip it*—that is, resell it to another buyer or to the public at a higher price.
5. To *strip it*—that is, liquidate its assets, let its people go, shutter windows and lock doors, and leave the former owner with an empty bag where a subordinated note used to be.

There are perils in exposing your operations and financial statements to a strategic buyer, but you can protect yourself against this with *confidentiality agreements*. A financial buyer may want you to hold a large amount of *paper* or seller's notes, which are subordinate to a strenuous level of leverage, while he or she relies on you and your management team to run the company leaner and meaner than ever before. The back-end payment may never get paid to you if the leverage is too great. I hope to be able to help you avoid the possible pitfalls of the show-and-tell period and provide you with tactics to make this inning of the game go well for you.

Fortunately, since the late 1980s, an industry of strategic buyers has emerged known as the *acquisition fund* industry, these buyers use quasi-leveraged buyout techniques; they will pay prices that are somewhat above financial buyers' prices but with more of the purchase price paid up-front.

Negotiating

As in all deals, buyers are loath to make their best offer first. Part 3 delves inside the buyer's mind and explains the price that the buyer eventually intends to pay and how you can get him or her to tell you. Strategic buyers will generally pay a higher price, but their motives may conflict with the owner's objectives. For example, a strategic buyer might plan to buy a company to obtain its market niche, goodwill and intellectual know-how but close the factory and terminate the employees. Clearly, that buyer should pay a premium for *economic injury* to the community. Financial buyers frequently offer "sticks" to the retiring owners in the form of a small amount of cash with the balance of the purchase price paid over time and "carrots" to in-place management in the forms of equity, bonuses tied to performance and improved insurance plans. The intent of this form of negotiation is to have existing management put pressure on the owner to take a less attractive deal.

Once you have read Part 3, you will know most buyer strategies long before the buyers arrive and how to counter them, increase the price and improve the terms. Chapter 9 is all about increasing the price of your company by implementing a handful of cost-saving and cash-raising tactics before the sale. These tactics will be implemented post-acquisition by most buyers, who will reap the benefits twofold if the seller trivializes them pre-acquisition. "Nothing propinks like propinquity," wrote Ian Fleming, and propinquity to an all-cash deal at 75 percent of your target price is where you want to be.

The Closing

Once price and terms are agreed to and the deal seems fairly well set, the buyer will issue to the seller a letter of intent that sets forth the basic terms of the deal and allows the buyer 60 to 90 days to perform financial and legal due diligence. This due diligence includes performing appraisals, audits and employee interviews, and engaging counsel to draft closing papers known as the agreement of purchase and sale. During this time the company is taken off the market.

Deals can abort during the period between the letter of intent and the closing. Lawyers can kill deals. Accountants can kill deals. The cadence can change from *allegro* to *ponderoso* as agents on both sides experience delays in delivering documents, records and money. Part 4 provides an authentic letter of intent and a real purchase agreement—documents that you could some day be presented with—and discusses ways of holding the deal together and the risks and costs that can be avoided.

Endnotes

1. *The Babylonian Talmud*, New York: Philosophical Library, Inc., 1944, p. 193.

2. Redfield, Robert, *The Primitive World and Its Transformations*, Ithaca: Cornell University Press, 1958, p. 6.

3. Boas, Franz, ed., "Mythology and Folklore," *General Anthropology*, New York: D.C. Heath and Co., 1938, p. 619.

4. Deacon, Arthur Bernard, *A Vanishing People in the New Hebrides*, New York: A.A. Knopf, 1934, p. 49.

5. Malinowski, Bruno, *Argonauts of the Western Pacific*, Boston: Beacon Press, 1922, p. 19.

6. Boas, Franz, *The Potlatch*, op. cit.

7. Davis, William C., *Jefferson Davis: The Man and His Honor*, New York: HarperCollins, 1991, p. 194.

8. *Ibid.*, p. 195.

9. *Ibid.*

Part

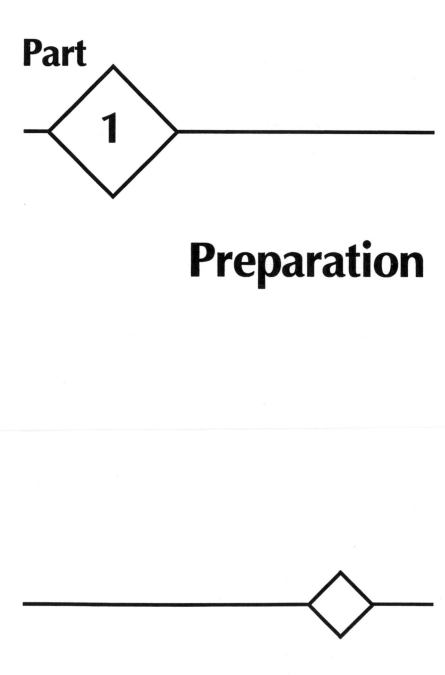

1

Preparation

The Best Time
To Sell

◆◆◆◆◆◆◆◆◆

Life is a roulette wheel. The steel ball does not always drop into the number we have bet on when we have made our biggest bet of the evening. For that matter, it does not drop into our slot for most of the evening. Thus, it is wise to avoid playing roulette with the valuable assets and actions in our lives. The decision to sell a company is one of those actions and one of those assets with which we do not gamble.

The Decision To Sell

The sale of a business is an intellectual process. You can maximize the price and the cash portion of the price by careful planning and by asking lots of questions—most beginning with the word *why*—of professional advisers. Even when the decision to sell does not coincide with the optimum time to sell, you can still obtain a good price by acting carefully and asking the right questions. There are a number of compelling reasons for selling a company.

The Niche Product

Your company produces and sells one product that is popular in a small but expanding niche in a large, growing market. The product can be easily added onto the product line of a larger, multiproduct marketing company in the same field and pushed through the large company's distribution channels for lower marketing costs than you are expending. A well-known example is the sports drink Gatorade, which was acquired by the breakfast cereal producer Quaker Oats. Other examples include Jaguar, which was purchased by Ford Motor Company, and IDS, the mutual fund marketing and management company acquired by the Shearson Lehman Brothers division of American Express.

The Capital Investment

Your company needs to invest in more manufacturing space or equipment to keep up with customer demand or to prevent your current product line from becoming obsolete.

An owner contacted me late last year with a problem. His company made a craft product that would improve the quality and appearance of consumers' homes. This $5 million-a-year (revenues) business operated out of one location that housed both the manufacturing facilities and administrative offices. The building was hemmed in on both sides by a well-established pickle manufacturer on the left and a nursing home adjoining the building on the right.

The crafts company was operating at one and one-half shifts at its present volume when Wal-Mart Stores, Inc. placed an order for $3 million per year and agreed to provide about six feet of shelf space for the company's crafts line in 2,100 stores. The profit to the company from the Wal-Mart order would be 20 percent after operating expenses, $600,000 per year. The owner had two choices: Turn away other business and make Wal-Mart one-half to two-thirds of his revenues, an extremely risky proposition; or build a larger facility that would permit the company to expand to $8 million and beyond, a costly and disruptive proposition.

The owner of the crafts company decided to give someone else the "headaches of expansion" and sell the company. When I visited him, he was filling the Wal-Mart order without eliminating other customers by operating a full second shift, paying workers time-and-a-half to work on the weekends and moving the packing and shipping departments out onto the street—and praying that it would not rain! You don't know the meaning of the word *chaos* until you have seen an order from Wal-Mart descend on a company that lacks the space or time to fill it.

Owners Disagree on the Company's Direction

Partners often disagree on the direction a company should take once it has passed its entrepreneurial stage and is fairly mature.

This year I visited a seafood processor with sales of $20 million per annum; the two owners were feuding over the question of strategic plans. Each owner had children involved in the business. One owner, perhaps under his children's influence, wanted to develop a branded product line to be sold to supermarkets and compete with Mrs. Paul's and other well-capitalized brand names. The other owner was content to process seafood for other packagers and earn a smaller but more reliable profit. The debate developed into an uncompromising conflict. Unable to raise the capital to buy one another out, the owners sold the company and went their separate ways.

Estate Planning

Among the most common reasons for selling a company is to diversify the assets in an owner's estate so that the company is not the dominant asset. As an owner becomes older and his or her children choose other fields of endeavor, the company is frequently sold to provide the owner with income during retirement years. Business dynasties in which the children follow the entrepreneurial parent into the business and demonstrate equal or superior skills are rare. The Pritzkers (Hyatt Hotels), Watsons (IBM), Rockefellers and Fords are some obvious examples. However, it is more common (except in recently emigrated families where the children are employed in the family's business) for children to forsake the family business for the arts, the sciences or to walk behind a plow hundreds of miles from a smokestack.

No Plan of Succession

How many times have we seen a thriving company headed by an aging but active owner who has failed to develop a management team capable of succeeding him or her? Sometimes the heir apparent is the son or daughter; sometimes it is a 20-year to 30-year loyal employee.

Yet the owner is loath to sell to the next-in-line because he or she doesn't have the money to buy out the owner.

This attitude is foolish. The leveraged buyout is a common device for transferring ownership but not as widely used in management-led buyouts of small-sized and medium-sized companies as it could be. A management team can buy out the owner by borrowing on the assets of the company and repaying the debt with the company's cash flow if—and here's the catch—the company's assets are not pledged to secure loans.

I have visited numerous businesses whose owners wished to sell but were so deeply in debt that there was no opportunity to releverage the assets. In these instances I tell owners that they have already sold the company—they can't do it twice. In borrowing on the company's assets and putting the loan proceeds in his or her pocket, the owner sold the company once. Although the money was reinvested in the business, the owner drew out a higher salary and enjoyed other perks rather than paying off the loan. Thus, until the business has been deleveraged, it cannot be sold *again*.

It is difficult to sell a company burdened with debt for any price other than the amount of the debt plus, perhaps, a back-end consulting fee. Most buyers from the outside will not pay the company's worth *plus* agree to assume the debt. An inside buyer may be more comfortable working off the debt and paying the owner something extra out of excess cash flow. But if the owner has personally guaranteed the borrowings, he or she will probably not be freed of that risk and obligation no matter who buys the company.

How To Paint Yourself into a No-Exit Corner

To destroy your plan for selling your company to key employees or to an outside group, here is all you need to do:

◆ Borrow the maximum on all the company's assets.
◆ Personally guarantee the loans.
◆ Drain the excess cash flow for your personal uses.
◆ Do not pay back loans.

If you take these steps, you will be assured of developing either a no-exit strategy or an unprofitable one. The worst-case scenario will be the most likely: You will transfer ownership because you have worried yourself into the hospital but remain sufficiently alert to harass your employees who invest their savings or use the money in the *employees stock ownership plan* (ESOP) to buy you out for a price equal to "We'll pay your debts if you will just go." This deal will put you in the intensive care unit.

Summary of Reasons for Selling

The five most common reasons for selling a company and the most common types of sales are as follows:

Cause	Effect
1. Niche product in a large and growing market	Strategic acquisition by a larger company in a similar or related field
2. Capital investment requirement	Strategic or financial acquisition by a buyer who recognizes the size of your "opportunity"
3. Owners disagree on the company's direction	Strategic or financial acquisition by a buyer who can make the tough decisions devoid of family emotions
4. Estate planning	Financial acquisition, unless the company has developed an important and expandable niche; then strategic acquisition
5. No plan of succession	Financial acquisition by a buyer, frequently a key employee, who assumes the debt burden

An acquisition of the entire company is not the only exit strategy. You can consider other alternatives:

- ◆ You could spin off a peripheral division by selling it to its management and employees or to a strategic buyer.
- ◆ Given the right temperature on Wall Street, you might be able to take the company public.
- ◆ If you have made significant contributions to the company's profit-sharing plan over the years and invested the cash wisely,

you might be able to trade the securities and cash in the employees' profit-sharing plan for ownership in your company.

◆ You can borrow on the assets of the company with your management team signing the notes, put the cash in your pocket, and ownership of the company is theirs.

The alternatives for optimizing a profitable exit strategy are many—it takes some planning to find the best one.

Timing the Sale

The best time to put your company on the market is in the second or third year of an upward trend in earnings, with a fourth year that gets off to an even stronger start. You will receive more offers, higher prices and superior terms if you are offering to sell a company whose future prospects look superior to its historical results.

The most widely used measurement of value in the stock market is the *price-earnings* (P/E) *ratio*. Publicly held companies with bright future earnings prospects, such as environmental engineering and pharmaceuticals, have higher P/E ratios than do cyclical, out-of-favor or mundane companies, such as defense contractors and housing component manufacturers.

Figure 1.1 shows a comparison of P/E ratios and market-to-book value ratios of a composite of craft products marketing companies and insurance companies. Crafts are growing in popularity as people seek new means of adding to their income by establishing home businesses in fields such as sewing, knitting and T-shirts. The insurance industry is in the midst of upheaval with the demise of several major insurers, creating greater opportunities for the survivors.

As strange as it may seem, the public market in the summer of 1992 valued three crafts companies—Crown, ERO and Natural Wonders—at more than their sales. That means for every dollar that entered the cash register of a Natural Wonders store (retailer of archaeological wonders), the stock market investor would bid the company's price up by $2.34. That, of course, was hysteria—not reason. Nonetheless, timing is extremely important in the sale of a person's company, and to ignore the importance of timing is to fail to grasp the unique way in which values are created.

The insurance industry was also a favorite of public investors in 1992, but the valuations were much smaller than for crafts companies.

◆ **Figure 1.1**   Five-Company Composite: Fabric and
Crafts Companies: Common Stock and
Financial Data

Company	Mkt. Price 7-29-92	Latest 12 mos. EPS	Current P/E Ratio	Mkt. Value ($MM)	Sales ($MM)	M.V./ Sales
Crown Crafts	17 5/8	$0.93	19.0 x	$143.9	$121.9	1.18 x
ERO	13 1/4	0.67	19.8	134.2	87.5	1.53
Fabri-Centers	12 3/4	1.82	7.0	113.8	468.9	.24
House of Fabrics	14 3/8	1.58	11.0	205.7	565.0	.36
Natural Wonders	19 1/4	0.42	45.8	131.7	46.4	2.34
5-Company Avgs.			20.5 x			1.13 x

Figure 1.2 shows the valuation of nine medium-sized insurance companies in 1992.

If a crafts company and an insurance company were each for sale
at the same moment in time, if each had $1 million in after-tax earnings
and if price were based on a multiple of earnings, the crafts company
would fetch a price more than twice that of the insurance company.
That could change if the prospects for insurance companies brightened
and the prospects for crafts companies dimmed. Consumer preferences, the state of the economy, the degree of government regulation
and other factors could cause a major seesawing of values. Few of us
can predict these macro changes, their timing and magnitude.

Privately held companies are not valued on a P/E ratio scale
because that valuation method measures after-tax earnings and privately held companies are managed in a manner that minimizes income
taxes (hence after-tax earnings) while the opposite applies to publicly
held companies. The key measure of value of private companies is
adjusted earnings before interest and taxes (*adjusted EBIT*)—an
important phrase in your new lexicon of achieving a profitable exit
strategy. Before considering anything else, buyers will ask your
merger and acquisition broker three questions:

1. What business is it in?
2. What is its adjusted EBIT?
3. Will management remain?

◆ **Figure 1.2**   Nine-Company Composite: Insurance Industry Common Stocks

Company	Market Price 12/15/92	52-Week High	52-Week Low	% Change from 52-Week Low	Mkt.Val/ Book	P/E Ratio 1992E*
American Travellers Corp.	8 1/4	$14.00	$5.00	65.0%	80.4%	7.8 x
Central Reserve Life Corp.	9 3/8	9.63	5.23	82.9	142.2	11.3
Employee Benefit Plans, Inc.	12 3/8	60.50	8.50	45.6	144.6	44.2
Mid-South Insurance Company	9 1/4	10.00	5.84	58.3	111.4	7.9
Penn Treaty American Corp.	11 3/4	17.99	9.50	23.7	78.3	n.a.
Pioneer Fin'l Services, Inc.	5 3/8	9.13	4.00	34.4	61.6	11.7
United Insurance Cos., Inc.	18 7/8	20.75	12.63	49.5	156.5	n.a.
Westbridge Capital Corp.	6	6.88	1.25	380.0	145.2	24.0
Washington National Corp.	22 3/4	23.50	14.25	59.6	73.5	13.7
9-Company Averages				58.3%	111.4%	11.7 x

*E = Estimated

These three questions will elicit the principal characteristics of any company. The answers define the nature of the company's business, its degree of success in its field and whether or not the buyer must invest in a new management team post-acquisition. The answers describe a company with an important *franchise*—reason for existence—or a company that should perhaps cease to exist and allow its competitors to carve up its market share. A company with a franchise serves an expanding customer base, makes a solid profit year in and year out and has a management that is willing to remain. This company is usually seeking an acquisition because of the niche market or capital requirement reasons previously described.

The company in an overcrowded or shrinking industry such as mail-order personal computers or machine shops that make components for missiles is unattractive to buyers. An unattractive company cannot generate consistent profits due to shrinking margins and has an old, bickering or not particularly competent management team.

Values for private companies range from three to eight times adjusted EBIT[1] for the most recent 12-month period; for an average of the last three years or for the year in progress; or for an average of the last 12 months plus the year in progress. Buyers will audit your company during the due diligence process in order to test the integrity of EBIT, then adjust it for the elimination of owners' salaries and perks, savings in expensive overhead items, elimination of duplicate departments, and the addition of the buyers' costs of inventory or managing the company post-acquisition. You will never see the buyers' adjusted EBIT numbers, but knowing how they are arrived at will help you know the value your company should fetch in the marketplace.

Adjusted EBIT-D and DA

A "sleeper" in the valuation process—the EBIT-D and EBIT-DA mean *earnings before interest, taxes and depreciation (and/or amortization)*—will enable you to obtain an even higher price for your company. If your company is depreciating the cost of equipment at a high rate or amortizing goodwill or product development costs at a high rate, your depreciation or amortization is pure cash flow to the buyer. The buyer *has* to pay for it as if it were earnings, and it can demonstrably affect price in a positive direction.

If you assume that an appropriate multiple for your kind of company is five times adjusted EBIT-D, the effect on price of a high rate of depreciation can be seen in Figure 1.3.

To accept a price less than $6.75 million—the buyer's measure of value—is to leave $1.5 million in the buyer's pocket rather than yours.

Addition by Subtraction

You can further increase the valuation of your company by studying the components of your company's operating expenses and subtracting the expenses that a new owner would not have to incur. Give this process serious attention since every excess or one-time-only $1,000 or $10,000 expense that you find when multiplied by the buyer's valuation multiple is money in your pocket. Following is a summary of where most of the add-backs are hidden.

Overstatement of Cost of Goods Sold

If you own a privately held company, you are probably taking many steps to minimize income taxes. To build a cushion into cost of goods sold, some owners overstate their inventory costs. Both sales-persons' commissions that are based on gross profits rather than sales

◆ **Figure 1.3**   Price Offered at 5 x Adjusted EBIT-D

($000s)	Without Depreciation	With Depreciation
Net profit before taxes	$ 700,000	$ 700,000
Add-backs		
Owners' compensation	200,000	200,000
Owners' perks	25,000	25,000
Reduction in overhead exps.	65,000	65,000
Monitoring costs	(30,000)	(30,000)
Interest exps.	90,000	90,000
Depreciation	—	300,000
Adjusted EBIT-D	1,050,000	1,350,000
Price at 5 x adjusted EBIT-D	$5,250,000	$6,750,000

and income taxes to federal and state governments can be lowered by reducing gross profits. The effect of this on the *operating statement* is lower *net operating income*, and the effect on the *balance sheet* is an overstatement of inventory.

To balance the books, some owners write off lots of inventory as "unsalable" or "worthless" when in fact the goods remain in the warehouse and are still for sale. If this practice has been ongoing for many years, there could be millions of dollars' worth of unexplained inventory in the warehouse. The seller has a potential problem with the Internal Revenue Service if there is ever an audit that the buyer does not want to assume and for which he will demand in the *purchase agreement* to be indemnified against.

I have seen this demand for indemnification become a deal-breaker because it comes up during the buyer's due diligence and, when the seller is confronted by it, he or she becomes defensive. As with the example of the owner who loads up his or her company with debt and then tries to sell it, so it is with the owner who has squirreled away profits for 10 or 20 years in the form of tax savings from inventory overstatements—it is preferable to be forthright about it.

In fact, in preparing the company for sale, I recommend that you restate inventory over several years and credit cost of goods sold, which understates costs, increases earnings and requires you to pay higher taxes to the government. This will provide a more accurate financial statement, clean up an obligation to the government and avoid the issue of a punitive indemnification clause in the purchase agreement. The buyer should be informed of this adjustment and will reflect it in his or her calculation of adjusted EBIT-DA.

Discounts Not Taken

If your company is cash poor and unable to take some or all the discounts offered by suppliers, this adjustment is worth subtracting out of cost of goods sold and adding back to adjusted EBIT. For instance, assume your company has sales of $8 million per year and that it purchases $4 million in raw materials. Further, let's say that your company's suppliers customarily offer terms of 30 days net with 2 percent discounts if the invoice is paid in 10 days. However, because your customers pay in 55 days on average and factoring costs are more than 20 percent, you have elected not to take the discounts. A financially stronger owner would take them because the savings is $4,000,000 x .02, $80,000 a year, which can be put into add-backs.

Overstatement of Commissions

Some owners pay themselves a commission on sales as a means of compensating themselves even though they are not directly involved in sales. This occurs when the owner was responsible for bringing in an important customer that has continued to renew the relationship with the company year after year.

Excessive Insurance Costs

As you prepare your company for a sale, you might audit your insurance costs. Chances are that you have dealt with the same insurer or agent for several years and have not been exposed to competitive insurance products in the areas of property and casualty, workers' compensation and employees' health insurance. There are many alternatives to traditional health insurance, such as self-insurance except for catastrophic illnesses, for which you pay a significantly lower rate; and a preferred provider organization, which will negotiate lower rates for your company. Take advantage of savings in this area, and transfer the differential into add-backs.

Excessive Legal Expenses

If you spent last year in litigation with a supplier or former employee or in a patent dispute, be sure to subtract the related legal expenses from operating expenses. Also, this is an excellent time to review the rates your lawyers have been charging for services provided. Has your company been an *annuity* for its law firms? Like the giant corporations who have been negotiating lower hourly rates from their law firms, there is no time like the present to do the same. If you are successful, put the savings into add-backs.

Professional Fees

The same applies to the fees of accountants and consultants. Ask *why* their rates are as high as they are. Ask whether they would rather not have you as a client if you insisted on a 25-percent reduction in fees. They will likely lower their rates; if so, divert the savings to add-backs.

Excessive Advertising Expenses

In the spirit of the 1990s, and because you are preparing your company for sale, you should shop for lower advertising rates. Agencies that place companies' advertisements in trade journals get a whopping 15-percent fee for making a telephone call. There is no time like the present to ask for a lower rate and to shop the account with other advertising agencies. You might get a fresh approach and a more successful message by shopping ad agencies. If you are successful in lowering the rate, put the savings into add-backs.

Communications Costs

Without a doubt alternative long-distance carriers will offer you a lower rate than you are presently paying if you ask them to compete for your company's long distance business. Most of them are into *affinity marketing*, that is, offering their customers copying equipment, facsimile machines, frequent flyer points, and hotel and car rental discounts if you sign up with them. Once you have negotiated a savings in communications costs, project the cost savings, and transfer the savings to add-backs.

Profit-Sharing Contributions

If your company has been setting aside a percentage of its profits every year since the millennium, the annual charge to earnings should be added back as well.

Don't overlook these add-backs. If you neglect this area, the buyer will pay you less and take the savings after he or she owns the business. Rather than stating the cost savings as hypothetical add-backs, I will illustrate in Chapter 9 how to effect the cost savings and benefit twice—once with cash in your pocket and the second time with five times the cash in your pocket when you sell.

The Absence of Earnings

In the absence of earnings, the owner of a privately held company will receive substantially less for his or her company. The buyer will probably apply a valuation multiple at the lower end of the three times to four times adjusted EBIT range (if there is any E on an adjusted basis) because the future prospects, based on past results, are dim. The company may be worth only liquidation value.

However, sometimes owners of a company must sell the business even though the time is not the best, and other features must be highlighted to obtain an acceptable price. These features may include off-balance sheet assets such as customer lists; assets that have been written off but have going-concern value; intellectual properties such as tooling, blueprints, trademarks, copyrights and patents.

If your company has lost money only recently but has been profitable in prior years, take an average adjusted EBIT with all the add-backs that you can truthfully muster, and seek a valuation based on a multiple of average adjusted EBIT over the past four years.

The Importance of the Upward Trend in Earnings

An upward trend makes the statement that the future prospects for the company are brighter than the past. This persuades buyers to offer purchase prices at the higher end of the three times to eight times adjusted EBIT range. The stock market works the same way. Shortly after the Iraqis began burning the Kuwaiti oil fields, the P/E ratios of publicly held companies that manufacture oil field equipment moved up from an average of 12.4 times to 17.5 times, an increase of over 40 percent. A P/E ratio of 17.5 times is equivalent to an adjusted EBIT ratio of 10.5 times, assuming a 40 percent tax rate.

Summary

The best time to sell is when earnings are trending up. However, even if you have losses, there may be adjustments in the cost of goods sold and operating expenses that can be added back to produce a positive adjusted EBIT. Moreover, if you are in business, your company has franchise value. It *owns* a piece of its market. It has a customer list and possibly intellectual properties. These have value and, like the 49ers who found gold in the streams of the Sierra Nevadas, you have to dig out the *add-backs*.

Endnotes

1. Note that buyers place lower values on companies than do public investors. For instance, take the high-end multiple paid by private buyers of eight times and multiply by the reciprocal of the sum of state and federal income tax rates. It comes to an after-tax multiple, or P/E ratio, or 13.3 times. This is considerably below the average P/E ratio of stocks currently trading on the New York Stock Exchange of approximately 19.0 times. The reason for the disparity in valuation multiples is the public's cockeyed optimism about its investments coupled with the ease of selling them, or liquidity, in the event that stock prices fail to move up.

Agents To Call On

◆◆◆◆◆◆◆◆◆

The process of selling your private company begins with locating, interviewing and selecting agents to represent you. You will need three teammates—a merger and acquisition broker, an appraiser and an attorney experienced in the purchase and sale of businesses, known as a *deal lawyer*. The broker will bring qualified buyers to your door, the appraiser will put a value on your fixed assets and the deal lawyer will see that you are protected with squeaky clean contracts.

Legal Specialists

You may value the advice and counsel of your company's attorney as it concerns the stewardship of your company. He or she may be excellent in handling commercial disputes, negotiating warehouse leases and settling insurance claims, but if the attorney has never been involved in the sale of a company, he or she could inadvertently break a deal for you.

There are lawyers, and then there are *deal lawyers*. A deal lawyer is a facilitator—someone who is hired to protect the seller's interests and to effect rather than block the sale. Further, your company's counsel may want to keep you as a client and may selfishly block a sale to keep you in his or her billfold. A final reason for hiring a deal lawyer to represent you in the sale of your company is that the buyer has made many acquisitions and you are going through the exercise for perhaps the first time. You need a good deal lawyer—one who is well-known to the acquisition funds industry and has drafted and reviewed dozens of purchase agreements.

I asked the most active acquisition funds in the United States to list the best deal lawyers in the country—the ones they use to buy companies. The ten most frequently mentioned deal law firms are listed in Figure 2.1; the complete list of frequently recommended legal superstars appears in Appendix B. I recommend that you select one of these experienced deal lawyers to handle the sale of your company rather than your regular company legal counsel because they have been through hundreds of deals, the buyer has been through dozens of deals and you have probably never been involved in one. Selling a business is like going into a battle over the value of property. Arm thyself accordingly.

Appraisers

At some point in the process of selling your company, an appraisal of your company's property, plant and equipment may become necessary. If a financial buyer is the likeliest candidate to acquire your

◆ **Figure 2.1**   The Ten Most Highly Regarded Deal Law Firms in the United States

Name	Headquarters City
Altheimer & Gray	Chicago
Kirkland & Ellis	Chicago
Hutchins & Wheeler	Boston
Latham & Watkins	Los Angeles
Testa, Hurwitz & Thibeault	Boston
Kelly, Drye & Warren	New York/Los Angeles
Dechert, Price & Rhoads	New York
Mayer, Brown & Platt	New York
Perkins Coie	Seattle
Jenkins & Gilchrist	Austin

company, the buyer will probably borrow on the assets of your company to raise the cash to pay you. The buyer's lenders will ask him or her for a *market value* appraisal of the property and plant and a *liquidation value* appraisal of the equipment. You can pay for the appraisals and present them to the potential buyers to review. However, let them know that if they buy the company, they will have to reimburse you for the appraisal costs.

The *best* appraisers are not necessarily the ones who arrive at the highest values for your hard assets. Indeed, those who consistently overstate values are quite possibly unacceptable to lenders; and if you hire them, you may find that their work must be redone by more acceptable appraisers. I asked members of the asset-based lending community (lenders that finance leveraged buyouts) and the managers of the nation's acquisition funds (investors who frequently hire appraisers and rely on their values) to provide the names of the best appraisers in the country. Figure 2.2 shows the ten appraisal firms most frequently cited.

Expenses

You may be shocked at the costs of appraisals and the rates charged by deal lawyers. However, in my opinion, based on working on nearly

◆ **Figure 2.2** The Ten Best Equipment and Real Estate Appraisers in the United States

Name	Principal Location
MB Valuation Services, Inc.	Dallas, Texas
Murray Devine	Philadelphia, Pennsylvania
American Appraisal Association	Princeton, New Jersey
The Manufacturers Appraisal Co.	Philadelphia, Pennsylvania
Norman Levy Associates	Boston, Massachusetts
Daley, Hodkins & Co.	Melville, New York
Thomas Industries	New Haven, Connecticut
Accuval Associates, Inc.	Mequon, Wisconsin
Rosen & Company	Cleveland, Ohio
Best Appraisers, Inc./Best Auctions, Inc.	Louisville, Kentucky

200 acquisitions, you will be rewarded by using mature, experienced professionals to advise you in the sale of your company. Their fees and costs will come back to you in the form of a higher purchase price.

Appendices I and II provide detailed information concerning the most highly regarded deal lawyers and appraisers. If maximizing your exit price and receiving the best terms are important to you, go with the best teammates you can find.

Summary

Successful execution of your exit strategy will be determined by the professionals whom you select to help you. The three teammates—a merger and acquisition broker, an appraiser and a deal attorney—must each have demonstrable, proven ability in the purchase and sale of privately held companies. Check their track records with both references that they provide and references that we provide in the directories at the back of this book.

Dealing with Merger and Acquisition Brokers

◆◆◆◆◆◆◆◆◆◆

The merger and acquisition (M&A) broker who has sold companies in your industry and has an outstanding list of buyers of companies such as yours is the broker you want to find. Even if a broker asks for an up-front fee or *retainer*, it is irrelevant in the total scheme of things if the fee is less than $6,000. What is important is the broker's buyers—the broker can either bring you to strategic buyers or acquisition funds, or he or she cannot.

The M&A Broker's Contract

You need to look for a number of factors in the M&A broker's contract. The first, and perhaps most important, is whether the broker has an *exclusive* or *nonexclusive* arrangement with your company. In an exclusive arrangement, the broker collects a fee whether or not he or she finds the buyer. In a nonexclusive arrangement, if the buyer comes through someone else, you do not owe your broker a fee.

Fees

The most common fee structure is the *Lehman Formula*, which is best described by the following scale.

5% x the first $1,000,000
4% x the second $1,000,000
3% x the third $1,000,000
2% x the fourth $1,000,000
1% x amounts more than $4,000,000

For example, on the sale of a company for $7.5 million, this translates into the following finder's fee.

First	$1,000,000	x 5%	=	$ 50,000
Second	1,000,000	x 4%	=	40,000
Third	1,000,000	x 3%	=	30,000
Fourth	1,000,000	x 2%	=	20,000
Fifth	1,000,000	x 1%	=	10,000
Sixth	1,000,000	x 1%	=	10,000
Seventh	1,000,000	x 1%	=	10,000
Balance	500,000	x 1%	=	5,000
Total	$7,500,000		=	$175,000

Modified Lehman Formula

If you believe your company will fetch a large price (i.e., more than $10 million), it is appropriate to ask the M&A broker to take a lesser fee. This is frequently done by modifying the Lehman Formula.

There are many variations of a *Modified Lehman Formula*, including beginning with 4, 3 or 2 1/2 percent, depending upon the size of the transaction. The closing fee is lower if the M&A broker charges a high retainer to write the *descriptive selling memorandum* and higher if the retainer is lower or nonexistent. In fact, if the M&A broker charges no retainer, pays for out-of-pocket expenses and limits the time for earning a fee for finding a buyer, he or she may ask for a finder's fee of 8 percent to 10 percent of the purchase price.

Also, the smaller the transaction, the higher the closing fee. If your company is likely to sell for less than $500,000, you can anticipate being asked to pay a higher closing fee.

The Payment of Up-Front Fees

Some M&A brokers ask for no fees in advance, and others ask for more than $30,000 to value the business and prepare the descriptive selling memorandum. How do you determine whether to pay an up-front fee and, if so, how much should it be?

When my investment banking firm represents a seller, we charge an up-front fee and enter into a nonexclusive contract because exclusive contracts can be unfair to the seller and too confining. If we cannot find a buyer in 12 months and someone else locates a buyer, we do not collect a fee.

The up-front fee separates serious from nonserious sellers. If the business owner wants to find out how much his or her company is worth but is not interested in selling, the broker wants to know that in advance. One way to determine intent is to ask for an up-front fee. Family-owned businesses are more inclined to test the valuation waters than corporations that are interested in spinning off divisions or subsidiaries. For these corporations, which have usually been given board authorization to sell at any price, a no-up-front-fee-plus-exclusive agreement is satisfactory.

Michael Milken's Changes to the Rules

Much has been written about the brilliant, but now embarrassed, investment banker Michael E. Milken. Yet no one has explained the enormous fees that he charged his clients for selling their divisions and subsidiaries. Milken altered the fee structure of middlemen by crafting a way to earn *six fees per client*.

Michael Milken's Instructions

Milken was employed by Drexel Burnham Lambert, a small investment bank that had no important corporate clients. Status on Wall Street directly correlates to fee income—the more prestigious the investment banker's client list, the more it can charge for its services. Top-drawer investment banks derive enormous fees from raising capital and advising on mergers and acquisitions for their Fortune 500 clients. As the 1980s approached, Drexel Burnham Lambert's clout and profitability appeared destined to remain small because the leaders of American industry wanted their financial transactions to carry the imprint of Wall Street's finest—which did not include Drexel.

Milken changed the financial markets and industrial management for years to come—with a product, the *junk bond*, in a service industry. (Service spinoffs of product companies succeed more often than do product spinoffs of service companies.) The junk bond is a high-interest-rate (more than 16 percent), usually unsecured bond with interest and principal repayments that are uncertain at best and impossible to meet at worst. Milken introduced junk bonds as the means of overpaying for takeover targets in corporate raids.

Before Milken, companies were taken over by financial buyers via leveraged buyouts that involved borrowing on the assets of the takeover target and repaying the borrowings out of the company's cash flow. The excess asking price typically exceeded the amount that could be borrowed on the company's assets by 5–10 percent of the purchase price and was funded by the financial buyer's savings or the seller taking back a small note. If the cash flow of the takeover was insufficient to service debt, pay back the risk equity and provide the financial buyers a reasonable return, a lower price was offered, or the buyers walked away. Money rarely chased deals before Milken.

Milken introduced the idea of overpaying for companies—not by 4 or 7 percent but by 100 percent—and paying for the excess price with cash raised by the sale of junk bonds (so named because there was neither cash flow nor assets to support them). Buyouts were an extension of what Milken had been doing since 1977 when he began helping his clients leverage their balance sheets with high levels of debt through the issuance of junk bonds. By dramatically overpaying for deals—more than twice the amount that could be borrowed on the target company's assets—Milken created a win-win-win situation for all participants in the takeover market.

Secured Lenders

Regular lenders in the leveraged buyout market were pleased with the takeover activity because their loans were fully secured and they could make more loans.

Junk Bond Buyers

Mutual funds, pension funds, insurance companies, and savings and loan institutions happily loaned money at more than 16-percent interest. They were told that when an interest or principal payment came due but could not be paid out of cash flow, Milken's firm would find a source of payment.

Managers of Takeover Companies

Although some managers put up a semblance of a fight for public consumption, most had *golden parachute deals* that would make them multimillionaires after the takeover. Furthermore, the takeovers were frequently at stock prices that they could not hope to generate in five years of the most adroit management.

Shareholders of Takeover Targets

Shareholders of takeover targets were happy to be offered a dollar for something that the most efficient auction market in economic history said was not worth more than 50 cents. Shareholders of nontargets in the same industry benefitted as well when their holdings rose in sympathy with their breakup value—the projected aggregate price at which their company's parts could be broken up and sold off.

Investment Bankers

The best deal fell to the investment bankers, of which Drexel Burnham Lambert became the most proficient, most highly regarded and most profitable. Whereas investment banks traditionally earned one or two fees for arranging acquisitions for their corporate clients, Milken multiplied the number of fees to at least six per transaction and increased their size. His fees included:

- a finder's fee for introducing the target.
- a valuation fee charged to the buyer for stating that the price was fair.
- a financing fee for raising the money to buy the company.
- an equity fee, or part ownership in the takeover target, for being its initiator.
- spinoff fees (several, depending on the number of spinoffs earned by selling off divisions to raise cash).
- fees to refinance the junk bonds when it was clear to all that the debt could not be serviced.

The Junk Bond Bandwagon

Other investment banks jumped into Milken's enormously profitable arena (his personal income at times exceeded $500 million per year). The competition to do Drexel-type deals to generate fees pushed the takeover game to such extremes that spinoffs and refinancings could not be handled fast enough. Commercial banks did not collateralize themselves properly. Financial buyers did not manage companies to maximize cash flow; as a result some of their trophies ended up in bankruptcy.

The premise of the junk-bond-backed LBO binge of the 1980s was quite simple: Let's overprice takeovers and see who buys the program. Nearly everyone who was called signed up for Milken's deals even though the financial buyers the junk bonds were financing had no proven management ability. Names included Ronald Perelman, who acquired Revlon; Nelson Peltz, who bought Triangle Industries; Carl Icahn, who purchased TWA; T. Boone Pickens, who attempted to take over Phillips Petroleum; and Bobby R. Inman, who acquired Tracor.

There have been some junk-bond-backed LBO bankruptcies, but for the most part the jury is on the side of the financial buyers of the late 1980s. Putting aside the economic validity of the Milken-inspired age of takeovers and the felonies he committed during this period, the *deal* that he conceived, developed, implemented and sold to some of the most astute lenders and investors in the country is awesome!

In a rational world, money managers entrusted with billions of dollars of savings and pension funds simply do not buy junk bonds that yield 16–18 percent per year if the financial statements clearly indicate that there is inadequate cash flow to service the debt. Institutional investors are *fiduciaries*. Justice Louis Brandeis defined a fiduciary as someone to whom money is entrusted and who is supposed to exert greater care in its management than in the management of his or her own money. Why did these caretakers of the nation's savings take such incredible risks?

The "Godfather" Proposition

Milken (and the competitive investment bankers who tried to play catch-up to Drexel from 1985 to 1989) made institutional investors a series of offers that they could not refuse. First, the bank received a *commitment fee* upon subscribing to buy junk bonds. Thus, if the deal was lost to a competitive bidder, if the takeover broke down or if the full amount of the financing could not be raised, the subscribing financial institution received payment for reading the offering circular and documents. The commitment fees ranged from $3/8$ of one percent to $7/8$ of one percent. Thus, a $10 million commitment resulted in a payment to the institution of approximately $50,000 for reading the deal and voting yes.

Milken's junk bond offering circulars were shipped to institutional money managers in tightly bound manila envelopes that literally screamed: *Open me, ye who seek undreamed of riches!* The investor had to respond to a Drexel deal within 24 to 48 hours. Although institutional investors were not used to being ordered about by investment bankers, they took orders from Drexel. They could either subscribe to the deal in two days and see more junk bond deals in the future, or they could pass and probably not see any more Drexel deals.

Milken changed buyer-seller dynamics. He positioned junk bonds as solutions to the problems faced by institutional investors, that is, their need to earn sufficiently high yields to cover operating expenses and payouts to policyholders, pensioners and passbook holders to whom they were offering high yields. Before Milken, if an institution could lock in average yields of 12 percent per annum, it made ends meet. Junk bond yields of 16–18 percent permitted operating expenses (read: management salaries and bonuses) to rise without jeopardizing statutory payouts. An investment officer in a large institution, who frequently receives a bonus if his or her portfolio yields more than a predetermined target rate of return, could boost his or her $100,000 salary by an additional $100,000 by investing in junk bonds. That is a strong inducement!

Finally, Milken promised junk bond buyers that, if the borrower was unable to pay interest or principal on the debentures when due, Milken and his team would either refinance the initial junk bond with a new one that offered superior features or sell a peripheral division of the borrower to raise cash to meet the payment deadlines. Drexel had a highly skilled investment banking crew that could roll over the debt when it came due with debt restructurings or cashouts.

Drexel's promise to refinance junk bond principal when it came due was tantamount to a *guarantee* that the buyer would make, and not lose, money. As long as Milken was around to honor that guarantee, the institutions did not lose money; he replaced their old debt with new. However, in 1989, when Milken was removed from the industry that he created, it began to unravel.

In an effort to catch up, Drexel's competitors offered higher and higher prices to takeover targets and embellished the junk bonds with equity kickers, higher interest rates and improved terms.

During the party that became known as the "Great Takeover Bash" of the late 1980s, all participants made more money than they had dreamed possible. Shareholders were selling out at double their investment. Managers jumped out of target companies and floated to the lush fairways of Scottsdale, Arizona, and Tarpon Springs, Florida, on golden parachute deals. Institutional investors showed more profits than at any time in their history, and their money managers' billfolds bulged with the rewards of their financial acumen. Financial buyers built empires and net worths as large as their Social Security numbers. Investment bankers generated six to seven times the traditional business fees, and Milken alone made more money than the gross national product (GNP) of half the countries in the United Nations.

Little thought was given to the ability to repay more than $260 billion in junk bonds. Some takeover targets defaulted. Some fraudulent inside trading by high-profile *arbitrageurs* (investors who bet on takeovers) sent jitters through the institutional investor crowd. Legislators who caused the savings and loan industry debacle by voting in 1982 to deregulate it without proper "speed bumps" needed a scapegoat, so they blamed the Milken crowd and the junk bonds they "forced" on institutional investors. As quickly as the party began, it ended. American industry went into recession. The takeover business cost some jobs when layoffs were required to service debt, but junk bonds were not solely to blame.

The junk bond-backed leveraged buyout boom of the late 1980s may or may not return. Many of those junk bonds sold to institutional lenders and to the public are now acceptable investments held by respectable institutions. As the trustee for the endowment fund of an educational institution in Santa Fe, New Mexico, I voted in 1990 to buy several of these once-vilified bonds whose underlying cash flow had now caught up to and exceeded debt service. Thus, I suspect the age of overpaying for companies is over.

Summary

Some M&A brokers will ask for an up-front fee plus a closing or success fee if they locate a buyer satisfactory to you. The object of the up-front fee is to determine that you are a serious seller and not merely attempting to ascertain your company's value. But if you pay an up-front fee, do not give the broker an exclusive engagement. That is, the broker must find the buyer to be paid the closing fee.

Managing the Process

◆◆◆◆◆◆◆◆◆

Clarity Up Front

Before engaging a broker, it is extremely important to clarify your expectations and his or her commitment. To help clarify matters up front, you should ask a number of specific questions:

- ◆ Do you think you can sell my company?
- ◆ What price do you think you can get for my company?
- ◆ To whom do you think you will sell it?
- ◆ How long do you think it will take?
- ◆ Who will be assigned to my company?
- ◆ How frequently will you report to me?
- ◆ When should I inform my key people that I am selling the company?

Do You Think You Can Sell My Company?

To this question the majority of merger and acquisition brokers would answer: Yes. After all, why kill a sale as the customer is entering

29

the shop? The more important question is: Why do you *think* you can sell my company? To which you would expect (or hope for) the answer to be: Because my firm has sold several companies in your industry, and we have an extensive list of buyers of companies such as yours.

In fact, if the broker cannot demonstrate a track record of success in selling companies such as yours to buyers that you would like to have own your business, then you should search for another broker—one with a verifiable track record who fits the bill. You should be able to contact the broker's clients to confirm that the broker found buyers for their companies in a reasonable amount of time and at a satisfactory price.

Figure 4.1 provides names, addresses, and telephone and fax numbers of a handful of industry-specialized M&A brokers.

◆ **Figure 4.1**   Representative List of Industry-Specialized Merger and Acquisition Brokers

---

Apparel
Arnold S. Cohen
110 E. 57th St., Ste. 16-F
New York, NY 10022
212-753-1490
Fax: 212-753-2983

Automotive
Corporate Strategies, Inc.
Richard D. Pulford
3000 Town Center, #540
Southfield, MI 48075
313-354-1445
Fax: 313-352-4030

Banks
D. Latin Securities, Inc.
Donald E. Latin
600 N. Pearl St., Ste. 333
Dallas, TX 75201
214-220-1214
Fax: 214-220-1277

Biotechnology
L. William Teweles & Co.
L. William Teweles
777 E. Wisconsin Ave.
Milwaukee, WI 53202
414-273-4854
Fax: 414-273-8140

Cable Television
Malone & Associates, Inc.
Robert G. Malone
1401 Seventeenth St., #1550
Denver, CO 80202
303-298-7700
Fax: 303-295-6447

Chemicals
Findtech, Inc.
Chem J. Listner
165 Passaic Ave.
Fairfield, NJ 07004
201-227-6262
Fax: 201-227-6291

Department Stores
Financo, Inc.
Gilbert Harrison
535 Madison Ave., 3rd Fl.
New York, NY 10022
212-593-9000
Fax: 212-593-0309

Environmental
Scully Capital Services, Inc.
Larry J. Scully
1133 - 15th St., N.W., Ste. 700
Washington, DC 20005-2701
202-682-3434
Fax: 202-687-3422

Floor Covering
Torwest Companies
R. M. Torre
One Park Plaza, #530
Irvine, CA 92714
714-474-8140
Fax: 714-474-1849

Food and Dairy Processing
Anderson/Roethle, Inc.
John D. Roethle
733 N. Van Buren St.
Milwaukee, WI 53202
414-276-0070
Fax: 414-276-4364

Furniture
Maxey International, Inc.
L. Keith Maxey
PO Box 8804
Roanoke, VA 24014
703-345-8796
Fax: 703-982-8796

Health Care
Cleary & Berlew Associates
David Cleary
218 N. Lee St.
Alexandria, VA 22314
703-548-3140
Fax: 703-549-1095

Hospitality
Fogel International, Inc.
Larry Fogel
2222 E. Camelback Rd., Ste. 222
Phoenix, AZ 85016
602-957-1130
Fax: 602-954-2633

Insurance
Trent (Richard O.) & Associates
Bill James
7201 Classen Blvd.
Oklahoma City, OK 73116
405-848-2641
Fax: 405-848-2650

Laboratory Instruments
Strategic Directions Int'l., Inc.
Lawrence S. Schmid
6242 Westchester Pkwy., #100
Los Angeles, CA 90045
310-641-4982
Fax: 310-641-8851

Leasing
Intercontinental Capital
  Associates
Jeffrey Furman
885 Third Ave., #2400
New York, NY 10022
212-751-4110
Fax: 212-826-5617

◆ **Figure 4.1**   Representative List of Industry-Specialized
Merger and Acquisition Brokers (Continued)

Oil and Gas
Triumph Oil & Gas Corp.
R. Stuyevsant Pierrepont
1270 Ave. of the Americas,
    Ste. 605
New York, NY 10020
212-307-6870
Fax: 212-307-6977

Paints and Adhesives
Einhorn Associates, Inc.
Stephen Einhorn
2323 N. Mayfair Rd., #490
Milwaukee, WI 53226
414-453-4488
Fax: 414-453-4831

Printing
Probus Enterprises, Inc.
Robert St. Pierre
Harvard Bldg., PO Box 2005
Pinehurst, NC 28374
919-295-2288
Fax: Call first

Publishing
Veronis, Suhler & Associates, Inc.
John S. Suhler
350 Park Ave., 20th Fl.
New York, NY 10022
212-935-4990
Fax: 212-935-0877

Russian-Related
Palms & Company
Michael Mandeville
6702 - 139th Ave., N.E., Ste. 760
Redmond, WA 98052
206-883-3580
Fax: 206-881-6125

Security Guard Services
Robert H. Perry & Associates
Robert H. Perry
PO Box 67
Greensboro, NC 27402
919-272-2266
Fax: 919-272-1142

Temporary Employment
Alan Gelband Co., Inc.
Alan Gelband
30 Lincoln Plaza
New York, NY 10023
212-245-2911
Fax: 212-355-2414

Title Insurance
Corporate Development Services,
    Inc.
Lawrence E. Kirwin
996 Old Eagle School Rd., #112
Wayne, PA 19087
215-688-1540
Fax: 215-688-5174

The industry-specialized brokers listed in Figure 4.1 are representative of the degree to which the buying and selling of companies has become a specialized business. For example, Bill James of Richard O. Trent & Associates, Inc., a specialist in the purchase and sale of life insurance companies, attends at least five industry seminars and conferences per year and, at any one time, is conducting seven or eight *searches* for specific life insurance companies—credit life, universal life, group life, term life, annuities and so forth. In most instances, during the initial interview, Mr. James can tell a seller the price that he can obtain for the business, the likely terms of the purchase and the probable buyers. He is representative of the professionalism that an experienced M&A broker can bring to a cautious seller.

What Price Do You Think You Can Get for My Company?

Most experienced brokers can provide an approximate valuation of your company if you provide them with adequate information in the initial interview. They will ask about the company's current earnings and those in the most recent fiscal year. Brokers will inquire about the amount that you take out of the company each year in salary, *perks* (short for perquisites) and interest payments; they will ask if there are other charges to earnings, such as inventory adjustments, excessive write-offs of bad debts or depreciation.

Perks refer to personal expenses charged to the company. Nepotistic payments should also be included in the perks category. These amounts will be added back to earnings or losses to arrive at adjusted EBIT-DA. The broker will mentally multiply by a factor of between three and eight depending on the strength of your franchise, the overall outlook for your industry, location, size and whether or not a good management team is in place (information that you can provide in the initial conversation).

Although at first blush, location and size may not appear relevant, companies conveniently located near major airports or metropolitan areas are popular among buyers. Additionally, the larger a company is, the greater the number of potential buyers that will be attracted to it. A regional manufacturer of low-calorie Italian pasta might interest a dozen major food processors if its sales are more than $50 million per year; but if its sales are $10 million or less, it will more than likely appeal to financial buyers who will seek to buy it, grow it and sell it to a large company in five years.

Some brokers may not wish to be pinned down on the question of price, but you need to know that the price will exceed liquidation value or, at a minimum, be liquidation value (tangible net worth or what you could put in your pocket by closing the company down, collecting its receivables, selling its assets and paying off its debts) plus one year's cash flow. To get an approximation of liquidation value, you may want to call in an appraiser. A comprehensive "Directory of Equipment, Real Estate and Industry Appraisers" is provided in Appendix II.

To Whom Do You Think You Will Sell It?

Most brokers will not provide their list of potential buyers prior to their engagement. However, the more experienced brokers will probably know if the business is more likely to be acquired by a strategic or financial buyer and should be willing to tell you that. Because strategic buyers are preferred buyers, some brokers will restrict financial buyers from seeing the descriptive selling memorandum until they have exhausted their contacts with potential strategic buyers. A financial buyer will likely borrow on your company's assets to pay you. If that amount is inadequate, the buyer may have the additional cash or, if not, ask you to take an earn-out, subordinated note or some form of term payout that you may never see because of the tremendous debt your company will be carrying. The pros and cons of selling your company to strategic and financial buyers will be reviewed throughout this book.

How Long Do You Think It Will Take?

This depends on the attractiveness of your company, the supply of companies like yours that are on the market, the perception of the future prospects for your industry and, most important, the quality and quantity of the lists that your broker will use to locate buyers. If your company produces products or offers a service to a niche segment within a rapidly growing market (such as local area network computer systems, security guard services or environmental products), if that niche can be expanded with more marketing muscle, and if the broker knows the market and has a good list of potential buyers, the process may take less than 180 days.

But if your company is dominant in a slow-growth, saturated market characterized by shrinking gross profit margins and excessive government regulation (such as gas-powered lawn mowers, aluminum siding for houses or lead-filled radiators), no matter how fresh the broker's list, selling your company may take as long as three years.

In some industries companies are sold back and forth like commodities. Television stations, radio stations and insurance companies are relatively easy to broker because the names of company owners are published in readily available directories. A community of M&A brokers specializes in media and insurance companies. Figure 4.1 provides the names of dominant brokers in these and other industries.

In any event this book will help you shorten the selling process to 12 months. If your business cannot be sold within a year, there may be some flaws to overcome. The slow-selling company may lack franchise value, be unprofitable, be in a decline, be in the wrong industry, lack a skilled management team to run the company, or its owners may be seeking a too ambitious a price.

Who Will Be Assigned to My Company?

To monitor the selling process so that a sale will occur rapidly and at a good price, you should ask a lot of questions up front, including:

- ◆ Who will I be interfacing with at the merger and acquisition firm?
- ◆ Who will be writing the descriptive selling memorandum?
- ◆ What does he or she know about my company?
- ◆ Will he or she be coming out for a due diligence visit?
- ◆ How can I be helpful to make sure the memorandum is as good as it can be?

Be sure to meet the person with whom you will be interfacing and establish a mechanism for remaining informed. Check that your broker is actively working on selling your company at least four days a week. Any company can be sold if enough qualified buyers are contacted— the operative word is *qualified*.

Involving yourself in preparing the descriptive selling memorandum is an important stage in maximizing the selling price and lessening the time required to sell your company. Nobody knows your company as well as you do. You know what makes it tick, and it is critical that you communicate this to the broker.

For instance, assume that you have been in business for more than 20 years and have 2 decades of significant supplier relationships and 2 decades of customer relationships. Further, assume that your company can be liquidated for $3 million, according to appraisals of its inventory and equipment, but its earnings are a relatively flat $400,000 per annum. Is your company worth liquidation value plus one year's earnings—$3.4 million? It's worth that *plus* the cost that the buyer would have to pay to create your customer list plus supplier relationships. These *off-balance sheet* assets might add another $600,000 to the purchase price. However, unless you communicate that to potential buyers in the descriptive selling memorandum, it may be difficult to convince buyers to reach for higher values.

How Frequently Will You Report to Me?

The broker should contact you each time he or she has a qualified or potential buyer who wishes to receive a copy of the descriptive selling memorandum. You must have the right to approve or disapprove a prospect qualified by the broker. After all, if the descriptive selling memorandum falls into the wrong hands—those of a competitor or supplier—serious damage could be done.

Whether or not there is a prospective buyer, telephone contact should occur at least weekly. Ask the following questions:

- What did you do for me this week?
- How many mailings did you send out?
- How many calls did you make?
- Did we get any turndowns this week? If so, who? Why?
- Should we change the memorandum?
- Do you need updated financial statements?

If something unusually positive or negative occurs to the company, you should inform the broker immediately. For instance, if a major contract is awarded or lost, if the chief financial officer resigns or if profits are unusually large or small in a particular month, tell the broker. It could impact his or her discussions with a prospective buyer.

Encourage tenacity in your broker. Remember that your company is the broker's inventory—it is not making him or her money sitting on a shelf in the office. Be sure that the broker is mailing memoranda to qualified buyers. On average, it takes six readers of a memorandum to find one potential buyer sufficiently interested to visit the company; it takes four different visitors, on average, to find a buyer who offers the right price and terms.

When Should I Inform My Key People That I Am Selling the Company?

To avoid a blitz of rumors and concern that the company is *on the block*, you can and should keep the sale of your company a secret for as long as possible. Rumors of a company's sale, overblown into crisis proportions, cause productivity to suffer. The broker should mail correspondence to your house and alert you before faxing important papers.

When the broker makes a due diligence visit, he or she can be introduced to key personnel as a banker, insurance broker or management consultant. However, when the broker appears two months later with two other people, you should inform certain key people that you are considering "bringing in some investors." When the prospective buyer becomes sufficiently interested to want to interview department heads and senior management, be certain that the buyer has set forth his or her price and terms, or at least a range, in writing to avoid announcing a prospective deal that will never happen.

Managing the Broker

The process of generating interest in an acquisition candidate requires discretion and professionalism. The broker elicits interest in his or her client on a no-name, no-location basis by mailing, telephoning and faxing information about the company without revealing its name or location. An experienced broker will mail the no-name, no-location *teaser* to lists of potential buyers that have the same or similar *Standardized Industrial Codes* (SIC) and other lists including acquisition funds, acquisition companies and conglomerates. Note that, in the following three example teasers in Figure 4.2, it is virtually impossible to determine the names of the companies that are for sale.

Competitors or companies that might wish to learn about the acquisition candidate for reasons other than to acquire it cannot identify the company from the teaser. They might try to persuade the broker to send them the descriptive selling memorandum, but this must, and can, be prevented if the owner and broker maintain active communication several times a week.

◆ **Figure 4.2** Three Sample Teaser Letters

Example 1: Auto Parts Manufacturer

The company manufactures numerous branded auto parts in two locations and sells through WDs and conventional retail channels— Auto Zone, Pep Boys—as well as via mail order. Revenues exceed $30 million and EBIT-DA is $1.75 million. The company is a subsidiary of a NYSE-listed conglomerate. Board has authorized the sale.

Example 2: Credit Life, Credit Accident and Health Insurance Company

The company is a publicly held, diversified insurance company that sells credit life and credit accident and health insurance. The company is licensed to sell and underwrite insurance in 14 states but is active in only 6 of them. It has more than 180 production sources, about half of them commercial banks and the other half auto and truck dealers. The target company has 30 employees, most of whom have been with the company for more than 15 years. Key financial information is summarized as follows:

($000s)	For the Most Recent Fiscal Year-End
Total income	$15,545
Adjusted EBIT	785
Total assets	26,400
Capital and surplus	12,332
Loss ratio	.45
Combined ratio	.98

Example 3: Roofing Materials Distributor

The company is the largest distributor of roofing materials in its region with sales of $37 million per annum and EBIT-DA of $2.2 million. It is more than 20 years old and has 7 branch locations. Revenues have grown at the rate of 15 percent per annum over the last 5 years. The owner seeks to retire; the children are not interested in the business and middle management lacks the capital. Asking price: $6.6 million.

Defensive Selling

To manage the solicitation process, yet lessen the risk of the descriptive selling memorandum falling into competitors' hands, the broker *must* obtain the seller's approval before sending the teaser to an interested buyer. The broker sends the owner a description of the prospective buyer—including name, location, size, history of acquisitions and how the prospective buyer came to be known to the broker or how he received the teaser.

It is critical that the broker know as much as possible about buyers who request copies of the descriptive selling memorandum. Failure to do this could be grounds for terminating the M&A broker.

The Confidential Disclosure Agreement

A certain percentage of teasers will result in requests from potential buyers to see a copy of the descriptive selling memorandum. It is the broker's professional obligation to *qualify* potential buyers. This is, at best, a difficult assignment. A competitor of the acquisition candidate may hear of the sale and ask its investment banker or a friend at an acquisition fund to obtain a copy of the descriptive selling memorandum. The results could be disastrous.

To mitigate damages, experienced brokers use confidential disclosure agreements that put the recipient of the memorandum on notice that he or she is liable if he or she uses the memorandum in a manner that causes economic injury to the target company. A competitor could make a serious bid to lure key employees from the target company by telling them that the company is being sold. In one instance a competitor received a copy of a target company's descriptive selling memorandum from an unscrupulous intermediary, then gave a trade journal a false story that the target company was the subject of a "fire sale" to avoid a Chapter 11 filing. It took several months for the owner of the company to squelch the rumors and restore smooth relations with suppliers and customers.

Figure 4.3 shows an example of a typical confidential disclosure agreement.

The broker may send the descriptive selling memorandum *only* to potential buyers that have signed the confidential disclosure agreement. These agreements should be signed by *principals*, not by their

◆ **Figure 4.3**   Sample Confidential Disclosure Agreement

(To Be Typed on Company Letterhead)

Date

Mr. A. David Silver
President
ADS Financial Services, Inc.
524 Camino del Monte Sol
Santa Fe, NM 87501

Dear Mr. Silver:

We are interested in the potential acquisition of the auto parts marketing company (the "Company") that you described to us. This interest is, of course, subject to further due diligence on our part and the mutually acceptable completion of negotiations.

We understand that, with our interest in acquiring the Company, we will be furnished with certain materials that include information that is either nonpublic, confidential or proprietary in nature. Such information, in whole or in part, together with analyses, compilations, studies or other documents prepared by you, or by us or our representatives, that contain, otherwise reflect or are generated from such information and our review thereof, is hereinafter referred to as the *Proprietary Information*.

In consideration for the information that will be provided for our use in evaluation of the Company, we agree to the following:

1. The Proprietary Information will be kept confidential and shall not, without the prior written consent of the Seller, be disclosed by us, our agents or employees, in any manner whatsoever, in whole or in part, and shall not be used by us, our agents or employees, other than in connection with the transaction of acquiring the Company. Moreover, we agree to transmit the Proprietary Information only to those who need to know the Proprietary Information for the purpose of evaluating our possible interest as described herein. We will be responsible for any breach of this agreement by our representatives or employees.

2. We agree that we will not have discussions of a business nature with any employee, officer or director of the Company or its other affiliates except where specific permission to do so is granted by the Seller. We further agree that we will not hire or seek to hire any employee, officer

or director of the Company for a period of three (3) years from this date without the express written agreement of the Parent.

3. We agree that we will not disclose the fact that discussions concerning the potential acquisition of the Company are being held, unless required to do so by law or regulation and to that extent agree to notify you prior to doing so.

Yours very truly,

Company Name

By: _____

Title: _____

Date: _____

---

agents or intermediaries. The owner must approve all recipients (even if they have signed confidential disclosure agreements), and he or she should receive copies of all signed confidential disclosure agreements.

Retainers

Should you pay your broker up front? Although some merger and acquisition brokers do not charge monthly retainers plus expense reimbursements, most do. Those who do not will ask for significantly higher closing fees, perhaps as high as ten percent. Those who do will normally request a closing fee within the Lehman Formula.

One of the more aggressive M&A brokers charges an up-front fee of approximately $35,000. It attracts many clients because it has numerous regional offices that generate clients through seminars and cold-calling. A retainer of that amount is extraordinary because it provides a profit to the broker before he or she has earned it.

A more typical retainer is several thousand dollars per month for three to six months plus conventional expense reimbursements. The broker should be required to obtain your approval for all expenses above $500 per month. The broker should not travel at your expense without your approval, and you should not approve a trip unless it is to attend a due diligence or price negotiation meeting in your office with a prospective buyer. You should motivate the broker with a small retainer and expense reimbursement agreement but not encourage lassitude by overpaying for his or her time.

Exclusive versus Nonexclusive Agreements

If a broker asks for an exclusive agreement, then no matter who finds the buyer—the broker, your Uncle Phil or your accountant—the broker is paid a fee at closing. However, your Uncle Phil may expect a fee as well. This could lead to paying a double fee or ten percent of the consideration that you receive. This is an excessive price to pay, particularly since the federal and state governments will receive more than 30 percent of the purchase price. Exclusive agreements are not a good idea.

Nonexclusive agreements are more common. As an insurance policy, the broker will ask for a retainer to cover costs. In the event that Uncle Phil finds a buyer and the broker does not collect the closing fee, he or she will not be out several thousand dollars. The retainer will cover time and money spent on a descriptive selling memorandum (writing, proofing, editing, modifying, printing and binding), mailing hundreds of teasers, making and taking dozens of telephone calls, and managing the process of sending confidential disclosure agreements. If a broker does all of this without an exclusive agreement or a retainer plus expense reimbursement arrangement, he or she is probably naive. And you do not need naiveté working for you.

Hence, the rule of thumb is: Give an exclusive arrangement or pay an up-front fee.

Spare Me

Some owners are too cheap, too egotistical, too secretive, too dishonest in terms of tax avoidance gimmicks, too proud, too reliant on the free advice of their accountant and lawyer and too stubborn for me to represent in the sale of their companies. These sellers have often run good middle managers away because they failed to retire and let younger people take charge. The more isolated an owner becomes, it seems, the higher the price he or she asks.

I remember dealing with a couple who would not permit meetings at their company's facilities for fear that the employees would get wind of a pending sale and not be as productive. These same people were cheating the government out of several hundred thousand dollars a year in taxes while thanking God that they had sired doctors and lawyers who did not need to inherit the business. The company was unprofitable without the tax avoidance schemes; hence, medical school and law school were paid for by a noninterest-bearing forgivable loan from Uncle Sam. The couple would not pay a retainer to any M&A broker because their pride did not permit them to value anyone's contribution before the fact. Spare me the hyper-proud owner.

Summary

The M&A broker whom you select should be monitored carefully and closely. Make certain that he or she requires all prospective buyers to sign confidentiality agreements. Assist him or her in writing the direct mail teaser and the descriptive memorandum. Speak with the broker once a week without fail. Keep him or her focused on finding a buyer for your company.

Part

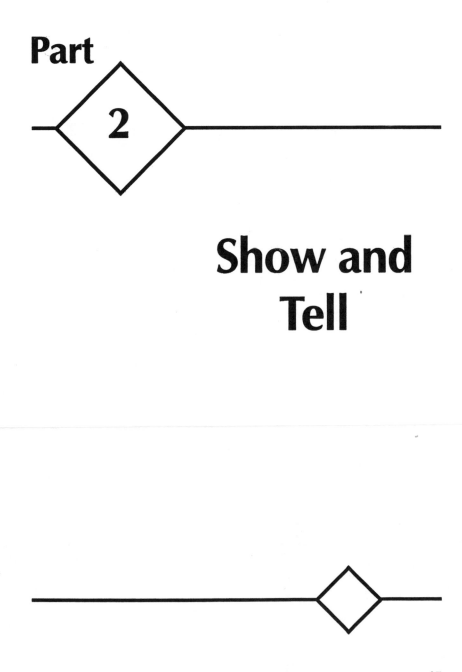

2

Show and Tell

Strategic versus Financial Buyers

◆◆◆◆◆◆◆◆◆

There are essentially two generic groups of potential buyers of the privately held company: The strategic buyer wants the company for its *opportunity*; the financial buyer wants the company for its *cash flow*. Naturally, the strategic buyer will pay more.

Strategic Buyers

When Eli Lilly & Co. paid 15 times revenues for Hybritech in 1987, it did so to obtain a presence in genetic engineering. When Pillsbury paid 26 times earnings for Steak 'n Ale in 1980, it did so to add a dinner-house chain to its restaurant division. When Medtronics paid 8 times revenues for Versaflex in 1990, it did so to broaden its product line by reducing its focus on pacemakers.

Something unusual takes possession of strategic buyers' minds. Passion drives them to overpay for a niche business. Egos encourage them to take over small, interesting niche and regional businesses with the intent to make them large, interesting, national and, sometimes, international.

Feeding their need to overpay is the fact that opportunity has actually met reality in a few instances. Sara Lee Corporation grew from a regional bakery to an international food marketer by acquiring expandable, medium-sized food businesses. In one week in September 1992, Bacardi, Ltd., a rum producer, acquired Martini & Rossi, a European vermouth producer; Gillette Company bought Parker Pen Holdings Ltd.; RJR Nabisco, Inc. purchased Stella D'Oro, a family-owned cookie maker; and General Mills acquired the Shredded Wheat cereal brand from RJR Nabisco. These deals elicited the following responses from industry experts and consultants: "The great brand names of today are very valuable because they almost guarantee you very good cash flow into the future," said Karl van der Heyden, chief financial officer of RJR Nabisco.[1]

"The buzzword in business now is back to basics," said Jack Trout, president of Trout & Reis, marketing consultants. "The perception is that the cost of building a brand name from scratch is too high relative to purchasing one. From a risk perspective, many managers cannot defend the uncertainty of building a brand name from scratch," said Milina M. Lek, a Chicago-based marketing consultant.[2]

One of the great battlegrounds in business today is supermarket shelf space. (This applies to drug stores, liquor stores, hardware stores and office supply stores as well.) America is saturated with retail outlets. Acceptable real estate for building yet another retail outlet is virtually unavailable. Thus, the war is in the store—the more a consumer-products producer collects smaller companies with consumer brand awareness and existing shelf space, the more profitable it will be.

Pigs in Pokes

There are equally stunning examples of overpayment and catastrophe as well. In the mid-1970s Xerox Corp. paid $800 million for Scientific Data Systems Corp.(SDS), a mainframe computer manufacturer with sales of around $60 million. When SDS's founding entrepreneur Max Pavlesky was asked how he got Xerox to pay $800 million for a five-year-old computer company, he said, "One of my backers, Tommy Davis, told me, going into the room, to have a number in mind when they asked me to name my price. So I said, '$1 billion.' Xerox haggled me down to $800 million." SDS went out of business in a year.

It is not that Pavlesky pulled the wool over Xerox's eyes. SDS made an excellent computer—equal at the time, many would say, to those of Digital Equipment Corp. and Data General Corp., two other early-stage computer makers of the same genre. But copiers are not computers—copiers do not obsolete as rapidly as do computers.

Retail "Statements"

Once when I invested in a retail computer chain start-up, I learned the hard way. The company went public early, with only four stores in operation, to provide a currency other than cash for making acquisitions. In less than two years, the company had increased to 18 stores from Southern California to West Texas. However, IBM Corp. introduced a new and faster personal computer. With its ubiquitous Charlie Chaplin-type, user-friendly ads, IBM made virtually all the inventory in all 18 stores plus the warehouse obsolete, and there was no cash on hand to buy new models. Plus, we lacked a *raison d'être*—a statement that differentiated us from other computer retailers.

By eliminating the company in which I had invested plus all but the strongest computer retailers, IBM opened the door for alternate channels, such as direct mail marketing of computers. Now, ten years later, this same channel threatens IBM's dominance with entrepreneurial companies that build superior computers at much lower prices.

If your company is a retail business that is making an important and unique *retail statement* or is operating profitably in a region of the country that a strategic buyer would like to enter, it could be sold to a strategic buyer. Successful retailing is somewhat like surfing—the goal is to catch the right wave before it breaks. If a retailer catches the next consumer trend before it hits, he or she will own a gold mine.

This happened with tennis and basketball shoes, fast food restaurants, home-delivered pizza, and specialty kitchen utensils stores. Many strategic buyers are searching for unique retail chains that make a novel statement. Hospital companies have acquired clinics; food store chains have purchased restaurant chains; K mart, a large discount chain, bought Waldenbooks.

This has happened with many consumer products or services. Bookstores need rethinking—margins are low, and many books are returned unsold to the publishers. Carpets and rugs could be sold more imaginatively using videos and computer-assisted design. Art galleries are dinosaurs when it comes to innovative marketing strategies. For instance, sending art collectors videos or CD-ROMs to project artwork on their walls, is one way for art galleries to increase sales and cash flow.

Selling the Opportunity

The point of this seeming divergence is to say that you may own a company in Broken Spoke, Pennsylvania, that sells a consumer product, and you may be thinking that it is a conventional, necessary, ordinary consumer product. But in New York or Los Angeles, your product line may be regarded as unique, i.e., an *opportunity*. Your company, which may have conventional value to you, may offer *opportunity value* to a strategic buyer. And opportunity value is worth more to you because the buyer pays with his or her ego as well as his or her brain. A strategic buyer looks at all the possibilities of your business and pays for the opportunity to own your company to give his or her genius a proper brush and canvas.

When selling your seemingly boring company, remember two things:

1. *The poor boy sandwich*   Always tell the buyer that you never had the capital to implement some of the ideas that you had for the business.
2. *The gourmet feast for others*   Always tell the buyer how much more money he or she could make if he or she implements one or two of your plans.

A strategic buyer has capital and ego. Your business has franchise value plus upside opportunities. To get to the opportunities, the buyer must pay you more than the company is worth.

Let's assume that you operate a wholesale floral supply business in a medium-sized city and that you have sales of about $3 million per annum but are not very profitable. A conventional buyer would pay you, perhaps, the liquidation value (tangible net worth) plus $100,000 for the franchise value, a total of $420,000. This strikes me as low, notwithstanding that the company has not grown in years and does not seem to have a direction. Figure 5.1 shows the floral supply company's historical financial statements.

Although most owners of businesses such as this would be pleased to sell for $400,000 to $450,000, it leaves a lot of money in the buyer's pocket. If the owner of this business listed the opportunities that, with a little capital, he could have taken advantage of, he would be waving a red flag in front of the bull. A strategic buyer likes nothing more than *opportunity*.

Following are some suggestions the floral supply wholesaler should make in his descriptive selling memorandum and support in conversation with the buyer:

◆ Figure 5.1 Historical Summary Financial Statements Floral Supply Wholesaler

Balance Sheet Data ($000s)

	12/31/91	12/31/92	2/28/92
Applicable assets			
Current assets	$423	$506	$513
Less: curr. liabs.	368	425	408
Net working capital	55	81	105
Plant, eqpt. - net	193	209	202
Other assets	13	11	13
Total applicable assets	$271	$301	$320
Capitalization			
Long-term debt	—	—	—
Shareholders' equity	$271	$301	$320
Total capitalization	$271	$301	$320

Operating Statement Data ($000s)

	FYE 12/31/91	FYE 12/31/92	2 Mos. 2/28/92
Revenues	$3,450	$3,516	$661
Cost of goods sold	2,415	2,461	430
Gross profit	1,035	1,155	231
Operating expenses	925	1,077	205
Net optg.income	110	78	26
Int. exps. (income)	60	48	7
Net prof. before taxes	$ 40	$ 30	$ 19
Add-backs			
Owner salary & perks	$ 40	$ 45	$ 12
Depreciation	20	18	2
Int. exps.	60	48	7
Total add-backs	120	101	21
Adjusted EBIT-DA	$ 160	$ 131	$ 40

- *Franchising the company's know-how and operational skills* to launch wholesale florists in other regions of the country.
- *Information marketing,* i.e., the sale (or the give-away) of a newsletter and its sale of ad space to customers and noncustomers (through rented lists). This newsletter should describe horticultural and decorative items that can be purchased from the company.
- *Subscriptions and memberships* to *plant-of-the-month clubs*, information products, tours of beautiful gardens, seminars and related products and services.
- *Rental of floral-quality plants* to local businesses and for events such as conventions and seminars.
- *More efficient use of the company's vans.* Used primarily in the mornings to make deliveries to the company's customers, the vans are idle for much of the remainder of the day. The vans could be contracted to retail florists for making their deliveries, which occur primarily in the afternoon.
- *Expanding the florist section of retail food stores to include floral arrangements.* The company could explore the opportunity of making retail florists out of chain store personnel assigned to the floral area. This strategy would require the company's floral arrangers to make the arrangements and deliver them to the chain stores.
- *More efficient use of the company's physical space.* The parking lot, which has 2,000 square feet of excess space, could be converted to a nursery yard to permit expansion into that market segment. The second floor of the facility, about 4,000 square feet, could be used to sell cards, coffee and other products to its retail customers while they wait near the checkout counter.

These suggestions translate to the strategic buyer as: *I can do it.* The strategic buyer's ego, coupled with his or her experience in implementing strategic plans effectively, causes the strategic buyer to *pay up* for opportunity values. An example is Pillsbury Company, which purchased the Burger King chain in the 1970s. Feeling positive about its food service skills, the company then acquired Steak 'n Ale, a small dinner-house chain for 35 times earnings. Hubris pays! Eventually, Pillsbury itself had to be taken over and shrunk to a better size.

Several of these ideas, such as converting delivery vans into an afternoon delivery business for retail florists to increase revenues and cash flow, are not capital intensive. The seller can explain his or her lassitude for never entering this business with: *We never got around to doing it.*

Financial Buyers

If strategic buyers don't come knocking at your door, or if they do but you can't convince them to buy, you will probably have to deal with financial buyers. These entrepreneurs, with a couple bucks in their pocket and an understanding of how to accomplish leveraged buyouts, want to own the business their fathers never left them. Their goal is to borrow on the assets of your company and repay the debt with the company's cash flow.

Quasi-Strategic Buyers

Fortunately, over the last ten years many financial buyers have raised capital from large financial institutions—pension funds, insurance companies and university endowment funds—and have hundreds of millions of dollars of equity capital with which to make acquisitions, along with the asset-based lenders that provide them with leverage. Hundreds of these acquisition funds are in the marketplace, ferreting out middle-market companies whose owners are seeking buyers. See Appendix III for a list and descriptions of these acquisition funds. The tactics for buying companies are similar to those used by financial buyers.

Let's assume that you own an electric sign manufacturing company with $12 million in revenues. The financial statements submitted to the financial buyer are shown in Figure 5.2. The financial buyer makes two quick examinations to see if a leveraged buyout is feasible: (1) to determine how much can be borrowed on the target company's balance sheet, and (2) to determine if the target company's cash flow will support the debt service. Assume that the buyer intends to offer you five times *net adjusted EBIT* (adjusted EBIT *less* the cost of replacing you)—$5 million.

Using conventional borrowing ratios, the financial buyer estimates the amount of debt that can be borrowed on the target company's balance sheet, as presented in Figure 5.3.

◆ **Figure 5.2**   Outdoor Electric Sign Manufacturer Vendor
Balance Sheet

Balance Sheet Data ($000s)

Assets		Liabilities & Net Worth	
Current assets		**Current liabilities**	
Cash	$ 100	Accounts payable	$1,400
Accounts receivable	2,000	Accrued expenses	600
Inventory	1,400		
Total current assets	3,500	Total current liabilities	2,000
Fixed assets		**Long-term debt**	
Plant (net)	500	**net worth**	
Equipment (net)	400	Common stock	500
Other assets	100	Retained earnings	2,000
		Total net worth	2,500
		Total liabilities &	
Total assets	$4,500	Net worth	$4,500

Operating Statement Latest 12 Months ($000s)

	Latest Fiscal Year
Sales	$12,000
Cost of goods sold	8,700
Gross profit	3,300
Operating expenses	2,300
Net operating income	1,000
Provision for taxes	350
Net profits after taxes	650
Add-backs	
Owner's salary	200
Owner's perks	100
Depreciation	50
Inventory adjustment	150
Total adjusted EBIT	$ 1,500

◆ **Figure 5.3** Leveragability of the Seller

Asset	Book or Liquidation Value	x	Loan Ratio =	Amount of Loan (in Dollars)
Accts. rec.	$2,000		.80	$1,600
Inventory	1,200*		.50	400
Plant	500**		.75	375
Equipment	250**		.75	187
Total				$2,562

* Work in process inventory has been netted out. Borrowers will only lend against finished goods and raw material inventory.

** Estimated liquidation value, that is, the amount that the assets would bring at auction, a dollar amount that you can determine by hiring an appraiser. (See Appendix II.)

The financial buyer's desktop analysis indicates that a little more than one-half the price he or she intends to offer can be borrowed. When the entire estimated purchase price is multiplied by 13 percent (financial buyers borrow *above* the prime rate and assume that rates will increase rather than decrease to mentally hedge their bet) and approximately $500,000 per annum is added to that amount for annual loan repayments, he or she can measure it against pretax earnings to determine if the debt can be serviced.

$5,000,000 x .13 = $ 650,000
Plus term loan repayments +500,000

Total annual debt service $1,150,000

The company's net adjusted EBIT is inadequate to service the debt: i.e., $1 million is not as large as $1.15 million.

There is more. The target company has been overstating cost of goods sold by approximately $650,000 per year, which the financial buyer discovered during his or her due diligence visit. Thus, the company's net adjusted EBIT-D is $1.65 million, which is comfortably above debt service: $1.5 million/$1.65 million = 1.1 x.

Next, the lender will ask the financial buyer to put up at least 20 percent of the purchase price so he or she will have something at risk. If your asking price is $5 million, the combination of the financial buyer's loan of $2.5 million and equity investment of $1 million (the buyer's 20 percent investment) totals $3.5 million. The balance of the purchase price is likely to be in the form of a back-end payment to you, such as a $1.5 million noncompete agreement.

A noncompete agreement, which will be discussed in Chapter 10, is like a subordinated, unsecured note without interest that you will receive in annual installments for five years. The financial buyer loves this instrument because the annual payments can be written off against earnings, thus reducing taxes; and showing goodwill on the balance sheet can be avoided, which would amortize over 25 years rather than 5 years for the noncompete agreement. Noncompete agreements save taxes and cash for the buyer.

In this example, if you sell to a financial buyer, all that you can be certain of is the $3.5 million cash received up front minus the broker's fee. That amount is roughly equal to net worth plus one year's earnings. The balance of the purchase price may be paid to you out of your company's earnings over five years—if there are earnings. You are at risk for 30 percent of the total purchase price. It is not the deal you wanted, but it is the only deal you may be offered. We will discuss methods for improving the terms in Chapter 10.

The principal difference between acquisition funds and financial buyers is that the former have pools of cash to add to the purchase price and the latter may not have more than $100 in cash to their names. Thus, in the above example, rather than the $1 million that the buyer puts up in the way of equity, the "poor boy" financial buyer may ask you to put up $900,000 of it via a subordinated note or sale lease back of the equipment or building. Try to find healthier buyers than this.

Tradeoffs

The strategic buyer may use a scorched earth military strategy in taking over your company. He or she is likely to close down your operation and move it to one of his symbiotic facilities in another town. Your employees may lose their jobs. The community may suffer. Or the strategic buyer may leave your facility in place but supplant management personnel and transfer the checkbook and power to his or her headquarters in another city. Your company will lose its locally

◆ **Figure 5.4** Overhead Reduction Tactics That Financial
Buyers Use To Increase Cash Flow

Personnel cuts	The number of accounts receivable clerks and accounts payable clerks will be reduced by half. Production personnel will be reduced by 10 percent or more.
Advertising	The financial buyer will bid out this work and seek lower-cost agencies with fresher ideas.
Legal fees	A new law firm, which will agree to work at a discounted rate and use faster, more experienced professionals, will be hired.
Accounting fees	The same applies to accountants. The low-bid, highest-quality accountant will win the account.
Health insurance	If your company is not part of a preferred provider organization with low-cost, catastrophic-based coverage, the financial buyer will move the company into one a millisecond after the closing. Health insurance costs are usually one of the highest overhead items.
Communications costs	Expect a new carrier, which will lower long-distance costs by 10 percent or more, and a lower cost overnight courier to be engaged.

owned flavor and community-mindedness, but most of the production
jobs will be saved.

The financial buyer will retain most of your key personnel. Indeed,
he or she will likely reward your managers with earnings bonuses and,
in some cases, equity incentives. This is because the financial buyer,
in most instances, understands finance but not operations and does not
intend to get involved with operations—that is, as long as his or her
monthly management fee is received. The financial buyer will make
deep cuts in overhead expenses to make certain the debt can be paid
down out of cash flow, thus protecting his or her personal guarantee
and management fee.

Figure 5.4 shows the overhead reduction tactics that you can
expect to be implemented almost immediately by the financial buyer.

For additional cost savings that you can do *before* the buyer takes the keys, see Chapter 13.

The Local Buyer

If neither the strategic buyer, the financial buyer nor the acquisition fund appears on your doorstep, you may have to sell the company to your management team or to a local investor who chooses to back your management team. In this instance you are probably going to hold a lot of paper, maybe 50 percent of the purchase price, and be paid out over 5 or more years. You may even get your company back in a few years laden with debt.

Selling your company to someone in the community who has a couple bucks in his or her pocket and the ability to shake a few more out of the local banks and golf club cronies is usually a terrible idea. More frequently than not, he or she will make a mess of the company and blame you for failing to disclose some important facts. You will be embarrassed when the business is forced to shut down, and local community leaders will beg you to come back, take it over and turn it around. This will mean that the money you received in the sale will probably have to be reinvested to turn the company around.

The Management Buyout

The *management buyout* (MBO) is similar to the leveraged buyout (LBO) in every respect save one. Your management team probably doesn't have the necessary capital and will either have to ask you to put up the $1 million of equity, using the electric sign manufacturer example, or raise it from an acquisition fund. If it does the latter, you will probably receive 70 percent of your target purchase price in cash, as in the financial buyer example above, and hold a 30-percent unsecured note or noncompete agreement for the balance.

If the management team is unable to locate an acquisition fund to put up $1 million in equity, it may ask you to *hold more paper*. This could be done in several ways, the most popular of which are as follows:

◆ Seller keeps the cash, accounts receivable and inventory as part of the purchase price.
◆ Buyer collects the accounts receivable for seller.

◆ Buyer sells the inventory for seller. When this is accomplished, the buyer has paid the seller $3.5 million.

◆ Seller takes a $1.5 million five-year note secured by plant and equipment for the balance.

This is not such a bad deal for the owner, especially if he or she knows and trusts the management personnel who will be responsible for paying the back-end payment. And if he or she is confident that the accounts receivable are collectible and the inventory is salable, the owner will probably see the full $5 million. Plus, by not securing the back-end payments with a lien on the current assets, the buyers will have a line of credit to buy raw materials with and carry new accounts receivable. If the seller demands that the company's assets secure his or her term loan, he or she breaks the deal because, without a line of credit to run the business, the managers will be starved out for lack of cash, and the business will fold.

The ESOP Purchase

If you have set aside a large amount of money in the employees' profit-sharing plan, you could elect to sell the company to your employees. In the *employee stock ownership plan* (ESOP) buyout, the role of the acquisition fund is played by the employees. They must agree to use their hard-earned retirement money to buy stock in the target company. This means transferring liquid, safe, publicly held government and corporate bonds, in many cases, for illiquid, highly leveraged stock in the company for which they work. Many employees—especially those nearing retirement—should not agree to this trade. They should elect to be cashed out or have their account transferred to an annuity fund at the time of purchase. For younger employees the ESOP buyout may be a good idea. It has worked very well for Avis Car Rental, an employee-owned company. It has not worked quite as well for Wierton Steel, another company where ownership was transferred via an ESOP buyout.

Summary

Figure 5.5 shows the five potential, logical buyers for every company, ranked in terms of maximum profitability and minimum risk to the seller.

◆ **Figure 5.5** Ranking the Universe of Buyers by Profitability to the Seller

---

Buyer Summary of Pluses and Minuses

Strategic buyer	Pluses	◆ Pays the highest price.
		◆ Pays all or mostly all cash.
	Minuses	◆ May move the entire company or every part of the company except production, to another city.
Financial buyer	Pluses	◆ Pays at least half the target purchase price in cash.
		◆ Retains your top managers and department heads and rewards them with stock incentives and/or bonuses.
	Minuses	◆ Asks you to finance some of the purchase price; generally over too long a time and without tangible or adequate collateral.
Acquisition fund	Pluses	◆ Pays more than the financial buyer but usually not the full price in cash up front.
	Minuses	◆ Generally offers a back-end payment of three to seven years without collateral.
Management buyout	Pluses	◆ Good people who know the business will be left to run it.
		◆ You transfer ownership to people you trust and respect, and whose feelings are likely to be mutual.
	Minuses	◆ You may receive less than half of the purchase price in cash.
		◆ Your back-end payment is dependent on the management team leveraging the current assets to the hilt, which puts the company and your payout at risk.

ESOP buyer	Pluses	◆ Good people who know the business will be left to run it.
		◆ If the ESOP is large, you may receive 70 percent or more of the target purchase price in cash.
	Minuses	◆ With almost every employee a shareholder, and most employees not knowing very much about management, the company could be torn with strife as soon as you turn in your keys to the front door.

The Strategic Add-On

You will find in Appendix III, the "Directory of Acquisition Funds," a description of some of the portfolio companies of the acquisition funds. These are companies that the acquisition funds have previously acquired and currently operate.

Once the managers of the acquisition funds have stabilized the companies in their portfolios, they search for strategic add-ons. These are small-sized and medium-sized companies that compete with or are in similar businesses as their portfolio companies. If you fit that criteria, you may receive an offer for your company that bears the price earmarks of a strategic buy but has some of the terms of a financial buy.

Endnotes

1. Gilpin, Kenneth N., "Brands Still Easier To Buy Than Create," *The New York Times*, September 14, 1992, C-1.
2. Ibid.

Communications with Employees

◆◆◆◆◆◆◆◆◆

A seriously interested suitor is going to visit your business and walk through the facilities at least three different times. By the third visit, the suitor and his or her colleagues will want to interview key personnel. The potential buyer will likely send in auditors and an appraisal firm. That's a lot of strangers wandering through your shop, and your employees will ask questions. If yours is a union shop, fireworks could erupt.

The Union's Concern

Most union officials know by now that, if the company for which they work is purchased on an *assets* basis, its contract could be canceled. If it is purchased on a *stock* basis, its contract cannot be altered because all contracts are transferred to the new owner *in situ*. In some parts of the country, union officials are quite sophisticated in the means by which they can abort acquisitions, using very basic tactics. Let me tell you of a personal experience.

The Wheelbarrow Test

Slashing excessive labor costs (i.e., firing people, throwing out the union and changing benefit programs) may be the only economic justification for a purchase. If the buyer can roll back labor costs 20 percent, he can service debt; if he cannot, the acquisition cannot be justified. You will find acquisition candidates with these characteristics among capital equipment manufacturers in the Rust Belt.

For buyers who grew up on John Wayne and Randolph Scott westerns as I did, they may have a romanticized vision of their ability to walk into a steel forging plant; ask the hulking head of the union (an ex-Pittsburgh Steeler middle linebacker) to step outside for a minute; and then explain to him why canceling the union contract, lowering wages and increasing the earnings-based, profit-sharing plan will make him and all other employees happier. The buyer had better have a lot of courage and charm to willfully go face to face with the toughest guy in the plant. Put it this way: After the confrontation, the buyer should not take a nap under a tree outside the plant!

The union head knows that in an asset sale the buyer can terminate the collective bargaining agreement. As soon as someone discovers that the rental car in the parking lot belongs to a potential buyer, word will spread through the plant like wildfire: *The plant's about to be sold. We'll be working for peanuts again. There'll be layoffs.* If a buyer is not built to tough it out with labor, he or she had better not buy a capital equipment manufacturer with the intent to capture cash flow by busting the union.

A Poetic Warning

I put on my best Randolph Scott mask one day and entered a plant outside Chicago to see how 160 people stamped out steel parts on 1,500-ton presses. The plant was put up for sale by a man we will call Ralph, and although it was earning $2.9 million EBIT, I could obtain a cash overadvance on asset-based loans and fully leverage the acquisition by doing an asset sale, busting the union and rehiring 120 out of 150 plant workers at $11 per hour versus the $15 per hour that Ralph was paying them. I had visited the mayor of the town and arranged for an Urban Development Action Grant to finance a new addition to the plant; thus, after a year of being the industry's lowest-cost manufacturer, I would rehire 60 to 80 plant workers. But a year of unemployment lines is not a reason for rejoicing in an abandoned mining and textile town of the Rust Belt. The citizens there have endured the mushroom-growing scenario before—mushrooms are grown in dark basements where manure is thrown on them at regular intervals.

After walking through the plant with Harold, the manager, I spent some time with Phil, the purchasing agent, and Flo, the chief administrative officer in charge of union negotiations. It was a few days before Christmas, the little town was cheerful and I was beginning to feel welcome. I bedded down in the local hotel and slept comfortably, dreaming about the Van Gogh of LBOs—the fully leveraged financing and excess cash flow after debt service. It was a financier's dream come true—buying a $2.9 million EBIT business with table money only, limited risk and enough cash flow to pay myself a $500,000 annual management fee.

The next day I drove into the parking lot of the plant and sashayed into the building to what I thought would be a red carpet sprinkled with gardenias and lined with plant workers singing, *Joy to the world, David hath come.* What I got was the following poem, written the night before by a plant worker who had pieced together the story. The poem was posted all over the building.

The Night before the Sale

'Twas the night before the sale when all through the plant,
The union was crying. . . he won't. . . he can't.
And Ralphie and his bank were waiting with care,
In hopes that the money soon would be there.
The employees were nestled all snug in their beds,
While visions of bankruptcy danced in their heads.
And Harold and the office kept it under their cap,
While the radio and newspaper fed us their crap.
When out of New Mexico there arose such a clatter,
He wants more money. . . make his wallet fatter and fatter.
Reporters were running, and flew like a flash,
Ralphie's not happy. . . he must have more cash.
When, what to our wondering eyes should appear,
But a jet from out West, let's see what we hear.
More rapid than eagles his offers they came,
And he whistled, and shouted, and called them in vain.
Now Ralphie, now Harold, now Phil and Flosie,
I'll give you more money, you will be quite cozy.
Now Silver was trying, and started to crawl,

But Ralphie must have it. . . he must have it all.
So to the village, Silver he flew,
And talked to the mayor, and commissioners too.
While Ralphie's parts were being stacked to the roof,
The union knew nothing. . . they felt like a goof.
He was dressed all in leather, from his feet to his head,
And you knew in a minute. . . this cowboy's well fed.
A bundle of papers he had flung on his back,
And he looked like a peddler just opening his pack.
His droll little mouth was drawn up like a bow,
And up till now. . . the sale was all show.
A wink of his eye and a twist of his head,
Soon gave the mayor to know she had nothing to dread.
He ran off his mouth, and went straight to his work,
But she was not sure. . . was he smart. . . or a jerk?
And laying his finger aside of his nose,
He got her attention. . . and she hoped he'd propose.
He sprang from his chair, and she gave him a whistle,
And away they flew like the down on a thistle.
But they heard him explain as he drove out of sight,
"I'll buy the plant, then we'll party all night!"—Author Unknown

There is not much more that I can add to the poet laureate of Chicago, who said it better than I could: *If you're going to buy a plant and bust the union, you're walking on the fighting side of me.*

Another union-busting buyout in which I was involved took place in a pork processing plant, and the warning that the plant foreman gave to me from the union representative had the flavor of cut-up parts stuffed into a hot dog grinder. *You tell Silver,* the note said, *that if I ordered 20 carloads of SOBs and they only sent Silver, I'd still pay for the order.*

Union busting to generate cash flow is a miserable experience, and you had better have the mental and physical armor to do it. If you intend to union bust, remember to buy all three kinds of insurance when you rent a car.

Whom To Tell What

As soon as you have decided to sell your company, the objectives and reasons for the sale should be presented to key members of management. The reasons for explaining this up front are several: (1) to offer them the opportunity to acquire the company; (2) to discuss the transmittal of this information to employees; and (3) to gain their support in making the transfer of ownership as smooth as possible.

When To Tell

Business is war. Sun Tzu wrote over 5,000 years ago that you win by putting yourself into the mind of the *opposing commander* and countering his next move with a preceding move of your own. The opposing commander is the *buyer*. Victory is getting your price with as much cash up front as possible. Total victory is getting your price— all cash and all up front.

You do not achieve this by telling your employees that the company is for sale until you have the cash nearly in hand. If they ask you what these people in the rental cars and tasseled loafers are doing walking through the plant, you can say, without being untruthful, that they are considering making an investment in the company.

The general must tell his lieutenants about the war, and this should be done up front to prepare them for interviews by one or more buyer groups. It is possible that the lieutenants will conspire with each other to tell horror stories to the buyers to scare them off and buy the company for themselves. Although this is not likely to happen, due to the general lack of sophistication of lieutenants in medium-sized companies, it is worth mentioning. You could head off a mutiny by offering each lieutenant a bonus equal to a percentage of the sales price above a base number.

To avoid the potential of a *coup d'état*, do not call all the lieutenants into the conference room at the same time. Speak to them one at a time and tell each one that he or she is important to you and that you would not want to go through a change in ownership process without his or her direct involvement. You should also say that this information is strictly confidential and should not be repeated, except to the potential buyers.

The lieutenants, after all, may not like you. They may not regard you as a wise, kind, sensitive and brilliant leader. They may think you are an old scrooge who wouldn't give a dime for the well-being of the employees who have given their lives, souls and hearts to the company. Behind the smiling "Good morning, Mr. Smith" may be gritted teeth hiding the words of Lady Macbeth, "Out, out, damn'd spot." There may be a Polonius behind the tapestry of every department head whom you must inform about the pending sale so that the due diligence process can go smoothly.

What To Tell

If you could write the script for the interviews that the lieutenants have with the buyers, the emphasis would be on *opportunity*. Strategic buyers pay up for opportunities, and financial buyers pay up for leveragable assets and cash flow. The numbers cannot be embellished, but department heads should attempt to persuade even financial buyers that there are several elegant opportunities for revenue and cash flow growth once ownership has changed hands. Product extensions can be pushed through the company's existing marketing channels. New marketing channels should be opened to push the company's existing product line through. And inexpensive means of capturing more customers should be found.

"But why haven't the owners implemented these interesting strategic plans?" the prospective buyer may ask the department head.

"How many pairs of pants can the guy put on in the morning? I mean, he is pretty well off and has never seen the need to take risks to grow the business," the lieutenant answers. In many cases, that statement is certainly truthful.

You may not have a grasp on some of the marketing and cost savings opportunities of which your lieutenants are aware. Perhaps they attend more seminars than you do or read the trade journals more thoroughly. Therefore, spend some additional time with them, and ask them about changes they might implement if they owned the company and strategies they might put into place. Have them do some cash flow projections and *stress test* them; that is, raise the amount of capital needed up front and lower the revenue projections. If the projections still look good, tell your M&A broker about them.

Summary

Telling senior officers and key employees about the possible sale of the business is a delicate matter. It should be handled on a *need-to-know basis*. For example, if a buyer is coming for a preliminary due diligence visit, it may not be critical that he or she meet with anyone other than the owner. But if the buyer indicates that your asking price is fairly close to his or her idea of a fair price and if he or she has signed a letter of intent to that effect, then the buyer will want to interview key employees and senior officers. You will want to prepare them.

Putting the House in Order

◆◆◆◆◆◆◆◆◆

Appearance Affects Price

"Mr. Smith," said the buyer to one of my clients, "I have been in many factories in my day. I love them—the sounds, the smells, the oil and grit, the precision-like noises. You have all of that in your factory, yet there is an orderliness to your operations that I have not seen before."

I was taking the buyer through a company's plant where valves and water tanks were being manufactured—a messy, noisy operation at best. But the cleanliness of the seller's plant, the orderliness with which parts were maintained and scrap was stored and hauled and the absence of cheesecake photos and cigarettes dangling from the lips of oil-stained faces actually enhanced the selling price. The plant was presented in its best possible light: It was obvious that people took great pains to maintain the best working conditions.

A few months ago, I walked a buyer through a roofing materials distributor where the dust was an inch thick, the forklift trucks were covered with black oil spills and driven by young men who thought they were A.J. Foyt (the well-known race car driver), and the recordkeeping (although suited to the owner's chaotic management style) looked like a hurricane had hit a stationery store. The buyer said to me, "I haven't worked hard for 30 years to save a million bucks to buy a filthy, messy business. I want something with more order to it."

A business's appearance affects its price. Dust on the inventory immediately tips off the buyer that some of the inventory doesn't turn over frequently. Slow turning (or is it no turning?) inventory is worth less than fresh goods. An accounts receivable clerk with a full ashtray on the desk, an empty aspirin container in the wastebasket and a telephone handset that looks like it has been eaten into by an enraged Doberman will give the impression that the company's customers do not pay well or quickly.

Equipment that is being held together with oily rags and baling wire will certainly give the impression that megabucks will have to be spent in the near future to replace equipment. Inexpensively replacing the equipment before selling the company will bring in a higher selling price. Have your equipment appraiser walk you through the numbers.

Computerized Operations

It is increasingly difficult to sell a company whose administrative functions are not computerized. These include accounts receivable, accounts payable, inventory, payroll and general ledger. The price that American Express paid for mutual fund manager IDS was lowered 20 percent because the seller's operations were not fully computerized.

When a privately held company's inventory is not perpetually maintained on computer, this fact literally screams to the buyer that a serious understatement of income taxes exists, which will complicate and possibly prevent a sale.

Earlier, we addressed the issue of overstating raw material costs to reduce income and income taxes, and understating inventory with write-downs and reserves. The only way around this is to reverse the entries and pay the underpaid taxes. An alternative is to inform the buyer that cost of goods sold has been overstated and that you are willing to indemnify the buyer for underpaid income taxes in the event of an IRS audit. Count on an audit. The IRS flags recently acquired companies for audit. The IRS looks for indemnification language in the purchase agreement and comes after the buyer and the seller for underpaid taxes. The indemnification passes the buck to the seller. You could pay the full amount of the purchase price to the IRS if the transaction is audited and the IRS finds that you underpaid income taxes for several years.

It is best to put the excess warehouse inventory back into cost of goods sold over a period of three to five years, raise the profitability and pay the taxes that you have been saving. This is not as painful as you might think. Inflation has raised the price of goods in your warehouse; thus it will take fewer rolls of textiles or steel to make up the unpaid taxes that were avoided a decade ago. In effect, the IRS has made you an interest-free loan with a future payback. In presenting your financial statements to the M&A broker, be sure to explain this adjustment so that he or she can inform the buyers. The adjustment is a material fact, and you must be up front about it.

"You Have Sold the Business Once Before"

A company cannot be sold twice. If you have borrowed heavily on the company's assets and pocketed some or most of the loan through sales commissions, salaries and perks, a knowledgeable buyer will offer you $1.00 for the company's assets plus the assumption of liabilities. I have seen owners wax horrified looks when they cannot leverage the company to the hilt and then sell it for more than its debt. But that would be selling the company twice. It is best to repay as much debt as possible before putting the company on the market.

If the company owes you money and it appears on the balance sheet as *notes payable to shareholder*, you cannot reasonably expect to be compensated for the loan. Most buyers will look at the note as equity. If you owe the company money and it appears on the balance sheet as *accounts receivable from shareholder*, you cannot reasonably expect to be compensated for that asset. You have sold the business once before by borrowing money from it. An extraordinary amount of naiveté is displayed in leaving these items unattended to at the time of the sale, and naiveté will be reflected in less attractive offers.

There are exceptions. If you have borrowed on all the company's assets to develop an innovative and important niche product that fits into the marketing channels owned by a nationally known consumer products manufacturer, that buyer might be willing to pay off your loans and give you a bonus for patents, copyrights, trademarks and intellectual know-how. But strategic buyers are fewer and harder to bring to the table than financial buyers. They may pay twice what the business is worth on paper, but to convince them to do so, you must convince them of your sizable opportunities.

A friend of mine in the electronics contracting business bought a similar but smaller company in the early 1990s for a price equal to an assumption of the target company's short-term debt, but he left the owners' personal guarantees on the mortgages and equipment loans. The owners sold the company but remained personally obligated for about $1 million of term loans.

I asked my friend how he managed to pull that off.

He said, "It's the '90s. The guys would have gone under if I hadn't paid off their bank loans. But I wanted them to stick around, so I made them stay on some of the paper."

"But what's their advantage?" I asked.

"Bankruptcy avoidance," he answered.

Appraisals

There is no better time to update inventory, equipment, building and real estate appraisals than at the time the company is being offered for sale. Not only is it necessary for insurance purposes to keep your appraisals current, but if the appraised values of these assets are greater than the amounts shown on the books, you can obtain a higher price for the company. Up-to-date appraisals available for potential buyers to review also show your seriousness and professionalism.

You should contact your commercial bankers for the names of the most highly regarded appraisers in the community. Commercial bankers have a simple way of judging the quality of an appraiser. Have they cost me money in the past by coming up with inflated numbers?

I sent questionnaires to the most active buyers in the country, asking them to name the *best* equipment and real estate appraisers with whom they had worked. Their names, addresses, telephone and fax numbers, references and industries of specialization are provided in detail in Appendix I. Note that some appraisers act as auctioneers and liquidators. If you want to spin off some assets for cash prior to selling your company, you might hire one of the appraisal firms to do that.

The selection of these firms by acquisition funds is based on the fact that their appraised values hold up at auction more than those of other firms. This also implies that the valuations are for the most part lower than those of other firms because the appraisers want to retain the acquisition funds as clients.

Verbal Understandings

Prior to the sale of a business, all verbal understandings should be committed to written agreements. These may include salespersons' commissions, definitions of territories that salespersons cover, manufacturer's representative agreements, licenses, joint-ventures, supplier contracts and the like. If your business distributes widgets for a Korean manufacturer under a handshake agreement, a buyer will ask you to get that understanding in writing. To avoid alerting the supplier that the company is for sale, get a written agreement before the buyer asks for it. A written contract has value; a verbal understanding is not defensible in most states. Nobody knows this better than Sam M. Walton, the late founder of Wal-Mart Stores, Inc., who almost went under due to a verbal *understanding*.

Sam Walton's Surprise

In the late spring of 1950, the landlord of Sam Walton's Ben Franklin store in Newport, Arkansas, called at the store to have a business talk with his young tenant. What the landlord had to say sent a stunned and distraught Sam flying to his lawyer's office.

"My God, what's the matter?" asked Fred Pickens, Jr.

"My lease! My lease!" said Sam Walton. "It's up at the end of the year!"

"Well, just renew it. You've got an option to do that, I suppose."

The lawyer watched Sam Walton, the 32-year-old merchant *genius* of Newport, lower his head and stare glumly at the rug, shuffling his feet in agitation.

"No," said Sam Walton weakly, "I don't." (Sam's lease actually contained a renewal option *at terms to be negotiated*, which is really no option because the owner could set impossible conditions.)

Fred Pickens, Jr. rushed to the rescue and tried to negotiate a renewal of the lease. It was critical for Sam: No other location was suitable and available for a Ben Franklin store in Newport. If he couldn't hang on to his Front Street location, he'd be out of business.

The lawyer offered Holmes, Sr. higher rent; he refused. He tried to interest the landlord in various other terms but kept running into a stone wall. Finally, he grasped the real situation.

"It's no good," he told Sam. "I hope the next time you take over a lease from somebody, you check to make certain it contains a proper renewal clause. The landlord is not going to let you keep the store. The plain truth is he wants his son to run a Ben Franklin in that building! You've shown the whole town what a money-maker it can be."

Fred Pickens, Jr. watched the color drain out of his client's face. "Looks like you're finished," he said.

The lawyer saw Sam clenching and unclenching his fists, staring at his hands.

Sam straightened up. "No, Fred," he said. "I'm not whipped. I found Newport, and I found the store. I can find another town and another Ben Franklin. Just wait and see!"[1]

Supplier Relationships

You may not have reviewed your written distributorships or bank loan agreements recently. They may contain *notification* clauses in the event of a sale of the business or a transfer of ownership. Certainly, if the business is sold while a loan is outstanding and you intend to transfer the guarantor to the buyer, the bank needs to be notified and its approval sought.

Suppliers may rely on your continued involvement in the business to maintain a supply relationship. Further, you could be selling to one of their competitors, and they may not regard that favorably. If you need their approval to sell the company, this is not a negotiation to enter into until the buyer has spent some money and time on due diligence and has made you an offer in writing that is generally acceptable.

If you own a franchised business, you may be restricted from selling it to an outside buyer without offering it to the franchisor first. Other signed agreements have their own restrictions on selling the company. Your time would be well spent to review all the company's written agreements before the buyers ask to see documents.

Regulatory Approval

Note that if your company has been dumping waste into the soil around its plant for the last 30 years, its sale is going to be delayed by at least six months (longer if your business is located in New Jersey) until you obtain the approval of the state and/or federal environmental agencies. If you sell the company without this approval and the buyer is subsequently fined for your toxicity problem, you may end up returning the purchase price or losing it in litigation.

Summary

If you try to sell your company that is located in a rented building, if the building's owners dumped waste into the soil prior to renting it to you and if that waste has caused an Environmental Protection Agency violation, the sale will be aborted or at least delayed until the agency calculates the damages and the building's owner pays for a clean-up.

If you are selling a medical practice or a service business in which patient (or client) personal records are maintained, selling the patient (or client) records is a crime. These records are the intrinsic value of the business, yet they are nonsalable. Rather than sell them, you *transfer them for safekeeping* to the new owner who pays you a noncompete agreement, funded over time, for the business. A specialized broker is needed to sell a business in a regulated industry.

Endnotes

1. Trimble, Vance, *Sam Walton: The Inside Story of America's Richest Man*, New York: Penguin Group, 1990, pp. 56–57.

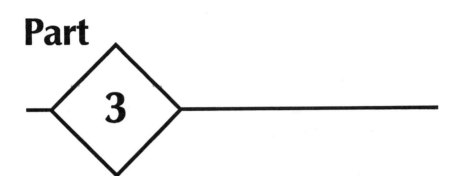

Part 3

Negotiating with the Buyer

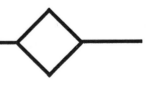

8

The Valuation Process

◆◆◆◆◆◆◆◆◆

Price

What is a company worth? It is worth what a buyer is willing to pay for it.

But the acquisition business is one in which price could be anywhere, depending on the buyer. Again there is much noise and very little signal. I will try to clear up the confusion.

Manufacturers of *nonproprietary products*—that is, no patent protection or no national brand name products—and distribution companies are worth 4 to 5 times the most recent 12-month adjusted cash flow (EBIT-D). The more value these companies add to raw materials, the more rapid their growth; the stronger their management team, the more important their *franchise* in the industry. The more their opportunities for expansion of cash flow and the larger their customer list, the greater the premium above 5 times adjusted cash flow that a buyer is likely to pay. The less value-added, the slower the growth of cash flow; the weaker the management team, the smaller its significance in the market; the fewer the opportunities it addresses and the smaller its list of customers, the closer to 3 or 4 times adjusted cash flow that a buyer is likely to pay.

Other factors that influence price are the length of time that the company has been for sale, the orderliness of its plant and warehouse, the existence of audited financial statements and crisp, orderly, accurate recordkeeping, the company's location, the absence of unsigned agreements, the existence of litigation and the urgency of the sale.

Divorce or the death of a spouse actively involved in the business creates a more urgent sale and deflates price. Messy recordkeeping deflates price as well, in the same manner that a car without a dashboard full of controls sells for less than one that has one. A company that has been on the market for some time sells for less than does one that has not been shopped. Two companies that are identical in absolutely every respect will be sold at two different prices if one is located more than a two-hour drive from the nearest metropolitan airport and the other is located in a metropolitan market of 250,000 people or more (location, location, location).

Adjusted Cash Flow

In the practical world of acquisitions, the words *profits* or *earnings* are not relevant measures of a company's economic validity. These words mean something in the public market; indeed, they are the most important measure of a company's worth to stock buyers, particularly as the numerator in fractions where revenues and net worth are the denominators. But in buying and selling companies, the most important number is *adjusted cash flow*: the amount of money available to service debt (in the case of a financial buyer) and the amount of money available to contribute to the buyer's cash flow (in the case of a strategic buyer).

Cash flow is derived by adding to net profit before taxes all noncash charges to the operating expenses. These charges are typically depreciation, depletion and amortization. In some companies many noncash charges are reinvested each year to replenish fixed assets. This occurs in rental companies, such as automobile renting or leasing, and with retail video stores. In calculating cash flow for these kinds of companies, only the depreciation of the fixed assets not held for lease should be added back—that is, fixtures, vans and leasehold improvements.

◆ Figure 8.1   Calculation of Adjusted Cash Flow

($000s)	Annual Operating Statements	
	Presentation by the Seller's Accountants	**Calculation of Adjusted Cash Flow by Buyer**
Revenues	$10,000,000	$10,000,000
Cost of sales	7,500,000	7,300,000(a)
Gross profit	2,500,000	2,700,000
Operating expenses		
Selling expenses	500,000	475,000(b)
Commissions	450,000	350,000(c)
General & admin. expenses	1,300,000	700,000(d)
Depreciation	200,000	—(e)
Total operating expenses	2,450,000	1,525,000
Net operating income	50,000	1,175,000
Interest expense	40,000	—
Net profit before taxes	$ 10,000	
Adjusted EBIT-D		$ 1,175,000

Add-Backs

(a) The owner also owns an affiliated company that buys some raw materials, stores them and delivers them to the target company at a $200,000 profit.

(b) The owner takes his wife to three trade shows a year and stays a week beyond each show for rest and relaxation.

(c) The owner receives a commission on all sales of 1 percent paid to his marketing services company.

(d) Numerous family expenses are paid out of the general and administrative category, including excessive rent, excessive insurance premiums to a brother-in-law, the owner's salary of $250,000 per annum, his car insurance and gasoline card and $25,000 in family expenses.

(e) Depreciation is on plant and equipment that does not need replacement.

Adjusted cash flow means adding to cash flow those costs that will not exist once the company is sold. These include the owner's salary, personal expenses of the owner paid by the company, perquisites— such as salaries paid to family members whose services are not vital, payment for trips or conventions in which a family member is taken along, rent paid to the owner over and above the market rate, and interest expenses on loans that will be repaid upon the sale of the company. Figure 8.1 shows an example.

If you are using five times adjusted cash flow as the determinant of purchase price, the company whose operating statement appears in Figure 8.1 is worth approximately $5.4 million. But wait. Don't rush into the broker's office with a price of $5.4 million chiseled into your brain. You haven't deducted from net operating income the *costs that the owner will incur to run the company* after you're teeing up the little white balls at Desert Mountain in Carefree, Arizona.

In the first place, you may be an important cog in the wheel that makes your company operate. The buyer does not need to pay your replacement CEO the $1 million per annum that you are pulling out in compensation, perks, commissions and benefits; but a full-time chief executive officer is a new and significant cost. The buyer may want to be that person or serve as a not-actively-involved chairperson and be compensated for providing advice, assistance and board-level services. New ownership will certainly incur additional travel or communication costs, and the new owner may feel a need for life insurance policies to fund a stock buy-back agreement with co-investors and more interchange with consultants and accountants. He or she may wish to increase the compensation of certain key managers who you may have underpaid but are vital to a new owner who will not be on the premises full-time.

Total these expenses, add a 20-percent margin for error and deduct them from $1.175 million. Let's say the net adjusted cash flow amount is then $875,000. The purchase price the buyer may feel comfortable in offering is $4.375 million, or five times $875,000.

The No EBIT Price

Although you can expect to be offered a price based on a multiple of adjusted EBIT, what can you expect in the way of a price if there is no EBIT? If you have losses and owe a ton to the banks, can you expect to sell the company and put any money in your pocket, or is that a dream? One sure way of adding more cash to the selling price is to begin selling information about your company's product or service.

The answer is that, if your company is in business, it has value. The value may be minimal—that is, the small amount of market share that your company is taking from its competitors. Or the value may be in your patents or trademarks. Biotechnology companies may have all their value in the future opportunities that their scientists are developing in the laboratories.

Yes, the company has value: But if it is in the company's potential, the seller will more than likely have to share some of the risk of the future potential being realized. This means a purchase price with very little cash up front and a lot of the purchase price tied to a percentage of the company's future sales or cash flow.

Summary

Valuation of the privately held company is based to a large extent on the reconstruction of cash flow. That involves adding back to income the expenses that will not be charged under new ownership. For example, your perks would be added back. In most instances a portion of your salary and other personal expenses would be added back.

If there is no cash flow or negative cash flow, the company will be valued on its balance sheet and off-balance sheet assets, such as customer lists, brand names, blueprints, intellectual know-how and people skills. These do not compute as easily as cash flow, but they have *opportunity value*—that is, what a new owner can do with them.

◆

9

Obtaining a
Higher Price

◆◆◆◆◆◆◆◆◆

The Strategic Buyer

In selling your company to a strategic buyer, emphasize all the opportunities for growth that exist but that you could not take advantage of due to not having *key people*. This plays directly into the large corporation manager's towering ego and will help obtain a higher price for your company.

Here are some opportunities to drop into the conversation:

◆ "We should be opening new marketing channels."
◆ "We have thought of the following but just haven't had the time or the personnel to do them."
◆ "We've been approached to bid on jobs in that industry but just haven't gotten around to it."

Upping the Price of a "Publishing Company"

One of the great franchises to own is a publishing company, particularly one that is the dominant provider of information to a particular region, market or industry. Newspaper and magazine publishers are frequently sold at prices not arrived at by deriving adjusted EBIT and multiplying it by the appropriate factor.

Rather, publishers are sold at a multiple of their number of subscribers. A similar multiplier applies to television and radio stations. The multiplier is listeners as measured by Arbitron or an independent data collections service. The factor used to measure price might be as high as $500 per subscriber or listener but is usually in the area of the price paid by the subscriber for one year's subscription.

What does this mean to you? You're thinking: I produce spaghetti. I don't have subscribers. That may be true, but every company has *publishing potential*. If you sell information about your product or service and maintain a list of subscribers to your newsletter or magazine, you can *double the price for which your business* is sold.

Subscriber lists and customer lists are off-balance sheet assets. Because a sophisticated buyer knows many ways to derive additional cash flow streams from your *information customers*, these lists are worth from $1 to $100 per name.

When a publishing company is taken over by a strategic buyer or a corporate raider, the publishing company's cash flow can be multiplied by opening the following channels:

- Resale of news stories to other publishers.
- Repackaging of stories as video tapes.
- Repackaging of stories as audio cassettes.
- Seminars led by highly regarded columnists.
- Capturing critical information on electronic media and reselling it as a "news utility," such as Reuters and the Telerate subsidiary of *The Wall Street Journal*.
- Books made up of special interest articles, such as *The New York Times Cookbook*.
- Articles on topical issues such as health care, diet, exercise recipes and gardening sold to small-town newspapers as "Sunday Features."
- Joint ventures with direct mail firms that seek to sell products via mail order to the newspaper's readers.
- Ownership of television and radio stations to spread the cost of gathering news stories.
- Target marketing—the gathering of health care articles in magazine form for resale to physicians for their waiting rooms.

◆ Newsletter publishing—the sale of special interest articles to selected consumers.

The strategic buyer also applies his or her own abilities and skills to multiply cash flow. This happens frequently, to the gratitude of owners who are fortunate enough to sell to large corporations.

A customer is a *user*. He or she buys your product or service and uses it. You may include an information package with your product; but if you are not asking for a response from your user, you are missing a profitable opportunity.

Users want to know that they are using your product or service to its greatest extent. They want to maximize their product satisfaction but generally derive only a portion of the benefits that are available. This is particularly true in the personal computer industry. To overcome that problem, computer manufacturers offer their customers the opportunity to join *users groups*. Moreover, they charge customers to join users groups, thus making money on the sale of the product and on the sale of information about the product.

Your nonpublishing company can also generate cash flow streams from selling information, thus raising its sale price. First and foremost, collect the names, addresses and other data about your customers.

To gather names of users, package with the product a *bounce back card* that captures the name, address, telephone number and other data about your customers. Once you have collected names and information about your customer in a computer, you are a direct response marketer and an information seller. You have doubled the value of your business.

Direct Response Marketing

Direct response marketing has profound leverage. It is the ultimate way to maximize sales for a number of reasons:

◆ It asks for a response.
◆ It captures the name, address and other information about the consumer.
◆ It enables the vendor to test the headlines and text of the mailer.
◆ It minimizes subjective judgments.
◆ It builds a list of nonconsumers.

The Basics of Direct Marketing

The first step is to rent several lists of names of consumers who buy products or services similar to yours via the mail. You can rent these lists from list brokers and test them by sending the same mailer to a random selection of names from each list.

The same procedure applies in telemarketing. The mailer (or caller) can describe the product or service and then ask for the order and/or provide a bounce back: "Send for our free catalog" or "To request more information, send for. . . ."

The direct response message can also be placed in a newspaper or magazine and on television or radio, where an 800 telephone number is provided.

By delivering the same message to a variety of lists or media and then using the best-responding lists (or media) to test variations of the message, the company can learn which consumers respond to precisely which version of the message, thereby minimizing subjective judgments. In the meantime a large list of generically interested nonconsumers is created from people who request the catalog or product information but do not buy.

List Costs   Names rent for five to ten cents each. If the names on the list recently ordered a product by mail order—within the last 90 days—and paid more than $100 for it, the names are worth closer to ten cents each. The cheaper names purchased a product via mail order within the last 12 months but paid less for the product. The older the list, the lower its value because consumers' addresses and circumstances change. It is better to spend a few cents more and rent a fresher list. Note: List brokers have a minimum order, usually 3,000 to 5,000 names.

You can eliminate duplicate names and avoid sending several mailers to the same address by having a list management firm do a *merge-purge-dupe-drop* run through its computer. Lists are rented on cheshire labels or computer printer paper, depending on the vendor's preference.

The cost of testing 5 separate lists, each with 20,000 names, and applying the lowest postage costs that we discuss in Chapter 12, is shown below:

100,000 x .075	= $	7,500
100,000 x .11	=	11,000
Presort costs	=	2,000
Stationery costs	=	3,000
Copywriting, design and production of mailer	=	7,000
Total		$30,500

This is roughly equivalent to the cost of buying one-quarter of a page in a popular national monthly magazine (plus a 15-percent advertising agency fee). Assume that the 5 lists produce a .5 percent response (500 orders) for a $100 product, or $50,000 in sales. If the vendor's cost of goods sold is less than $19,500 (39 percent), he or she would receive $30,500 investment back in cash and could test more lists, or the highest-responding list.

A direct response mailer, such as the one described here, could have generated a 3-percent response, that is, $300,000. The leverage on $30,500 is:

$$\$300,000 + \$30,500 = 9.8$$

The larger the response, the higher the leverage.

Telemarketing is the oral equivalent of a direct response mailer. A trained caller with a script calls a list of names that was selected because it has produced interest in the consumer's generic area in the past. This method is superior to direct response mailers because the caller can ask and obtain response to dozens of questions whereas the direct response mailer is limited to asking the respondent to order or request information about the product or service. The more expensive the consumer product—cars, tractors, homes, recreational vehicles—the more affordable telemarketing becomes.

Among the more compelling reasons to use direct response mailers or telemarketing is that they permit the vendor to acquire a great deal of information about the consumer and the nonconsumer. Traditional advertising lacks this feature and lacks the immediacy of the sale.

Ask yourself this question: When I sell my company to a strategic buyer, what will my sales force be worth? Probably very little because the buyer will have a bigger and perhaps better one. But what will my computer-based direct response marketing system be worth to a strategic buyer? Lots of money. The Information Age is not ephemeral. Information collection and processing systems are very valuable.

Artificial Intelligence as Marketing Support   If you utilize direct response mailers and telemarketing (with computer assistance) to lower costs and speed up data messaging, you will know, in some detail, your customers and their preferences. And you will gain the leverage that comes from that information. Some of the most fascinating developments in consumer testing are not happening in advertising agencies but in computer software firms. When their power is felt in large consumer products companies, advertising firms who have not adopted these methods as a primary research tool need to catch up quickly. Looking ahead to the next decade, I foresee a rapid downsizing of the advertising industry and a rise in *artificial intelligence-based telemarketing*.

Several strategically acquired companies have begun using *artificial intelligence* (A-I) to test consumer response to products and services and to ascertain what factors determine why a consumer buys a certain product and why he or she will or will not repurchase the product at a future date. The value of A-I in the *test* phase of consumer research is that the computer calculates large amounts of data rapidly and identifies trends that create *decision trees* to aid the user in developing follow-up questions and interpreting the data. "Look at the relationship," says the A-I software. "Mercedes-Benz owners used the word engineering an average of five times during the interview." Out of thousands of interviews, the A-I research software can pluck the response that shows that certain car owners relate to certain key words. I have seen a Mercedes-Benz dealer increase its sales 300 percent using A-I to enhance consumer research.

You might wish to investigate A-I software packages that are applicable to consumer research. But A-I is only as good as the telemarketing script.

Lexi: An Example of the Leverage of Customer Information

Robin Richards, CEO of Lexi International, Los Angeles, operates an A-I-based telemarketing consumer research company that tests products for nationally branded consumer marketing companies. Lexi has delivered sales increases of more than 400 percent for some of its clients while reducing their advertising expenditures. For a dealer in European luxury cars, whose advertising budget was roughly $500 per car sale, Lexi cut the cost to $375. Whereas the dealer had been selling an average of 5 cars per weekend, Lexi drove sales up to 20 cars per weekend in some instances.

Entering Lexi's offices on Sunset Boulevard, one is struck by the appearance and image conveyed by the hundreds of telemarketers sitting in front of PCs and speaking into headset telephones.

"Who are these people?" I asked Richards.

"They are actors and actresses between assignments. They are excellent communicators and enjoy the work because it is so much like acting," he said.

Lexi uses A-I to generate a substantial amount of background data on the consumer before the telemarketer is given his or her name and address. By accessing publicly available data, the telemarketer knows the consumer's address; whether he or she owns a house; the make, model and year of the consumer's car (from which a trade-in price can be established); if there is a swimming pool (from census data); if his or her home backs on a golf course or tennis courts; and more. The telemarketer can engage the consumer in conversation at any number of levels, and the computer can match responses against a personality characteristics grid. The telemarketer can close with a trade-in offer on the consumer's car and a special invitation to visit the showroom.

The invitation (the direct response mailer) is an engraved card with the consumer's name in calligraphy. The response rate to the special showroom has run as high as *80 percent*, and the close rate in the dealer's showroom is equally high, owing to the deep segmentation and prequalification accorded the process by A-I.

Lexi charges its customers less than the amount they would typically spend on a month's advertising to sell 40 cars, but with Lexi managing their marketing, the dealers sell over 120 cars per month. The Lexi system works for a wide array of consumer products—bank loans, home sales, consumer electronics, personal computer systems—as well as for industrial products and financial services.

Club Orange: An Example of the Value of Customer Data

Montreal-based Provigo, an innovative food wholesaler with 235 supermarkets and convenience stores in Canada and $6.2 billion in sales, introduced Club Orange in March 1989. Members must buy at least $50 of products and fill out a form that includes questions about family shopping patterns and demographic information.

In return, members receive a Club Orange membership, saving certificates, a bimonthly newsletter and nutritious menu suggestions. The savings certificates are redeemable at other merchants in the form of discounts on car repairs, fashion apparel and optical products. Provigo does not pay these merchants a fee; rather, it delivers customers to them and provides free publicity in its newsletters.

Other Club Orange benefits include advice on health and nutrition, menu suggestions, recipes, a toll-free hotline, classes on microwave cooking, a financial clinic during tax season and the use of a card that allows automatic debiting of the customer's bank account at the cash register. Provigo gave its shoppers a gift and asked for demographic information and family shopping patterns; in return, the shoppers willingly provided the information. And the testing is paid for by other merchants who honor the Provigo savings certificates.

Provigo has captured a 35-percent share of the Montreal market, substantially greater than its nearest rival. Its operating income in 1991 was $172.7 million (U.S.), an 8-percent increase over the previous year. The company gains profound leverage by taking advantage of its core flow of consumer transactions to generate new income streams at a minimal cost. Provigo's growth would not be possible without the computerized marketing strategy. The ability to harness electronics for consumer research can profoundly leverage the consumer.

Communicating To Turn People On   General Electric Capital Corporation, the financial services subsidiary of GE, the consummate lean-and-mean-managed company, sends its magazine to me as a member of the financial community. Although I may never bring a leveraged buyout to GE Capital because its criteria and my deal flow may not fit, you can be sure that I know that GE Capital wants my business. Though I am its noncustomer today, I could be its customer tomorrow; thus the company is willing to spend $5 every other month to send me an interesting newsletter.

Coopers & Lybrand, the public accounting firm, does the same thing with its interesting monthly newsletter, which is filled with tax and audit tips and interpretations of government rulings that affect businesses. This newsletter is sent to scores of client leads in an effort to turn noncustomers into customers. The other major accounting firms also publish interesting newsletters. In addition, Ernst & Young sponsors seminars and invites entrepreneurs to speak to venture capitalists—another way to turn noncustomers into new clients. Law firms are also doing this. Boyer, Norton & Blair, a Houston, Texas, law firm that specializes in lender liability lawsuits, publishes a monthly newsletter that is disseminated to noncustomers.

The lesson in all of this is that in as few as six times a year, you can accomplish three things:

1. Remind noncustomers that you still want to be their provider of products or services.
2. Demonstrate that service is a mainstay of your business.
3. Keep your mailing list updated.

Once you have an interesting newsletter going to your customers and noncustomers every month, the next step is to offer seminars, conferences and trade shows for your customers and noncustomers. These are called users groups.

Pyramiding the Users Group

Assume that you own or manage a pharmaceutical company and that one of your entrepreneurial managers has some solutions for the problem of corporate drug and chemical dependency. Assume also that the entrepreneurial manager is your human resources officer and that she became aware of dependencies among male middle managers placed under a great deal of pressure. Some wives and children of frequently transferred managers complained that they could not sustain meaningful relationships. Some children's schoolwork slipped badly. The middle manager and his wife found solace in drink or drugs. Wrenched by the notion of corporate America being torn apart emotionally by drug and chemical dependency, the human resources officer suggested to you that the families receive counseling.

You granted the human resources officer permission to do family counseling with employees to learn some antidotes for the problem. She became experienced in the field and began to make progress within the company, making you and your senior management more sensitive to this issue. You agreed that she could publish a newsletter to be mailed to other corporate human resources officers as long as it tied into creating more sales for your company's pharmaceuticals.

Building the Marketing Pyramid   The human resources officer began the new endeavor by sketching a pyramid of the market, which is based on the pyramid method of problem formulating (see Figure 9.1). The object is to convert as many of the 2,000 human resources officers into clients as possible. The goal is to widen the pyramid at the top by making the market aware of the problem.

Newsletter Start-Up   Many entrepreneurs begin business with a newsletter. It is a unique means of customer financing. The corporate chemical dependency newsletter is offered to 2,000 human resources officers on a subscription basis, 10 issues for $120. If 400 subscribe, your human resources officer has $48,000 in launch capital. It is possible to attract advertisers for a newsletter, but this particular newsletter does not immediately suggest any potential ads.

Seminar Marketing   Two or three months of publishing go by. Your human resources officer reports on the subject from every vantage point imaginable: the human angle, the legal angle, the moral angle and so forth. In the fourth month, believing that some of the subscribers are ready to discuss the issue, she announces a seminar. For $500 the

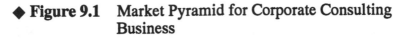

◆ **Figure 9.1**   Market Pyramid for Corporate Consulting Business

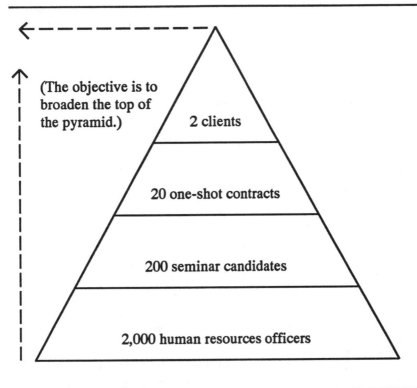

human resources officers can meet in Chicago for two days of panel discussion and lectures by psychologists and psychiatrists. Checks are received from 75 human resources officers, $37,500 in revenues. Your human resources officer spends $10,000 on a first-class seminar— good lunches, interesting speakers and a comfortable hotel (the guests pay for lodging). She makes this back by selling tapes of the seminar to nonattendees for $75 each.

Growth of Dependency Counseling Business   From the seminar your human resources officer gets 75 leads from corporations who are beginning to understand the extent of their problem. She offers each of them a small consulting assignment: one day's analysis for $1,000. Twenty corporations sign up over the next three months, providing further revenues of $20,000.

From these 20 consulting assignments she is awarded 2 performance contracts. She will counsel with all families that are suffering from the chemical dependency problem and recommend to the client corporation whether or not they can be salvaged with treatment. The contracts are worth $25,000 each, plus expenses for 1 year. Thus, after the first 12 months of operation, your human resources officer has generated the following revenues:

Performance Contracts	$ 50,000
Consulting Assignments	20,000
Seminars, Tapes	47,500
Newsletter	48,000
Total Revenues	$165,000

In the second year, the newsletter could double its revenues. There can be 2 seminars—1 on each coast—another 20 consulting assignments and 4 new performance contracts. As revenues approach $300,000, your human resources officer hires a staffer to publish the newsletter, assist with the seminars and keep the books.

Entering the third year, another human resources officer is brought into the company as a coworker. Growth continues, and your human resources officer finds other ways to permit growth of revenues without sacrificing quality, such as books and videos.

The pyramid method for tackling a new market that needs to be more problem-aware is an entrepreneurial creation. Your pharmaceutical sales grow as information about your products spreads. But you have also created a new profit center, a new cash flow channel: *the information division.* Look at its value: Net cash flow of $300,000 after two years times a multiple of five translates into an additional $1.5 million in purchase price.

Translating This to the Strategic Sell

Once you have built up the information channel and it is pumping cash flow along with your more conventional product and service sales, you can say to the strategic buyer, "We have two businesses for sale here: the manufacture and sale of our product and the sale of information about our product and our market. You will have to buy both to gain the full benefits of either."

The Financial Buyer

It is more difficult to obtain a higher price from financial buyers who seek to leverage everything in the company, then tighten their belt loops two notches to conserve cash to repay the debt. Rather than emphasize positive opportunities, which fall on the deaf ears of the cash-flow-conscious financial buyer, stress the places where expenses could be cut. Some of these include the following:

- Management salaries
- Management perks
- Space
- Administrative personnel
- Vehicles
- Lawyers
- Auditors
- Health insurance
- Commercial insurance
- Telephone
- Postage
- Courier
- Travel and entertainment
- Advertising

The financial buyer will use at least a dozen tactics to save cash flow, which will ultimately flow into the financial buyer's pocket. If you implement these tactics *before* the sale, your adjusted EBIT will increase, the savings will flow into your pocket and the price you receive for the company will be higher as well. These cost savings tactics are worth studying.

Reduce Advertising Costs

If you implement some of the direct response marketing ideas previously discussed, you will find that leads can be generated inexpensively, customer responses can be measured and weighed using the customer's money and sales can be achieved through word-of-mouth or testimonial selling.

In considering your advertising expenses, bear in mind the important distinction between finding potential customers (lead generation) and selling the prospects (marketing). The function of advertising is generally assigned to the former task. In certain instances, such as when a product's utility cannot be easily distinguished from its competitors, advertising has its role. If that situation pertains to your company's products or services, you can supplement advertising with public relations or video news releases, both of which are less expensive than advertising.

But if you have not implemented direct response strategies, it is important to cite some examples of how a more *energetic* owner could make a tremendous amount of money that could result in cash in his or her pocket. A phrase that catches the attention of financial buyers is: "I'm making enough money for my lifestyle. Why make changes?"

The financial buyer will generally have a much more expensive lifestyle to finance with your company's cash flow. Following are some expenses the financial buyer will slash to increase EBIT. You could point these out, for which you will receive a warm thank you. Better than that, you can begin implementing them today to raise adjusted EBIT and maximize your selling price.

To focus on hard numbers, assume that you are planning to sell a value-added distribution company with sales of $6.5 million, a 25-percent gross profit margin ($1.63 million) and 45 employees with an annual payroll of $900,000. Other facts are as follows:

Rental expense	40,000 square feet at $5.25 per annum, or $210,000
Health insurance	$450 per employee per month, or $243,000 per annum
Advertising costs	5 percent of sales, or $325,000 per annum
Accounting fees	$25,000 per annum for tax return and annual audit
Legal fees	$35,000 per annum, primarily for collection issues
Travel	5 salespeople, 300 airline trips per year, 300 hotel stays and car rentals for total travel costs of $210,000 per annum
Telephone, fax, courier and postage costs	$130,000 per year

After deducting overhead expenses from gross profit margin, the company's EBIT-D is:

Gross profit margin	$1,630,000
Less: Rent	210,000
Health insurance	243,000
Accounting fees	25,000
Legal fees	35,000
Travel	210,000
Advertising	325,000
Communications	130,000
Other overhead	100,000
Total SG&A expenses	1,278,000
EBIT-D	$ 352,000

If the estimated purchase price multiple is five times EBIT-D, the price you can expect to receive is a little over $1.5 million. Let's see how we can improve on this price.

Your Landlord Is Overcharging You

You will find that many *selling, general and administrative* (*SG&A*) *expenses* are high because providers of SG&A services usually set the price without negotiation. And we pay it. Landlords have been overcharging companies for decades on the theory: *Go for it. Maybe we can get away with it.*

Pull a copy of your lease. We will cut your company's office, plant and warehouse rental expenses. You are probably paying for *rentable* space when you should be paying for *usable* space. The difference between the two are the building's *common areas*. These include tenants' pro rata share of the lobbies, corridors, rest rooms, janitorial and electrical closets, vending and other areas that are shared by all tenants. If you are on an upper floor, your pro rata usage of the lobby is less than that of a first-floor tenant. Your firm should pay less for that common area. Are you paying less for the lobby? Read the lease.

Most landlords and leasing agents are reluctant to discuss the common area factor with tenants, but you should be armed to the teeth with all the facts. To the landlord, the common area is a *loss factor*— you want to absorb as little of it as possible.

The Common Area Factor   This is the square footage differential between rentable area and usable area. Again, rentable area includes the entire finished interior of a building's floor, including common areas such as rest rooms, lobby space, corridors and electrical and janitorial closets. Usable area is the entire interior square footage of office space available for the private use of the tenant. The *Building Owners and Managers Association* (BOMA) has established standards for measuring usable space. These standards state that usable space should be calculated by measuring from the inside surface of the dominant portion of the *permanent* outer building walls, to the office side of the corridor (or other permanent walls), to the center of partitions that separate the office from other usable areas.

Landlords typically calculate a pro rata share of the common area for each tenant and add that amount of space to the usable area to arrive at a number for the rentable area. Then they base the rent on this larger number. The landlord's *loss factor* (which properly should be called *excess profit factor*) is derived from charging for common area factors that the tenants simply never use, such as the janitor's closet and the air-conditioning equipment room.

Internal Space Measurement   The second problem is that the measurement of the space that your company is occupying for its office, plant or warehouse is probably inaccurate. The landlord more than likely took his or her measurements from a blueprint or from the outer walls. Remeasure the space from the inner walls, carefully measuring around the buttresses and excluding the electrical and telephone boxes. Then compare your total square footage number with the number in the lease. I will confidently bet that your number is the smaller one. Here are two examples of what you are likely to find:

1. Company ABC leases 5,780 square feet of office space at $19 per square foot. An in-house measurement indicates a discrepancy of 578 square feet, approximately 10 percent. Over a lease term of 5 years, the total recovery and/or savings could be $54,910. If taxes and ancillary services such as janitorial, security, insurance, utilities and parking are taken into account, the overcharge claim would increase. If Company ABC has 20 employees, that is a savings of over $2,500 per employee.

2. Company XYZ leases 30,500 square feet of warehouse space at $9.50 per square foot. An in-house measurement indicates a discrepancy of 3,050 square feet. Over a lease term of 10 years, the total recovery and/or savings would amount to $137,250, more with the ancillary services.

Renegotiating Your Lease   Once you have discovered that you have been overcharged by your landlord, you probably have two dollar amounts: one for miscalculating the usable area occupied by your office and one for overcharging your company for the common area. BOMA has standards for helping you roll back the first amount, but the second amount will require negotiation and cooperation with the other tenants. If there are no other tenants, you will have to negotiate lease rate reductions on your own.

The Lobby's Value   Who uses lobbies? Do they have as much value to a tenth-floor tenant as they do to one on the first floor? If there are shops on the first floor, the lobby is their walkway. If there are no shops, the lobby is a corridor to the elevator or to first-floor offices.

If I were on a high floor, I would be willing to pay for a space the length and width of the corridor from the front door to the elevator, but I would contest being charged a pro rata amount of the lobby space.

Full Service or Net-Net-Net   Before negotiating away the pro rata cost of the janitorial and electrical closets, examine your lease to determine if your company is receiving janitorial and electrical services as part of its lease.

A *full-service* lease includes all building services, maintenance, real estate taxes, janitorial services and utilities.

A *net-net-net* lease usually indicates that the tenant pays for all taxes, utilities, insurance and maintenance of the usable space and common area.

If your lease is net-net-net, it is appropriate to ask for some reduction in the costs of the electrical and janitorial closets because some of the services that relate to these closets are for areas that you are not paying for, that is, the parking lot, entrance area, building signs and basement storage.

Recapture   You calculate 8 years of overcharging of 2,000 square feet per year at an average rate of $4.75 per square foot. The landlord owes you $76,000 in back rent plus interest on the money, and your adjustment to annual EBIT is 2,000 square feet times $5.25 or $10,500. Multiply that times five and you have put $52,000 in your pocket.

Rethinking Your Communication Systems

The communications marketplace is muddled with alternative systems for sending messages and is further complicated by a cacophony of misleading claims about price and efficiency.

As a start-up investor in a leading long-distance telephone carrier, ALC Communications Corporation, in Birmingham, Michigan, I can attest to the dogged competition among carriers. And as a user of all the systems—snail mail (the U.S. Postal Service), E-mail (electronic mail or computer-to-computer transmission), overnight couriers, facsimile transmission and telephone, I can attest to the difficulty in selecting the least expensive method of sending a message.

Moreover, many marketers of communications systems act like Lily Tomlin's telephone takeoff: "I'm from the telephone company. I don't have to help you." When you try to correct an error in your bill or ask if there is a less expensive alternative, the "service" operator can be less than forthcoming. Fortunately, the marketplace eliminates those who fail to service their customers.

But cost savings are achievable in our communications budgets if we analyze the costs and benefits of each communications system.

Postage   If your business uses direct mail as a common advertising medium, wasted postage costs can add up to several hundred thousand dollars per year. Here are some tips to save postage costs.

1. Use an electronic scale to avoid the need for adding extra postage just to be safe.
2. Use a postage meter rather than stamps to limit your expense to the exact amount required.
3. Use *Forwarding and Return Postage Guaranteed* and *Address Correction Requested* on all mail. This is a relative inexpensive way to keep your mailing lists current.
4. Save unused postage stamps that were printed in error. They can be redeemed at 90 percent of their face value.
5. Use first-class presort when possible. For those mailings that qualify, savings can be as much as 25 percent.
6. Third-class bulk rates can save more than 60 percent for mailings of 200 pieces or more. In addition, sorting by carrier routes eliminates 3 United States Postal Service handlings, allowing faster delivery.
7. Include promotional pieces in your regular mailings of invoices and statements. Most letters mailed at the one-ounce rate weigh much less, so add a lightweight newsletter.
8. Keep a variety of envelopes on hand, and always use the smallest possible size. This will lower weight and avoid postage surcharges.

9. Use registered mail only when insurance is necessary. Certified mail is less expensive.
10. For promotional mailings, use a first-class post card rather than a first-class letter. A 4 1/2" x 6" single-fold piece will double your message area and can accommodate a business reply card.

Presorting Services Major mailers, such as credit card companies and mail order houses, sort their mail by zip code before taking it to the post office. The U.S. Postal Service offers them a 25-percent discount or 7 cents off a 29-cent mailing. An independent government commission that reviews postal rates says that the presorting discount is a bargain. (Understandably, the American Postal Workers Union, a 350,000-member union, argues that its members could do the job just as well and would like to see 2.5 cents of the discount in their paychecks.)

But what about companies that generate 500 pieces of mail per day or less? If that is your situation, you can call on 1 of 250 privately owned presorters located throughout the country. Presorters save you most of the seven cents, which can add up to several thousand dollars per year, depending on volume.

American Presort in Brea, California, was founded by Elodia Swenson after she quit her job in 1987. She rented 1,700 square feet of space in an industrial park, lined the walls with wooden cubbyholes and hired local high school students to sort the mail. She began calling on 500 companies in Orange County in her van, often bypassing the mailing department and speaking directly with the controller. Customers came slowly as American Presort gained credibility. Today, with TRW, Knotts Berry Farm and others as customers, Ms. Swenson presorts around 50,000 pieces of mail a day, which is a break-even level of operation.

Carrier Route Sorting If your company is in the field of direct mail marketing or sends out thousands of third-class envelopes each month, your postage costs are $167 per thousand pieces, or 16.7 cents per envelope. This assumes that you are presorting by zip code. You can lower the cost to $101 per thousand pieces, or 10.1 cents per envelope, a savings of 33 percent, if you sort the envelopes by carrier routes.

Regional post offices will provide you with the names of their carriers and the addresses they cover. Obtain census maps from the U.S. Commerce Department and enlarge them. Then hire high school students to sort the envelopes by carrier routes, bundle them with rubber bands and write the name of the carrier on the top of the bundle. Then mail the bundles to the post offices. Using carrier route sorting speeds up delivery.

Overnight Couriers   The major corporations pay considerably less than do small-sized and medium-sized companies to send an overnight package. The average cost to an ordinary user to send a one-pound package overnight is $14.50. Federal Express Corporation charges $20.25 for the same package, but it guarantees delivery by 10:30 A.M. the following morning. IBM and other large corporations are offered discounts of up to 40 percent by the air freight companies.

Jealous? You do not have to be because a package aggregator, UniShippers Association, Salt Lake City, Utah, has entered the marketplace and can achieve the same discount for your company. Figure 9.2 is a comparison of Unishipper's rates with three of its competitors.

What does this mean to your company? Let's say that your company ships 200 packages per year, about 1 every other day, and that the average weight is 2 pounds. If you use a carrier in Figure 9.2 other than UniShippers, you will pay $4,600 per annum. But if you ship via UniShippers, you will pay $3,000, a savings of $1,600 per annum. The real savings occur with big packages. Assume that you ship 200 packages each year and that each weighs an average of 50 pounds. Your savings via UniShippers will be $2,700 per year. In selling your company, every dollar saved is $5 earned.

Telephone   There are several ways to reduce telephone costs. As you know, there are alternatives to AT&T as your company's primary carrier. The alternatives and their fierce rival, AT&T, fill the media with claims of less expense, more clarity, superior computer links, more fiber optic lines and better conferencing. But these claims do not speak to the point. They are similar to beverage ads: There is so little distinction among the products that vendors resort to projecting images of satisfied users to attract users who wish to look or feel like these images.

Your company can purchase (or lease) interconnect telephone systems that have a feature known as *least cost* routing. (AT&T offers equipment that is competitive in most areas with those of interconnect or competitive telephone equipment manufacturers.) This feature relies on a microchip that automatically selects the least costly carrier for a particular long-distance call—WATS, AT&T, ALC, MCI, Sprint

◆ **Figure 9.2**   Rate Comparison for Overnight Air Freight
Service (Prices are subject to change.)

Weight (Lbs.)	UniShippers	Federal Express	DHL Express	Emery
Letter	$ 8.50	$ 14.00	$ 14.00	$ 14.00
1	14.00	20.25	25.00	23.00
2	15.00	23.00	25.00	23.00
3	18.00	25.75	28.00	25.75
4	21.00	28.50	31.00	28.56
5	23.00	31.25	34.00	31.25
50	68.00	95.00	89.00	95.00
90	103.00	145.00	129.00	145.00

or Telenet. If you are in the service business and your telephone calls
are billed to a client or customer—law firm, hotel hospital—you can
select an interconnect system with *call accounting/cost accounting*
that assigns each call to a specific telephone.

"Nothing so rapidly modifies the telephone behavior of employees
as announcing that a call accounting system has been installed," says
Donn Thielman, president of Aztec Communications, Palm Springs,
California, a consulting firm that services the telecommunications
needs of large corporations. "When we installed call accounting at
Hughes, Texaco and Lockheed, their monthly telephone bills dropped
30 percent," says Thielman.

Repackagers for Telephone Users   The concept of a repackager
operated by an independent company that has helped reduce air
express costs has been applied to telephone costs as well. In this market
a *repackager* is sometimes called an aggregator or reseller. This
intermediary, of which there are about 125 in the country, buys
hundreds of trunks at a reduced price each month from the major long-
distance carriers. The carriers sell telephone service for 11 cents per
minute; the repackagers pay a price of 5 cents per minute and resell
them for 8 cents per minute. You can use a repackager and buy (or
lease) interconnect systems that offer cost-saving features. Let your
fingers walk through the *Yellow Pages* to find aggregators in your area.

Codes Toll Restriction Interconnect systems also offer the ability to block certain telephones from calling particular area codes. For example, the accounts receivable department that calls the West Coast would be blocked from making calls to other regions of the country. "Codes toll restriction will slash another 5 percent off the monthly telephone bill," reports Thielman.

Telephone Affinity Cards Some credit card companies have begun to offer frequent flyer points on major airlines when certain long-distance carriers are used—the more telephone calls a company makes, the smaller its airline travel costs. Although the telephone affinity card can be used to reduce airline travel costs, be careful that telephone usage does not soar. Further, be clear with your fellow employees up front that the frequent flyer points will be contributed into a pot to be shared with all company travelers.

Recapture Your company switches overnight couriers for a savings of $3,000 per annum, changes long-distance carriers for a 10-percent savings of $8,500 (and the carrier gives you a free copier for switching) and uses half-page fax paper to save another $1,500 for total savings of $12,000 per year.

Cutting Travel Costs and Saving Time

No one travels with the cost efficiency of the financial buyer. Because time is money, especially when you are without the latter, the entrepreneurial financial buyer plays every conceivable angle to visit the most sources of cash on a single trip in the shortest time. These whirlwinds know:

- which airports will not send a towing bill for a rental car left at the departure ramp or what hardship tale to give to the rental car attendant to avoid a towing charge;
- where to sit on the airplane for the speediest exit;
- which car rental company will put them behind the wheel in the shortest time at 25 different airports;
- how to get the best discounts from car rental companies;
- how to maximize their frequent flyer points to earn the most free flights;
- which airports have the most pay telephones out by the gates; and
- how to get through the X-ray machine without delay.

But the greatest gift they have passed on to us is how to shave 25 percent off the cost of most airplane trips. For the company whose personnel make 400 airplane trips per year at an average round-trip cost of $750 per flight, that is an annual savings of $75,000 and perhaps $375,000 in additional purchase price to you.

The 25-Percent Airline Travel Savings   If you make a reservation 21 days or more in advance of the flight date, most domestic and some foreign airlines will offer you a 25-percent discount off standard coach fare. Assuming that the standard cost of the flight is $450 one way, the savings is $112.50, bringing the ticket price to $337.50. The catch is that if you change the time, day or carrier for that particular ticket, the airline will ask you to pay the $112.50 that you had saved.

However, when I polled a handful of frequent business flyers, most of them entrepreneurs, they said that they never lose the $112.50 when they change the time, day of the flight or the carrier (but still fly to the same destination).

Saving on the Hotel Bill   It is better to stay in the cheapest room in the best hotel than in the best room at the cheapest hotel. The differential ranges from zero to $25, but you frequently gain that back in the following ways: free shoeshine service, a more invigorating shower, a better mattress, free morning coffee, juice and the morning paper and fewer hidden charges.

The most annoying hidden charge is the telephone surcharge that hotels tack on when you make long-distance calls from your room using an AT&T calling card or the equivalent. Surcharges range from 50 cents to $2 but tend to be lower at the better hotels. Many hotels contract with private companies, known as alternative operator services, to handle outgoing calls. When you check in, ask if there is a surcharge; if there is, inform the desk clerk that you intend to make any calls on your calling card and if you are charged for these, you will protest to the FCC. A large number of complaints to the FCC will result in the elimination of surcharges. For a very large bill, say over $100, the FCC may mediate and help you recover your money.

Saving on the Restaurant Bill   Shrewd business restaurant patrons are paying 30 percent less for their dinners thanks to barter companies that offer meal discount cards. These barter companies market discount cards to frequent diners who pay for their dinners with conventional plastic but receive the discount on their monthly statements.

The member restaurants gather the dollar amount of the discounts they have given out for the month and send them to the barter company, indicating the services they would like for their money. These often include advertising in magazines and on the radio or airline travel for the restaurant owners and their employees. The barter company deals in lots of money collected at its tollgate. Accordingly, it pays less for restaurant advertising and holds on to the 15-percent agency fee. Plus, the barter companies sell their discount cards on a subscription basis for as much as $50 per member per year. It's a win-win situation.

Barter companies are a good deal for the traveler. You might wish to contact the following ones for discount cards:

Advantage Charge Trading Corp.
114 E. 32nd St.
New York, NY 10016
212-779-SAVE

IGT Services
22 E. 29th St.
New York, NY 10016
800-4-IGT-USA

Citibank CitiDining Card
(available only to holders of
Citibank Visa or MasterCard
and acceptable at over 1,000
restaurants in 16 cities)
800-221-7444

Travel World Leisure Club
225 W. 34th St.
New York, NY 10122
800-444-TWLC

Transmedia Network
509 Madison Ave.
New York, NY 10022
800-422-5090

Entertainment Publications
1400 N. Woodward Ave.
Birmingham, MI 48011
313-642-8300

Each card differs slightly in terms of the restaurants that it works with, annual membership fee and other features.

Saving on Rental Cars Car travel companies try to capture the business of large corporations, from whom it is easier to collect car rental payments, insurance claims and unpaid parking tickets by giving them discounts as high as 40 percent. For a one-day rental of a midsize car at Chicago's O'Hare International Airport, that is a savings of $26 on a $65 daily rental (before 70 free miles and 500 frequent flyer points). Assuming that your company's travelers rent 200 cars per year at $65 per rental, a 40-percent discount would save your company $5,200 annually. Although the bulk of their consumers come from small-sized and medium-sized businesses, they do not say publicly that discounts are available for the asking.

My own discount, a mere 15 percent, was obtained through a former controller of my company who was a member of the accountant's trade association. I blush with shame that I have been unable to improve on 15 percent. To save a few more dollars, I avoid the insurance coverages that my own automobile insurance policy covers, rent small cars, buy gas at discount gas stations if I have time and ask for frequent flyer points with each rental.

One of my first takeover and turnaround investments was in backing the strategic buyers who, 20 years ago, bought Genway Corporation, the car leasing company that services General Motors dealers and that launched General Rent-a-Car, an airport-based car rental company. The payoff to my co-investors, Central National Corporation and the partners of Kuhn, Loeb & Co., was about 50 times our investment in less than one year. Car rental companies such as Hertz and Avis have been bought and sold many times since, always with handsome rates of return to their buyers and investors. These companies have multiple cash flow channels—used car sales, insurance overrides, gas sales, cellular phone rentals—plus low tax rates due to depreciating their fleets, which enable them to greatly discount their rentals to large corporations.

Use the least costly rentals. The Budget Car Rental yard is much closer to O'Hare Airport than the others, perhaps ten minutes closer. The off-airport car rental companies are usually $2 – $15 cheaper per day than the other airport-based car rental companies (unless they are running specials)—and the time savings make them a first choice at O'Hare. At Los Angeles International Airport, Atlanta, LaGuardia and San Francisco, the airport-based car rental companies have practically no time advantage over the off-airport-based ones, so you might as well use one of the off-airport car rental companies. Figure 9.3 shows the comparative prices for a one-day rental of a midsize car at a major airport. (Dollar amounts are for comparison only and subject to change.)

Let's assume that your company's travelers fly into the major airports, rent their cars for one day and travel 100 miles and that your company has a 15-percent discount with all car rental companies. The travelers must be transported in a van to their cars; thus, transport time is assumed to be constant. The savings on 100 trips per year by using an off-airport company is shown in Figure 9.4.

◆ **Figure 9.3**   Comparable Car Rental Prices with Transport Time from Airport to Car Yard (Assumed Constant)

Company	Telephone No.	Weekday Rental Price (Per Day)
On-Airport		
Hertz	800-654-3131	$79.99 (70 free miles)
National	800-328-4567	64.95 (70 free miles)
Budget	800-527-0700	62.99 (70 free miles)*
Avis	800-331-1212	49.00 (no free miles)
Dollar	800-421-6868	39.95 (unlmtd. free miles)
Off-Airport		
Thrifty	800-367-2277	43.00 (150 free miles)
General	800-327-7607	39.95 (unlmtd. free miles)
Alamo	800-327-9633	39.95 (unlmtd. free miles)

* Or $72.99 with unlimited free miles.

With careful shopping, your company can save even more than $2,431 per year by using the off-airport car rental companies.

Frequent Flyer Points   To the many words already written on this subject, let me simply urge you to collect frequent flyer cards on all airlines and use them religiously. They are worth approximately one cent per mile should you wish to save them for a long trip or sell them to the merchants who advertise in the classified sections of *USA Today* and *The Wall Street Journal.*

The other advantages of frequent flyer cards are the discounts available at hotels, some as high as 50 percent. Citibank, American Airlines and MCI (the long-distance telephone carrier) are currently joint-venturing a clever package whereby an MCI caller who pays his or her bill with a Citibank Visa or MasterCard can gain frequent flyer points on American Airlines. A frequent flyer card also offers leverage at the check-in counter when the flight is overbooked and someone must be bumped.

Airline Club Memberships   The airline clubs are handy meeting places, particularly when you have a number of interviews in a single

◆ **Figure 9.4**   Savings with Off-Airport Company

	Average 1-Day Rental Price	Average Mileage @ $.10/mi	Less Discount	1-Day Costs	100-Day Costs
On-Airport	$64.25	$4.75	$(9.64)	$59.36	$5,936.00
Off-Airport	41.25	—	(6.20)	35.05	3,505.00
Difference	$23.00	$4.75	$(3.44)	$24.31	$2,431.00

city and the airport is a $40 – $60 trip from a downtown destination. You can make up the expense in a one-year club membership. Some airline clubs offer amenities such as personal computers, fax machines, free beverages and conference rooms. Note that, when an airline is taken over by a corporate raider, many of the once free amenities begin to have tollgates. TWA's conference rooms were free to the user before financial buyer Carl Icahn purchased the airline.

To economize on club memberships, become a member of a major East-West airline and a member of a major North-South airline—for $150 you will have covered most of the country. Put this little tip into your nonerasable memory chip: A special reservations telephone number is available to airline club members. When a severe blizzard shuts down an airport and leaves you stranded, the airlines' regular reservations telephone numbers are jammed with harried travelers calling to reschedule their flights. Not so with the special telephone number. You can usually get right through and reschedule on the first flight out in the morning.

Recapture   If you are diligent about saving on travel costs and policing this expense area, the salespersons become more careful about their travel expenditures and save 10 percent, $21,000, on tickets, rental cars, hotels and dinner costs. That could amount to more than $100,000 in your pocket.

Shopping Around for Auditors

The best time to shop for an auditor is two months before the close of your fiscal year. The worst time is between February and mid-April when accounting firms are working around the clock to prepare tax returns. If you are starting a new business, make one of your first hires a chief financial officer (CFO) who has experience either with a certified public accounting firm or who has been through at least two audits with a company that has used a CPA firm. Your company will earn back the salary of your chief financial officer in several ways.

1. The CFO will assist in interviewing audit firms.
2. The CFO will help negotiate a less costly audit.
3. The CFO will leave a perfect audit trail with squeaky clean documentation so that the CPA firm will do little more than read it, make sure that all of the numbers "foot" and sign it.

Where To Go for Your CFO   The best source of outstanding CFOs are the large accounting firms who have an out-placement service to assist their CPAs who want to work in industry. According to Don Bush, a partner with Coopers & Lybrand, Columbus, Ohio, "The ex-Coopers accountant knows the full range of our services—audit, tax, preacquisition review, data processing and consulting—and how to access these services for the least cost to the company."

The Utility Infielder   For small companies under 50 employees, a CFO with legal training is a double blessing because he or she can read and understand contracts, leases and bank loan agreements and also handle minor litigation items. The CFO cum lawyer can help negotiate these items and, because he or she is usually prudent by nature, spot errors, omissions, overcharges and vague language that could lead to future disputes.

Sure, you will pay more for a double degree, but the utility infielder will save the company twice his or her salary. Excellent recordkeeping and in-house counsel in one package are as important to a company as developing two marketing channels for one product.

Evaluating Your Audit Needs   Before you interview accounting firms, evaluate your audit needs. Are you a franchising company? Do you have several joint ventures or partnerships? Do you export? Are you planning to go public? In each instance you will want to identify a specialist within the accounting firm who is familiar with your kind of business. Small accounting firms will often have to climb onto the learning curve at your expense whereas the larger firms will provide creative accounting solutions—read *enhanced profits* and *reduced taxes*—in areas that are often puzzling.

Large accounting firms offer small-company prices to attract new business. Most of their new clients come from the entrepreneurial community, and the price of the first year's audit, assuming nothing extraordinary is required, will generally meet the bid that you receive from a smaller firm that lacks your specialty.

What To Ask before Selecting a Firm   Following is a checklist of questions to ask accounting firms during the first interview.

- What kinds of clients do you represent?
- Do you have clients of a comparable size and in a similar industry?
- What are the specialties of your firm?
- Have you ever done an audit for an initial public offering (or partnership or joint venture)?
- Might we have the names and telephone numbers of your clients who have needs similar to ours?
- Who will be doing the work on our audit?
- What are your billing rates?
- How many hours do you estimate the job will take?
- Do you offer special fee arrangements for special situations such as *initial public offerings*?
- What is your billing procedure? Will your bills itemize the accounting work done, including a description of the service, the date the service is rendered, the name of the person who rendered the service and the charge for the service?
- How might our company assist you in handling the audit?
- Will you defend your audit in court, if necessary, without charge to our company?
- Does your fee include a management letter?
- Who will be our partner-contact within your firm?
- Is your firm planning to remain in the community?

The last question may seem unusual, but accounting firms, such as other multi-office businesses, often open new offices, troll mightily for new clients and then fold their tents, forcing you to take your audit business elsewhere. Be suspicious of accounting firms who lowball their audit fee. They may be trying to win your account because they are straining under a regional office directive to generate new clients quickly or be shut down.

Be clear up front with the auditors that you will not pay for the time of one of their new employees to sit in on meetings for training.

Hiring the Auditor, Not the Firm   Although the resources of the firm that you hire can greatly affect the kind of service you receive, having a partner bring your business into the firm can help you establish a special relationship that can provide you with extra attention (off the clock). An ombudsman within the firm will more likely listen to your requests, route your inquiries and help you negotiate fees.

Further, when one of your staff requires a conference room in London, Los Angeles or Atlanta, the partner who earned the credit for bringing your company's business to his or her shop will usually arrange these extra benefits for you.

Obtaining an Engagement Letter   To avoid an open-ended fee arrangement, ask the accounting firm to submit an *engagement letter*. It should specify the scope of the assignment and its cost. It should state the amount of the retainer, if there is one, the number of hours, the people assigned to the task and their rates. The letter should specify that the audit will include a management letter. A partner of the firm should sign the letter, and the chief executive officer of your firm should countersign it.

Recapture   Three accounting firms are interviewed, and the winning bid is $17,000, a savings of $8,000 per annum.

Reducing Health Insurance Costs

Health benefit costs, the number-one component of overhead, devour earnings in one large gulp. They cost the big three automakers approximately $1,600 per employee, dependent and retiree per year. About $700 of health benefit costs are included in every car that rolled off of a U.S. assembly line in 1991.

Detroit is not the only troubled region. The National Association of Manufacturers reported in May 1989 that health care costs of its surveyed members are *out of control*. The study showed that the association's 2,029 members reported that their costs of providing health care represented an average of 37 percent of profit. Richard Heckert, formerly chairman of DuPont and the association's chairman, said that such costs "threaten the nation's competitive position."

Lee Iacocca, the retired president of Chrysler who bailed out his company with federal aid, now favors federal government intervention to help reduce health insurance expenses. But government intervention is not necessary. Federal regulation has a reputation for increasing the costs in most fields that it enters. And many companies pay much less than Chrysler for health care.

The Preferred Provider Organization   Rather than a federal rescue of corporate insurance programs, the solution lies with the *preferred provider organization* (PPO) and association-based health insurance plans. The PPO gathers under its umbrella many employers as its subscribers and then negotiates lower insurance rates with insurance companies. The PPO differs from the *health maintenance organization* (HMO) in that the HMO acts as an insurance carrier and negotiates with providers for lower rates. The PPO is a pure tollgate, playing one insurance carrier against another for the lowest rates. Some HMOs pay health care providers slowly—sometimes longer than 90 days—and therefore are unable to attract the providers that employees want to use. Because providers want rapid payment from major health insurance carriers (most of which seek the large number of employees that the PPOs can generate), physicians, clinics and hospitals sign up more readily with PPOs.

The competition between PPOs and HMOs has not produced a clear-cut winner to date. Many of the PPOs are private, and some are not-for-profit corporations; thus, their financial statements are not publicly available. However, quite a few HMOs are publicly held or are subsidiaries of publicly held insurance companies. Their financial statements are available, and they show more red ink than black.

Who's Making the Money?   With expenditures on health care in the U.S. running at $650 billion per year and underwriters of health care losing their shirts paying for it, who's making the money? Losses of this magnitude certainly mean profits to someone. The answer is the *providers*.

The pharmaceutical industry is intensely profitable. For the third quarter of 1992, the 12 major, publicly held U.S. pharmaceutical companies earned over $3 billion. Over the last 5 years their earnings have grown at an average rate of 16.5 percent per year. But according to the *New England Journal of Medicine* (March 1988), an estimated 24 percent of the drugs prescribed are useless.

The next largest beneficiaries of excessive health care expenditures are the manufacturers of diagnostic equipment. The 11 largest, publicly held producers of medical testing instruments earned $1.4 billion in the first three quarters of 1992. Further, their earnings have grown at the rate of 13 percent per year over the last 5 years. Does the American public need all the tests that it is getting? No, according to *Health Week*, which estimates that approximately 40 percent of the tests administered by physicians are unnecessary.

Many physicians claim that their fairly recent practice of over-drugging and over-testing their patients is a response to medical malpractice *lawyers*. This is reminiscent of the betrayal scene in Genesis 1, when Adam says to God, "She did it, not me, Lord." And Eve blames Adam, "But the snake made me do it."

Utilization Review Companies   As the debate rages over who is responsible for the multiplication of drugs and diagnostic testing, *utilization review* (UR) and *employee leasing* companies are selling protection to the beleaguered employers.

Utilization review companies are sleuths that use computers to track the procedures of physicians who are members of PPOs or HMOs. When they spot a blip on their screens, such as when more than half of the ob-gyn deliveries during a certain period were by cesarean section, they *remind* the doctor to bring costs back into line. The PPO is the tollgate and its subsidiary, the UR, the *enforcer*. Elliott A. Segal, president of National Capitol Preferred Provider Organization in Washington, D.C., told *The Wall Street Journal* that the woodshed talk is "a way of putting somebody on notice in a subtle but telling way."

Doctor, Your Patient Will See You Now   Healthcare Compare Corporation in Lombard, Illinois, a publicly held utilization review company with 1992 revenues of $150 million, has been monitoring physicians for five years on behalf of PPOs and insurance companies to eliminate unnecessary procedures. The UR helped Murray Industries, the Florida manufacturer of pleasure boats, reduce its health care costs 22 percent. Another client, Park 'n Fly Service, a parking lot operator in St. Louis, reported a reduction of 27 percent, without sacrificing quality of care.

Under UR, physicians use their traditional system of charging a fee for services rendered, but the procedures have to be approved by either Healthcare Compare or one of the other 300 UR companies (or divisions of PPOs) currently in operation. A typical UR fee is $1.25 – $2.00 per employee per month. URs have staffs of nurses and doctors, and in 60 percent of the cases the UR's nurses approve the procedures. The other diagnoses are reviewed by the UR's staff physicians. Emergency operations are done immediately without consultation.

Because HMO physicians charge a fixed fee, the continued growth of URs, which bird-dog non-HMO physicians, for the most part indicates the expansion of the PPO.

How Effective Is the PPO? Lockheed-Georgia, a 20,000-employee subsidiary of Lockheed Corporation, joined the SouthCare Medical Alliance PPO in 1988 and slashed its employee costs by $500,000, according to Donald Meader, coordinator of PPOs for Lockheed-Georgia. "We think that's only the beginning," Meader says. "We hope to do as well with dental, drugs and therapy costs."

"The answer to delivering lower costs to employers via the PPO system," says Larry Madlem, who manages SouthCare, "is to deal with physicians as if they were travel agents and hospitals as if they were airlines. The smart physicians know they'll sell the most tickets if they deliver the lowest cost fares and offer prompt, efficient service. Once you have that understanding, the smart insurance companies—the ones without HMOs—will line up for your business."

Association-Based Health Insurance Plans For employers with five or fewer employees, health insurance (including dental and maternity coverage) is available for approximately $100 – $150 per person per month, depending on employee ages and other factors. Employees and their families join an association with tens of thousands of other customers, and the association negotiates discounts on numerous products and services.

My company qualified for membership in USA for HealthCare, sponsored by National Health Insurance Company, Grand Prairie, Texas. Through USA for HealthCare, employees receive discounts of 12 percent on airline tickets, 50 percent on hotel rooms and 50 percent on car rentals, where available. That is only the beginning—discounts are also available on eyeglasses, prescription drugs, certain food items, theatre tickets and emergency road services.

Association-based health insurance is inexpensive because it is sold at group rates to individuals, but the group must be made up of five or fewer employees. However, if your company qualifies for association-based health insurance, you can literally turn health insurance costs into a profit center.

Recapture Using our company example, you interview several PPOs and association-based health insurers and the winning bid, without sacrificing benefits, a whopping annual savings of $62,100.

Rolling Back Legal Costs

Among U.S. corporations, legal expenses have become the second largest overhead item after health insurance costs. Financial buyers know how to roll back legal expenses from 15–20 percent of net operating income, to half that level. They demand cost cuts from their lawyers, or they take their legal business elsewhere. If you can slash legal expenses before you sell your company, you can put a substantial amount of money in your pocket.

How? I will tell you, but first a story.

A few years ago, I was sued in a California court for fraud, breach of contract and mental anguish. It was a nuisance lawsuit without substance, but lawsuits must be responded to within 30 days or the defendant loses the suit. My local attorney failed to respond, and I lost by default. The default judgment awarded $3 million to the plaintiff.

No people are more keenly aware of the relative skills within their trade than professional athletes and commercial litigators. Their box scores and wins and losses are published daily. Therefore, when I called the best litigators I knew in New York and Chicago plus those referred to me by business acquaintances, I asked them to recommend the sharpest commercial litigators in the San Francisco Bay Area.

Upon receiving the list, I narrowed it to three names based on immediate availability, hourly rates and confidence levels. I interviewed these three firms until I found the lawyer who I felt was the most (credibly) hopeful, intelligent and experienced—and who genuinely liked the case. His estimated fee was around $17,000, of which I agreed to pay half up front with the balance to be invoiced. Always try to obtain a flat fee quote for legal services in advance rather than an hourly quote—the latter is more susceptible to padding.

Within 30 days my lawyer turned around the default judgment and defeated the claim. I was, of course, relieved. He then asked me to send him a copy of the insurance policy my company maintains to pay for accidents. Curious about his strategy, I sent him the policy; within two weeks he returned the $17,000 I had paid him, courtesy of the insurance company. When I asked why, he said, "In California mental anguish is a personal injury, and your insurance policy covered my expenses because the lawsuit included a claim for mental anguish."

More   *To reduce legal costs, review all your company's insurance policies carefully to see how many risks are insured.* The process of insuring for essentially all business risks and having lawsuits and legal expenses paid by your insurers probably means that all litigious lawyers and clients will sue for every perceived injury until, eventually, there will be no insurance companies willing to indemnify any risk. But for now there exists, somewhere, an insurance company that will buy your company's risks and, in so doing, lower your legal expenses dramatically.

Directors' and Officers' Insurance   The best way to protect your company is with *directors' and officers'* (D&O) *insurance.* This policy indemnifies the company's officers and directors for errors and omissions in carrying out the objectives of the company. It does not protect the company in the event of fraud, misfeasance, malfeasance or gross negligence; but for honest errors and mistakes, D&O insurance is a necessary umbrella for a rainy day.

For example, suppose your controller makes a serious accounting error and fails to pay the company's withholding taxes for a year. The excuse: The controller thought that he or she was saving the company cash. But the IRS wants its $250,000 and is threatening to levy your company's bank accounts and other liquid assets.

A company without D&O insurance might call its lawyer who, for a $25,000 legal fee, will negotiate a settlement. (Unpaid withholding taxes can always be settled—but rarely compromised—and always stretched out. The IRS is comfortable with a six-month stretch, but I have heard of substantially longer installment plans.) Singer Willie Nelson's IRS bill was recently slashed in half by the IRS, and Mr. Nelson was given an installment payout plan, thus signaling a new era in IRS negotiations.

Depending on the terms of the D&O policy, the insurer may also pay approximately 90 percent of the unpaid withholding taxes. Thus, for $25,000 plus the cost of the policy, the withholding taxes plus legal fees will be paid by the D&O insurer *if* the nonpayment was not a fraudulent act.

D&O insurance policies are more expensive per capita for small companies than they are for businesses with 50 or more employees. Policies cost between $6,000 and $12,000 per year, and you should ask your insurance broker to research the marketplace for you.

Acting as Your Own Counsel   To take another bite out of legal expenses, have your most meticulous employees draft the more routine contracts needed to operate your business. Scottie Williams, a creative inventor with over 20 patents to his name, publishes a handbook that he sells for $26. It explains how anyone can file a patent and protect an invention in the U.S. for less than $600. Most patent lawyers will not talk to a company for less than a $2,500 retainer. Williams's pamphlet dispels all of the myths surrounding patents and takes the pain out of the process. For a copy of *Inventor's Workbook*, call Williams at 800-456-IDEA.

At the vanguard of the do-it-yourself law movement is Nolo Press, Berkeley, California, a publisher of self-help books for companies and individuals who seek to lower their legal fees. Nolo, which in Latin means *I do not choose to*, has 60 titles in circulation, and over 200,000 readers have bought its publications.

More Cuts in Legal Costs   Most companies use their lawyers inefficiently. For example, when a firm sends a team of three lawyers to explain a legal problem, the company's employees fail to ask two of them to leave the room. The scope of the legal services required can usually be determined by one lawyer in less than half an hour of billable time. Also, most companies do not put their legal requirements out for bid and then interview many lawyers at different firms. Nor when someone refers a lawyer to the company, do they ask why this particular lawyer will help your company. For all you know, the person making the referral may be earning psychological or social points but may not be putting you into the best hands. Probe for the reasons. Inform your company's law firm up front that you will not pay for incorrect advice nor will you pay to train one of their young employees.

Controlling the Billing   Discuss billing rates before the engagement. Discuss the way you wish to be billed—contingency, hourly rate paid monthly or per event. Many lawyers prefer that you pay a retainer up front (bankruptcy lawyers, quite properly, want 90 percent of their expected fee up front) and then work the retainer off in hours. This is an appropriate arrangement for a complicated lawsuit or for a matter that has an uncertain ending, such as an acquisition or public offering. It is inappropriate for the drafting of a contract. Prepare a budget with your lawyer before the task begins and monitor the budget.

Be sure to specify that you want fully itemized bills, ones that break down each hour or fraction thereof and describe how the time was spent. Question billed items that you do not understand. For example, your lawyer may not have to travel first-class. If he or she does not work for you while traveling, you should not be billed for travel time.

Roy H. Park, the innovator of Duncan Hines Days and now the owner of broadcast properties and newspapers, recommends telephone calls rather than visits to lawyers. He keeps a *talk sheet* by the telephone, invites members of management into the room and puts the lawyer on the speaker phone. When the conversation is over, the time is noted and the talk sheet is typed and filed in the legal costs folder, where it can be compared with the lawyer's monthly bill when it arrives.

When To Go In-House   If your company is consistently spending more than $75,000 a year on legal fees, it is time to consider hiring in-house counsel. However, most in-house lawyers can not handle the *big case* or the specialized issues—environmental, tax securities and antitrust—or litigation away from home.

If in-house counsel can be grafted on to other assignments such as corporate finance or fund-raising, you may get two tasks filled by the same person. Legal training is intensely analytical, and many lawyers are excellent acquisition analysts and financial planners. The EDS division of General Motors recently announced a reduction in outside counsel from 85 to 12 firms.

Cooperating with Competitors   Find other companies to share your legal costs on matters that affect a region or an industry, such as handling industrial wastes, environmental cleanups and massive tort litigation for inadequate labeling or product-safety features. The formation of coalitions is gaining popularity in administrative agency proceedings and local zoning matters.

Work with Your Competitors   Agree not to retain a law firm whose litigation department sues any company in your industry on a product liability or racketeering matter.

Using Arbitration Instead of Court Litigation   The American Arbitration Association handles 40,000 cases each year. It draws on the services of 60,000 arbitrators, many of whom are experts in a particular business or industry. An arbitrator has the authority to enter a binding, court-enforceable judgment from which only the most limited kind of appeal will be allowed. The fee for arbitrating a $10,000 case is $300.

When your company enters into a contractual arrangement with another company, be sure that any future dispute will be resolved by arbitration. For the contract the following language is recommended:

In the event of any dispute between you and (company), you and (company) agree to resolve them through the auspices of the American Arbitration Association in (city, state). Any award rendered shall be final and conclusive upon the parties. The prevailing party shall be entitled to his costs and reasonable attorneys' fees in connection with such arbitration and the enforcement thereof.

Rent-a-Judge   An alternative to arbitration is to hire a retired judge's services. Several companies now hire retired judges who decide cases more rapidly than the overloaded legal system can. In addition, legal fees are reduced because cases brought in private courts do not require as much documentation or as many procedural mechanisms. Parties must agree in writing to resolve their dispute either in this way or by arbitration and that neither will appeal the decision.

Recapture   Interview five local law firms and set the terms: Do not permit training of their junior people; make no payments for bad legal advice; ensure monthly time sheets agree with your time sheets; and establish a flat fee of $110 per hour for all work done. The winning bid: $20,000 per annum, a savings of $15,000.

Summary

It will take you less than 30 days to cut overhead. Changing your marketing strategy from an advertising budget of 5 percent of sales to more direct marketing and less advertising will take longer, and the results are not factored into this sample summary. But in pure overhead, the savings made for 30 days of diligent effort are as follows:

Savings in Overhead in 30 Days

	$ Annual
Rent	$ 10,500
Communications	12,000
Health insurance	62,100
Travel and entertainment	21,000
Accounting fees	8,000
Legal fees	15,000
Total	$138,100

At a purchase price multiple of 5 times EBIT, you have gained $690,500. If you do not recapture these savings, the buyer will pay you $690,500 less and put the $138,100 in his or her pocket. Plus, he or she will recover $76,000 of your money from the landlord.

Work Out the Best Terms

◆◆◆◆◆◆◆◆◆

"You Name the Price, I'll Name the Terms"

The terms of the sale are frequently as important as the price, particularly if your buyer is a financial buyer. To illustrate how you might obtain the best terms, Figure 10.1 shows three different acquisition candidates.

The fixtures manufacturer, the smallest of the 3 companies, can be acquired with 100-percent leverage because its assets are large in relation to its sales and cash flow. In older companies the fixed assets are frequently fully depreciated but quite usable and valuable to another buyer if the lender forecloses on the loan and requires auctioning off assets.

Although the fixture company can be bought with the financial buyer investing only $25,000 to $35,000, there is not enough cash flow to service the debt. The acquisition will need to be done with a substantial amount of seller financing; that is, the seller will have to provide most of the leverage. When and if cash flow increases, lenders

◆ Figure 10.1   Comparison of Acquisition Candidates

Name	ABC Company	DEF Company	GHI Company
Location	Huntsville, Ala.	Jackson, Miss.	Knoxville, Tenn.
Business	Manufactures air pollution control equipment that it sells to diversified industries	Manufactures compressors sold to oil and gas producers	Manufactures store fixtures, counters and racks sold to apparel, food, video retailers
Founded	1927	1958	1939
Management will remain	Yes	Yes	No
Customers	600	30	3,000
Users group	No	Yes	No
Sells abroad	No	Yes	No
Sells through			
Sales force	No	Yes	No
Reps	Yes	No	No
Catalog	No	No	Yes
Telemarketing	No	No	Yes
Advertisements	Yes	Yes	No
Trade shows	No	Yes	Yes
Videos	No	No	No
Sales last 3 yrs. ($000s) 1992	$6,500	$24,000	$2,300
1991	5,800	17,500	2,400
1990	4,500	15,000	2,550
Adjusted EBIT last 3 yrs. ($000s) 1992	$ 650	$ 2,800	$ 125
1991	435	1,000	300
1990	(120)	(1,500)	400
Shareholders' equity last 3 yrs. ($000s) 1992	$3,885	$ 9,000	$1,425
1991	3,815	8,200	1,680
1990	3,665	7,800	1,765

Asking price	$4,000	$30,000	$2,500
Debt to be assumed	—	5,800	—
Estimated leverage available			
Accts. rec.	$1,000	$ 4,000	$ 400
Inventory	500	2,000	500
Equipment	600	5,000	—
Plant	600	2,000	900
Total	$2,700	$13,000	$1,800
Cash flow available to service debt			
Adjusted EBIT	$ 650	$ 2,800	$ 125
Deductions			
Rent	—	—	—
Management	—	—	(80)
Monitoring	(75)	(75)	—
Total	$ 575	$ 2,725	$ 45
Estimated equity gap	$1,300	$11,200	—
Amount of debt that can be serviced (Adjusted EBIT/18%)	$3,194	$15,139	$ 250

can be located to prepay the sellers, perhaps at a discount. The timing is not right for this seller.

Among the many financing tactics, including a gross-profits royalty, an earnings royalty or a long-term note, the financial buyer might ask the seller to take some of his or her price from the sale of receivables and inventory. If unacceptable, the seller may be asked to consider a note secured by the assets of the company for a portion of the purchase price and a noncompete agreement paid out of a gross profits royalty for the balance. A noncompete agreement is frequently used to fill a portion of the equity gap. It prevents the sellers from entering the business in competition with the acquired company; and the consideration for not competing is a sum of money, often as much as one-third of the purchase price, paid monthly for a number of years. It is, in effect, a subordinated note without interest payments.

Noncompete Agreements

Financial buyers are likely to offer you a noncompete agreement (NCA) for a portion of the purchase price. Price Waterhouse & Company, a leading international accounting firm, estimates that this occurs in approximately one-third of all acquisitions. The noncompete agreement is similar to a long-term note paid to the seller, but without interest. You forego interest because the noncompete agreement is deductible from the buyer's taxable income.

Assume that a target company is purchased for $10 million, of which $2.5 million is allocated to a 5-year covenant not to compete. Further, assume that the buyer has a 40-percent tax rate and a 10-percent cost of capital or discounted present value factor. In Figure 10.2 we see that the cost of a $2.5 million, 5-year noncompete agreement is considerably less than full value.

One would think that the IRS would take a fairly staunch attitude about the use of noncompete agreements, especially because the deductibility portion of a note given to the seller is only the amount of interest on the note, whereas the noncompete agreement is fully deductible. The IRS has offered some guidance to buyers, and these are summarized as follows:

1. *Establish that the seller would likely come into the market as a competitor in the absence of the noncompete agreement.* Barriers that would prevent the seller from competing in the same market include health, geography, age or family reasons.
2. *Demonstrate the ability of the seller to compete.* This is evidenced by the seller's abilities, experience and knowledge of the target company and its market.
3. *Demonstrate via a business plan the competitive nature of the business.* It is important that the acquiring company develop a detailed and complete business plan in which the buyer explains in narrative form what it intends to do in the event of intense competition. The plan should explain that the entrance into the marketplace by another competitor with the experience of the seller would be serious and possibly destructive.

◆ **Figure 10.2**   Discounted Present Value of a $2.5 Million
Noncompete Agreement

($000s)	1	2	3	4	5
Payment of NCA	$ 500	$ 500	$ 500	$ 500	$ 500
Tax rate	.40	.40	.40	.40	.40
Tax savings	200	200	200	200	200
Present value factor at 10%	.9091	.8264	.7513	.6830	.6209
Present value	$ 708				

4. *Demonstrate that the dollar amount of the noncompete agreement is reasonable.* The acquiring company should prepare two cash flow models. The first should be a highly detailed, five-year business plan with cash flow projections that present the earnings capability with the noncompete agreement in place. The second cash flow model and narrative presents the company's earnings capability without a noncompete agreement in place. The two net cash flow streams are then discounted to determine discounted present value. The difference between the two should approximate the discounted present value of the noncompete agreement, as calculated in Figure 10.2 above.

Economic Reality

Noncompete agreements, in reality, lose their value in about three years. By then the buyer should have achieved the seller's level of experience and knowledge about the business. Economic reality dictates that a noncompete agreement should be paid up front (and amortized over five years) or paid in two or three years.

Further, a noncompete agreement should be *enforceable* under state law to meet the test of economic reality. Enforceability generally relies on the reasonableness of the terms of the noncompete agreement with regard to the number of years that the seller must remain outside the industry and the geographic circumscription. If the noncompete agreement is not legally enforceable, it cannot have much economic value; thus, it cannot be deductible from taxable income.

When Is the Noncompete Agreement of Greatest Value?

The least useful industries in which a high value can be assigned to a noncompete agreement are capital equipment manufacturing and consumer products. The high level of capital spending that creates a successful capital equipment company is itself an effective barrier to entry. Further, strong consumer interest in a line of products usually means that no single individual can significantly influence sales.

On the other hand, personal service companies, advertising agencies, consulting firms and businesses with a high intellectual content are perfect candidates to assign high values to a noncompete agreement. Once you open the trap door of accounting for the buyout, you encounter tax issues. That is why you may need to hire a tax adviser or have your accounting firm provide one.

When NCAs Are Used

As we can see from Figure 10.1 and the three target company examples, ABC Company, the air pollution control equipment manufacturer, has the best features for a leveraged buyout: diversified customers, growing cash flow, a sensible asking price, a considerable amount of available leverage and sufficient cash flow to obtain a cash overadvance or cash flow loan. The latter are term loans made for 12 months, secured by collateral as a secondary precaution but repayable out of cash flow. Note that the cash flow will support close to $3.2 million in leverage whereas the quick-test analysis of available leverage from the target company's assets is $2.7 million. If a cash flow lender can be located, the acquiring company is within $800,000 of buying the company, and the buyer, at this point, is likely to ask the seller to accept $400,000 of that amount in the form of an NCA. If the seller accepts, that leaves the buyer with a relatively small personal investment of $400,000 to purchase ABC Company.

DEF Company, the compressor manufacturer, must be sold to a strategic buyer or an all-cash buyer. Doing leveraged buyouts of cyclical capital equipment manufacturers is extremely dangerous—just ask Bobby Inman who bought Tracor Corp., a defense contractor with junk debt, only to watch it slide into Chapter 11 when revenues slipped shortly after *perestroika* in mid-1990. Financial buyers are loathe to acquire capital equipment manufacturers.

Although GHI Company, the store fixture manufacturer, has a very small cash flow, its net worth is fairly high—$1,425,000—because it has been around for so many years. The owner wants to receive $2,500,000 or more than 20 times adjusted EBIT. As we know, that will not happen. The real estate is worth $900,000, but the owner can keep the building and rent it to the buyer. Without the building the net worth is reduced to $525,000, which is about where the purchase price should be.

Of the $525,000 in purchase price, the buyer can ask the seller to keep the accounts receivables (they are supposedly worth $400,000), and the buyer will collect them for the seller. That leaves $125,000 in cash to be paid to the seller, which the buyer can raise through a quick sale of some finished goods inventory. The owner of GHI Company gets $525,000 plus a tenant for his building, and the buyer risks practically nothing. But, after all, the business is small and going south.

Summary

There are dozen of ways to structure the terms of a purchase once price is agreed to. One of the most popular devices is the noncompete agreement because the annual installment payments under the terms of this agreement are tax deductible whereas principal payments on installment debt are not. However, the IRS looks for abusive NCAs. If you are asked to take an NCA, make certain that it is for less than one-third of the total purchase price and three years or less in length.

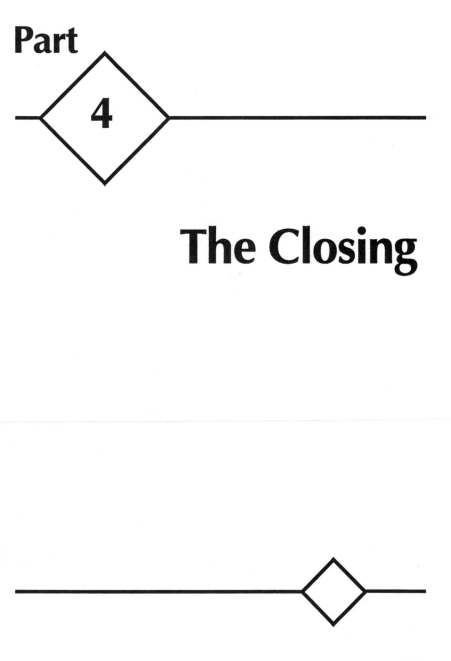

Part

4

The Closing

The Letter
of Intent

◆◆◆◆◆◆◆◆◆

As the closing approaches, the buyer gives the seller two documents: the letter of intent and the purchase and sale agreement. Figure 11.1 shows a copy of a sample letter of intent.

Let me explain the key elements of the letter of intent and phrases to be watchful for. First of all, this is a letter of intent from a financial buyer. You can tell this because paragraph 5 warns you that the buyer intends to use leverage. You do not want all the assets of the company to be used as collateral if you will be holding a subordinated note or a noncompete agreement for a portion of the purchase price. If the company goes under, your subordinated note or noncompete agreement will be worth zilch, and you will be handed your company back fully laden with debt. You should counter-propose that not more than two-thirds of the leverage value of the assets may be pledged to secure senior debt. In that way, if the *big-hat-no-cattle* buyer runs your company into the ground and you have to take it back because payments under the NCA cannot be met, you do not get it back fully laden with debt.

◆ **Figure 11.1**   Sample Letter of Intent

Date

Mr. Serious Seller
Chief Executive Officer
Target Corporation
Any Street
Middletown, AK 07000

Dear Mr. Seller:

This will confirm certain acquisition terms proposed by us on behalf of Target Holdings, Inc. ("Holdings"), a corporation to be formed and majority-owned by the undersigned and key employees of Target Corporation upon your acceptance of the terms herein. It is Holdings' intention to offer to purchase certain of the assets and to assume certain of the assets and liabilities of Target Corporation ("Target") pursuant to a formal purchase offer as described below, which Holdings will make to you. The offer would be subject to the following principal terms and conditions:

1. Holdings agrees to pay the sum of ten million dollars ($10,000,000) as the Purchase Price.

2. The Purchase Price will consist of $6,500,000 in cash at the closing and $3,500,000 in the form of a noncompete agreement payable to you at the rate of $58,333 per month over 60 months.

3. The assets that Holdings intends to purchase include every asset of Target on its financial statements as of the closing date, plus non-balance sheet assets including its trade name, customer lists, contracts, blueprints, technical know-how, and any and all other off-balance sheet assets.

4. The liabilities that Holdings intends to assume include every liability of Target on its financial statements as of the closing date, with the exception of notes payable to the bank, the management contract, the sales commission agreement with you and its airplane lease.

5. Holdings will obtain a portion of the capital for the purchase price at the closing from outside sources and from encumbering and borrowing against the assets of Target.

6. This offer is contingent upon further due diligence by Holdings, including an appraisal of tangible assets, a review of all Target contracts and agreements, and raising capital to consummate the purchase, which activities are expected to consume 60 days.

7. You agree that you will not withdraw cash from Target during the 60-day period, except to meet normal and recurring obligations of the business, and that you will not reduce, or cause others to reduce, the net worth of Target during the 60-day period below its level on the August 31, 1991 balance sheet of $5,500,000.

8. This letter is not intended to create a binding legal agreement or obligation, but to outline our intent to proceed in good faith on the general terms stated above. You will continue to provide full access to Target's financial records by Holdings' outside auditors, appraisers, personnel, and attorneys, and you agree to keep Holdings informed with respect to any matters material to the business of Target that would affect its willingness to go forward with this transaction.

9. We will both use our reasonable best efforts to consummate this transaction within sixty (60) days from today. We will proceed to instruct our counsel to draft a definitive purchase agreement for your review upon your signing this letter. If this transaction is not closed within sixty (60) days from this date, by written notice to the other party, either party hereto may suspend negotiations after that date and any further obligation to cooperate shall thereupon cease.

In the event of cancellation of this agreement after expiration of the above time period, each party shall bear its own expenses incurred in connection with this transaction.

10. You agree that you will not negotiate for the sale of Target, its assets or its stock until the period described in paragraph 9 shall have expired.

Sincerely yours,

_____

President

Target Holdings, Inc.

Date: _____

AGREED TO AND ACCEPTED BY:

_____

Chief Executive Officer

Target Corporation

Date:_____

Paragraph 6 is a further tip-off that the buyer is not financially strong. Moreover, the buyer is given the privilege of lowering the price following the due diligence period. You should demand a low-end range in the letter of intent—say $9,500,000—to prevent the buyer coming back after 60 days and lowering the price more than 5 percent.

The letter of intent lacks an earnest money deposit, but you are asked to remove your company from the market for 60 days. Although you could break the deal by demanding earnest money, you should have the right to continue finding buyers during the due diligence period; and to give the first buyer something of value, you can agree to inform him or her of any bona fide bids that come in during the 60 days and permit him or her the right to equal or exceed them.

Summary

When you are handed a letter of intent, most buyers will ask you to start to provide them with very serious information about customers, suppliers, prices and costs. Make sure that the buyer is serious (asking for nonrefundable deposits is usually a deal breaker). Thus, it is best to put some teeth into the letter of intent to give you some flexibility. And by all means, object to any buyer fully leveraging your company's assets then asking you to take an installment payment for the balance of the purchase price.

12

The Purchase and Sale Agreement

◆◆◆◆◆◆◆◆◆

The Legal Document

The purchase and sale agreement is the primary document that is signed by both parties at the closing. Figure 12.1 shows a sample purchase and sale agreement.

If your eyes are blurry after reading the six primary articles that make up a purchase agreement, I think you will agree with me that an experienced acquisitions lawyer is mandatory and probably worth your expenditure of money.

◆ **Figure 12.1**　Agreement for Purchase and Sale of Assets

Acquisition Agreement, made this 31 day of December, 1993, by and between HOLDINGS, INC., a Delaware corporation (herein called "Purchaser" or "Holdings"), TARGET CORPORATION, an Alabama corporation (herein called "Seller") and Mr. Sam Seller (herein called "Shareholder").

In consideration of the mutual promises herein contained, the parties agree as follows:

ARTICLE I

Purchased Assets; Price

1.01.　Purchase and Sale. Seller desires to sell and Purchaser desires to purchase all of Seller's assets or right, title and interest in and to the assets in consideration of the payment of the purchase price and the assumption by Purchaser of the liabilities of Seller all as set forth herein.

1.02.　Purchased Assets. Subject to the terms and conditions set forth in this Agreement, Seller will sell, convey, assign, transfer, and deliver to Purchaser and Purchaser will purchase from Seller on the Closing Date all of Seller's properties and assets (tangible and intangible) and its business as a going concern (the "Business"). The assets to be purchased are all the assets of Seller owned or used by it in the conduct of its business as of October 31, 1993 (the "Financial Statement Date") whether or not included in the Balance Sheets (as hereinafter defined) except as herein provided. The assets being purchased are herein sometimes referred to as the "Purchased Assets." Purchased Assets shall include without limitation the following at the Closing Date except for those assets which have been sold, transferred, or disposed of in the ordinary and regular course of business or with the consent of Purchaser between the Financial Statement Date and the Closing Date and shall include all assets which have been acquired whether or not in the ordinary and regular course of business prior to the Closing Date:

1.02.1.　Real Property and Leasehold Interests. All of Seller's right, title, and interest in and to the premises described in the deed _____ recorded [Date] and designated as Exhibit 1.02.1-A hereto and Seller's leasehold interests in and security deposits related to all properties occupied by Seller as tenant pursuant to the leases described in Exhibit 1.02.1-B hereto (the "Leases");

(Continued)

1.02.2. <u>Fixed Assets</u>. All of Seller's right, title, and interest in and to the machinery, equipment (including all registrations, applications, drawings, blueprints, tools, jigs, dies, designs, patterns, and samples pertaining thereto), motor vehicles, furniture, and fixtures and all other personal property and fixed assets owned by Seller (the "Fixed Assets"), including without limitation those assets listed in Exhibit 1.02.2;

1.02.3. <u>Books; Claims</u>. All of Seller's books and records (except minute books), business records, insurance policies, and claims and credits thereunder;

1.02.4. <u>Inventory</u>. All of Seller's right, title, and interest in all inventories and other supplies pertaining to the Business including raw materials, packages, work-in-process and finished goods (the "Inventory");

1.02.5 <u>Intellectual Property</u>. All of Seller's right, title, and interest in all patents, trade names, service marks, trademarks, software, inventions, and rights to inventions, trade secrets, and know-how, whether or not patentable, copyrights and copyright applications and registrations, and any other intellectual property used or useful in the Business, including, without limitation, those items described in Exhibit 1.02.5 (the "Intellectual Property");

1.02.6. <u>Contracts; Permits; etc</u>. All of Seller's right, title, interest in and privileges arising from (i) its unshipped orders, prepaid expenses, customer contracts, customer lists, outstanding offers, sales records, advertising materials, and all agreements for the sale, purchase, or lease of goods or services, (ii) all contracts, agreements (the "Contracts"), licenses, permits, and other intangible property rights (the "Permits"), (iii) all relevant documents pertaining to any operating location (including, without limitation, all certificates of occupancy, surveys, and construction drawings), pertaining to the Leases, Contracts, Permits, Inventory, Accounts Receivable, and Fixed Assets, and (iv) all retail price and product lists, historical account information, and sales records of Seller and all other things of value owned by Seller used or useful in the operation of the Business and not expressly excluded in this Section 1.02;

1.02.7. <u>Cash and Receivables</u>. All of Seller's cash and cash equivalents; all of Seller's right, title, and interest in all accounts receivable and all other receivables of any kind (the "Accounts Receivable") subject to such reserves, offsets, and deductions as are reflected in the October 31, 1993 Balance Sheet.

◆ **Figure 12.1** Agreement for Purchase and Sale of Assets (Continued)

1.03. <u>Purchase Price</u>. Subject to the terms and conditions of this Agreement and in reliance on the representations and warranties of Seller herein contained, and in consideration of the sale, conveyance, assignment, transfer, and delivery provided for in this Agreement, Purchaser agrees to pay to Seller a purchase price of Thirteen Million Dollars ($13,000,000), together with the assumption of all liabilities of Seller by Purchaser pursuant to Section 1.04 hereof to be paid at the Closing as follows:

(a) $13,000,000 less the credits set forth below by certified or bank check drawn on a New York Clearing House bank or federal funds transfer to the order of Seller; and

(b) $3,000,000 in the form of a note to Seller (Exhibit 1.03).

1.04. <u>Assumption of Liabilities</u>. Provided that the transactions herein contemplated are consummated and as a condition precedent to the sale of the Purchased Assets to Purchaser, at the Closing, Purchaser shall assume and indemnify Seller against all liabilities of Seller reflected on the Balance Sheet as of the Financial Statement Date or incurred subsequent thereto in the ordinary course of business or with the express written consent of the Purchaser, said assumption to be made pursuant to an Assumption Agreement, the form of which shall be substantially as set forth in Exhibit 1.04-A. Except as set forth in this Section 1.04, Purchaser will assume no other liabilities of Seller in connection with the transactions contemplated by this Agreement, whether fixed or contingent, known or unknown, relating to the operation of the Business or otherwise.

1.05. <u>Pension Plan Matters</u>.

(a) Purchaser shall assume all of the obligations and powers of Seller under each of the employee benefit plans identified in Exhibit 2.14 as being continued by Purchaser hereunder and for any unpaid amounts or underfunding in respect of such employee benefit plans; <u>provided, however</u>, Seller shall reimburse Purchaser for any medical, life insurance, or other employee benefit plan costs (a) for claims incurred before the Closing Date (regardless of whether such claims are filed before the Closing Date) and (b) with respect to any person not actively employed by Seller on the Closing Date because of an illness or other condition, claims

(Continued)

incurred with respect to such illness or condition before resumption by active employment with Purchaser. Purchaser shall not take or fail to take any actions that would result in Seller becoming liable for any such unpaid amounts or underfunding, including liabilities under the Pension Board Governing Commission, without previously providing such indemnities or bonds, or taking other actions, acceptable to Seller.

(b) No later than the Closing Date, Seller shall notify all trustees or insurance companies holding assets under the Pension Plan and all investment managers who are managing assets of such plan that Purchaser will be administering such plan and will be assuming all of Seller's obligations, rights, and privileges thereunder as of the Closing Date. Following the Closing Date, Seller shall cooperate with Purchaser in providing any such trustee, insurance company, or investment manager with any documentation they may require to effect the foregoing.

1.05.1. Additional Instruments. In addition, at the Closing, Seller shall deliver to Purchaser such endorsements, assignments, and other good and sufficient instruments of conveyance and transfer, in form and substance satisfactory to Purchaser and its counsel, as are effective to transfer to Purchaser or to record all of Seller's right, title, and interest in the balance of the Purchased Assets free and clear of any lien, security interest, charge, or encumbrance (except for any such lien, security interest, charge, or encumbrance the discharge of which cannot be affected by the payment of money by Seller and will not materially detract from the value or interfere with the present use of the Purchased Assets, or otherwise materially impair the conduct of the Business).

1.05.2. Consents and Permits. Seller will use its best efforts to obtain as promptly as possible, but in all cases on or prior to the Closing Date, written consents to the transfer, assignment, subcontract, or sublicense to Purchaser of all Leases, Contracts, Permits, Intellectual Property and all other agreements, commitments, purchase orders, contracts, licenses, rights, documents, and other assets being transferred pursuant hereto for which the approval or other consent of any other person may be required including the unqualified consent of ABC Leasing Co., the lessor of the Company's assets unless the parties hereafter agree in writing that it is not in their respective best interests to obtain any such approval or other consent.

◆ **Figure 12.1**   Agreement for Purchase and Sale of Assets (Continued)

ARTICLE II

Seller's and Shareholders' Representations and Warranties

Seller and Shareholder each hereby represents and warrants to Purchaser that:

2.01.   Organization and Good Standing. Seller is a corporation duly organized, validly existing, and in good standing under the laws of the jurisdiction of its incorporation as shown on Exhibit 2.01 with all requisite power and authority to own, operate and lease its properties and to carry on its business as now being conducted. To the best of Seller's knowledge, it is duly qualified to do business and is in good standing in each jurisdiction where the conduct of business or ownership or lease of property requires such qualification, as set forth in Exhibit 2.01.

2.02.   Intellectual Property. Except as and to the extent set forth in Exhibit 2.02, on the Closing Date Seller will own or be licensed or otherwise have the right to use all the Intellectual Property that is necessary for the operation of the Business as presently conducted and all tools, jigs, dies and forms whether or not located or maintained at Seller's premises. To the knowledge of Seller, no product, process, method, substance, part or other material presently contemplated to be sold by or employed by Seller infringes upon any rights owned by any other person; no claim or litigation against Seller is pending, or to the knowledge of Seller threatened, contesting its right to sell or use any such product, process, method, substance, part or other material; and to the knowledge of Seller, no patent, invention, device, application, principle or any statute, law, rule, regulation, standard or code is pending or proposed that would materially adversely affect the condition or operations of Seller.

2.03.   No Disposition of Assets. Unless otherwise disclosed herein, there has not been since the Financial Statement Date and will not be prior to the Closing Date, any sale, lease or any other disposition or distribution by the Seller of any of its assets or properties and any other assets now or hereafter owned by it, except in the ordinary and regular course of business.

(Continued)

2.04. <u>Capital Structure</u>. Seller Common Stock presently outstanding is validly issued, fully paid, and nonassessable; and there are no outstanding subscriptions, options, warrants, calls, commitments or agreements of any character affecting Seller's Common Stock or requiring the issuance of additional capital stock of Seller.

2.05. <u>Absence of Prohibitions</u>. This Agreement and the transactions contemplated hereby do not violate and are not prohibited or restricted, in any way, in whole or in part, by Seller's charter, bylaws or by any mortgages, liens, leases, indentures, agreements (written or otherwise), instruments, judgments, decrees, to which Seller is a party or to or by which Seller is bound or any law, regulation, or rule, except as shown on Exhibit 2.05.

2.06. <u>Tax Matters</u>. Seller has filed all tax returns that it is required to file; all such returns are true and correct; Seller has paid all taxes owed by it or which it is obligated to withhold from amounts owing to any employee, creditor or third party; Seller has not waived any statute of limitations with respect to taxes or agreed to any extension of time with respect to a tax assessment or deficiency; there are no material unresolved questions or claims concerning Seller's tax liability.

2.07. <u>Absence of Undisclosed Liabilities</u>. Unless otherwise disclosed herein, there are no liabilities (direct or contingent) of seller as to which a claim has been or may be made, that would adversely affect the assets and business of Seller, except those set forth herein or set forth or described in any Exhibits hereto.

2.08. <u>Litigation</u>. Except as set forth in Exhibit 2.08, there is no suit, action or proceeding pending or, to the knowledge of Seller, threatened against or affecting Seller, or which, if adversely determined, would materially and adversely affect the business, prospects, operations, properties or the condition, financial or otherwise, of Seller, nor is there any judgment, decree, injunction, rule or order of any court, governmental department, commission, agency, instrumentality or arbitrator outstanding against Seller having, or which, insofar as can be foreseen, in the future may have, any such effect.

2.09. <u>True and Complete Copies</u>. Copies of all agreements, contracts and documents delivered and to be delivered hereunder by Seller are and will be true and complete copies of such agreements, contracts and documents.

◆ Figure 12.1 Agreement for Purchase and Sale of Assets (Continued)

2.10. <u>Compliance with Law</u>. Seller has not failed or is not failing to comply with any applicable law or regulation where such failure or failures would individually or in the aggregate have a materially adverse effect on the financial condition, business, operations or prospects of Seller. There are no proceedings of record and to the knowledge of Seller, no proceedings are pending or threatened, nor has Seller received any written notice, regarding any material violation of any law, ordinance, requirement, order, rule or regulations enforced by any governmental agency or other entity (Federal, state or local) claiming jurisdiction over Seller, including any requirement of OSHA or any pollution and environmental control agency (including air and water).

2.11. <u>Capital Expenditures</u>. As of the Financial Statement State, Seller had no outstanding commitments for capital expenditures pertaining to it. After the date hereof, no capital expenditures or commitments in excess of $50,000 in the aggregate will be made by Seller except with Purchaser's prior written consent.

2.12. <u>Contracts</u>. Seller has delivered to Purchaser a schedule and true copies of all material Contracts (Exhibit 2.12) to which Seller is a party pertaining to the Business and Assets being purchased. The term "Contracts" as used in this paragraph means all loan agreements, guarantees, joint venture agreements, material purchase and sales agreements, collective bargaining, union, consulting and employment contracts. Unless otherwise disclosed herein, Seller has performed all obligations required to be performed by it and is not in default under or in breach of nor in receipt of any claim of default or breach under any such contract to which Seller is subject; no event has occurred that with the passage of time or the giving of notice or both would result in a default, breach or event of noncompliance under any such contract to which Seller is subject; Seller has no knowledge of any breach or anticipated breach by the other parties to any contract or commitment to which it is a party; and Seller is not a party to any materially adverse contract or commitment.

2.13. <u>Inventory</u>. On the Closing Date, the Inventory (including raw materials, work-in-progress, and finished products) will consist of items usable and saleable in the ordinary course of business and will be substantially similar in kind and quantity to the Inventory included in Seller's Balance Sheet, except as described in Exhibit 2.13.

(Continued)

2.14. <u>Lists of Other Data</u>. All Exhibits hereto contain in all material respects complete and accurate lists or summary descriptions of the information purported to be contained therein under this Agreement. All Schedules hereto contain in all material respects complete and accurate lists and summary descriptions as they pertain to the Business.

ARTICLE III

Representations and Warranties of Purchaser

Purchaser represents, warrants and agrees as follows:

3.01. <u>Existence and Good Standing</u>. Purchaser on the Closing Date will be a corporation duly organized, validly existing and in good standing under the laws of the State of Delaware.

3.02. <u>Restrictive Documents</u>. Purchaser is not nor will be subject to any charter, by-law, mortgage, lien, lease, indenture, agreement, instrument, order, rule, regulation, judgment, decree or any other restriction of any kind or character, that would be breached by the making of this Agreement or by the performance of the transaction contemplated by this Agreement.

3.03. <u>Governmental Authorities</u>. Purchaser is not required to submit any notice, report or other filing with and no consent, approval or authorization is required by any governmental authority in connection with its execution or delivery of this Agreement or the consummation of the transactions contemplated hereby. No consent, approval or authorization of any governmental or regulatory authority is required to be obtained by Purchaser in connection with the execution, delivery and performance of this Agreement.

ARTICLE IV

Covenants of Seller

Until the Closing Date, except as otherwise consented to or approved by Purchaser in writing, Seller and Shareholder each covenants and agrees that Seller will comply or he will cause Seller to comply with each of the following:

4.01. <u>Regular Course of Business</u>. Seller will operate its business diligently and in good faith, consistent with past management practices. Seller will maintain all of its properties in customary repair, order and

◆ **Figure 12.1** Agreement for Purchase and Sale of Assets (Continued)

condition, reasonable wear and tear excepted. Seller will comply in all material respects with the provisions of all laws, regulations, ordinances and judicial decrees applicable to the conduct of its business. Seller will not, except as otherwise permitted by this Agreement or consented to in writing by Purchaser:

(a) grant any powers of attorney to act for the Business;

(b) sell, terminate, assign or transfer any Lease concerning any property, or, except in the ordinary course of business, sell, assign or transfer any of the other Purchased Assets;

(c) cancel or terminate any contract, agreement or other instrument material to the Business; or

(d) amend, terminate or otherwise alter any of the employee benefit plans being continued by Purchaser under Section 1.05.

Seller shall from and after the date hereof up to and including the Closing Date:

(a) maintain in full force and effect the insurance policies set forth in Exhibit 4.01 hereto (or policies providing substantially the same coverage);

(b) take such action as may reasonably be necessary to preserve the Purchased Assets, wherever located, which are material to the Business;

(c) maintain its books and records in accordance with generally accepted accounting principles and in a manner consistent with past practices; and

(d) use its best efforts to preserve the organization of the Business intact, continue its operations at its present levels, keep available to Purchaser the services of the personnel of the Business, and preserve for Purchaser the goodwill of the Business, its customers, creditors and others having business relations with it.

4.02. Amendments. No change or amendment shall be made in Seller's Certificate of Incorporation or Bylaws. Seller will not merge into or consolidate with any other corporation or person, or change the character of its business.

4.03. Capital Changes. Seller shall not issue or sell any shares of its capital stock of any class or issue or sell any securities convertible into, or options, warrants to purchase or rights to subscribe to, any shares of its capital stock of any class.

(Continued)

4.04. <u>Dividends</u>. Seller shall not declare, pay or set aside for payment any dividend or other distribution in respect of its capital stock, nor shall Seller, directly or indirectly, redeem, purchase or otherwise acquire any shares of its capital stock.

4.05. <u>Capital and Other Expenditures</u>. Seller will not make any capital expenditures, or commitments with respect thereof, except as set forth in Exhibit 2.11. Seller will not make any loan or advance to any Affiliate and will collect in full any amounts outstanding now due from any Affiliate.

4.06. <u>Borrowing</u>. Seller shall not incur, assume or guarantee any indebtedness for money borrowed. Seller will not create or permit to become effective any mortgage, pledge, lien, encumbrance or charge of any kind upon any of its assets, except as contemplated by this Agreement.

4.07. <u>Other Material Commitments</u>. Seller will not enter into any material transaction or make any material commitment or cancel or be in default under any material commitment or receive notice, valid or otherwise, for any other person cancelling material contract.

4.08. <u>Full Access and Disclosure</u>.

(a) Seller shall afford Purchaser and its counsel, accountants and other authorized representatives reasonable access during business hours to Seller's plants, properties, books and records in order that Purchaser may have full opportunity to make such reasonable investigations as it shall desire to make of the affairs of Seller; and Seller will cause its officers and employees to furnish such additional financial and operating data and other information as Purchaser shall from time to time reasonably request.

(b) From time to time prior to the Closing Date, Seller promptly supplements or amends information previously delivered to Purchaser with respect to any matter hereafter arising which, if existing or occurring at the date of this Agreement, would have been required to be set forth or disclosed.

4.09. <u>Consents</u>. Seller shall use its best efforts to obtain on or prior to the Closing Date, all consents necessary to the consummation of the transactions contemplated hereby.

4.10. <u>Negotiations with Third Parties</u>. the parties have incurred and will incur by the nature of the negotiations and investigations regarding this Agreement substantial expenses with respect to the subject matter of this Agreement. Accordingly, Seller represents and warrants

◆ **Figure 12.1** Agreement for Purchase and Sale of Assets (Continued)

---

to Purchaser that Seller has ceased, and agrees that it will not commence or recommence, negotiating with any third parties for the sale of any or all of the Business, the Purchased Assets or the stock of Seller. Seller further agrees not to solicit any inquiries or proposals from or provide any information to any other person, firm or corporation relating to the sale of any or all of the Business or the Purchased Assets.

4.11.   Noncompetition Agreement. Seller and Shareholder each hereby covenants and agrees that for a period of five years commencing on the Closing Date it will not itself establish, own or operate, or authorize any other person to establish, own or operate, any facility that manufactures or markets products that are the same as or similar to the products currently manufactured or marketed by Seller. Seller further covenants and agrees not to use any corporate names, product names, trade names, trademarks or service marks that are similar in nature to or likely to cause confusion with any of the trade names, trademarks, or applications to the foregoing being conveyed pursuant to this Agreement as Intellectual Property.

4.12.   Brokers and Finders. Shareholder shall be responsible for any amount owed to Intermediaries or any other person on account of brokerage fees, commissions or finders' fees, and agrees to pay, indemnify, save and hold Purchaser harmless against any claim or liability for any brokerage fees, commissions or finders' fees due to Intermediaries or any other person arising as a result of agreement or actions by Shareholder in connection with the transactions contemplated herein.

ARTICLE V

Covenants of Purchaser

Purchaser hereby covenants and agrees with Seller that:

5.01.   Confidentiality. Purchaser will, and will cause its and its Affiliates' associates, principals, officers and other personnel and authorized representatives to hold in strict confidence and not disclose to any other party without Seller's prior consent, all information received by it from Seller, any of Seller's officers, directors, employees, agents, counsel and auditors in connection with the transactions contemplated hereby except as may be required by applicable law or to arrange the financing desired to effect this transaction or as otherwise

(Continued)

contemplated herein. If the transaction is not consummated, Purchaser shall return all documents received to Seller and shall not further disclose any information regarding Seller that has been made available hereto.

ARTICLE VI

Conditions Precedent

6.01. <u>Conditions Precedent to Purchaser's Obligations</u>. All of the obligations of Purchaser hereunder are subject to the fulfillment by Seller and Shareholder of each of the following conditions on or before the Closing Date:

    (a) <u>Representations</u>. All representations, warranties and covenants of Seller and Shareholder contained in this Agreement and in certificates and documents delivered pursuant to the terms hereof and in connection with the transaction contemplated thereby shall be true and correct in all material respects at and as of the Closing Date as if such representations and warranties had been made on the Closing Date, and Seller and Shareholder shall have delivered to Purchaser a Certificate, dated the Closing Date, signed by the President and Chief Executive Officer of Seller to such effect, in the form of Exhibit 6.01(a) hereto.

    (b) <u>Agreements</u>. All of the agreements, covenants and promises of Seller and Shareholder to be performed or complied with on or before the Closing Date pursuant to the terms hereof shall have been duly performed or complied with on the part of Seller and Shareholder and Seller and Shareholder shall have delivered to Purchaser a Certificate, dated the Closing Date signed by the President and Chief Executive Officer of Seller to such effect, in the form of Exhibit 6.01(b) hereto.

    (c) <u>Opinion</u>. Seller shall have furnished Purchaser with a favorable opinion, dated the Closing Date, of Shareholder's counsel, substantially in the form of Exhibit 6.01(c).

    (d) <u>Financial Tests</u>. The following financial results shall be obtained, and Seller and Shareholder shall deliver a Certificate signed by Seller's President and by its Chief Financial Officer (Exhibit 6.01(e), to the effect that Seller's financial statements as of the last day of the month preceding the Closing Date did reflect as, at and for the period then ended that:

◆ Figure 12.1   Agreement for Purchase and Sale of Assets (Continued)

(i) Seller's Shareholders Equity was at least $_____, Seller's Long-Term Liabilities did not exceed $_____, and Seller's Current Liabilities did not exceed the amount reflected in its October 31, 1993 Financial Statement.

(e) <u>No Material Adverse Change</u>. There shall have been no material adverse change since October 31, 1993 in the business, condition (financial or otherwise), operations or prospects of Seller. Seller shall have Accounts Receivable of at least $_____, at Closing. Seller shall deliver assurance to the effect ("cold comfort") from Seller's President and Chief Financial Officer in the form designed Exhibit 6.01(e).

(f) <u>Comfort Letter</u>. Purchaser shall have received a "comfort" letter from Seller's independent certified public accountants, dated the Closing Date, based upon a limited review (but not an audit) conducted no earlier than five business days preceding the Closing Date, substantially in the form of Exhibit 6.01(f) hereto which letter shall relate to the operations and financial conditions of Seller.

6.02. <u>Conditions Precedent to Seller's and Shareholder's Obligations</u>. All of the obligations of Seller and Shareholder hereunder are subject to the fulfillment by Purchaser of each of the following conditions on or before the Closing Date:

(a) <u>Representations</u>. All representations and warranties of Purchaser contained in Article 3 hereof shall be true in all material respects at and as of the Closing Date as if such representations and warranties had been made on the Closing Date and Seller shall have been furnished with a certificate of an Officer of Purchaser, dated the Closing Date, to that effect (Exhibit 6.02(a)).

(b) <u>Agreements</u>. All of the agreements, covenants and promises of Purchaser to be performed on or before the Closing Date pursuant to the terms hereof shall have been duly performed and Seller shall have been furnished with a certificate of an Officer of Purchaser dated the Closing Date to that effect (Exhibit 6.02(b)).

(c) <u>Resolutions</u>. Purchaser shall have furnished Seller with certified copies of resolutions duly adopted by the Board of Directors of Purchaser approving the transactions contemplated by this Agreement (Exhibit 6.02(c)).

(Continued)

(d) <u>Legal Opinion</u>. Purchaser shall have furnished Seller a favorable opinion, dated the Closing Date, of their counsel, to the effect that Purchaser is a corporation in good standing and has full power and authority to make and perform this Agreement, that this Agreement has been duly authorized by proper corporate action of Purchaser's directors and that this Agreement constitutes the valid and legally binding obligation of Purchaser, enforceable in accordance with its terms (Exhibit 6.02(d)).

(e) <u>Seller Consulting Agreement</u>. Sam Seller and Purchaser shall have entered into the Noncompete Agreement.

6.03.   <u>No Proceeding or Litigation</u>. No action, suit or proceeding before any court or any governmental or regulatory authority shall have been commenced or to the best of Purchaser's knowledge threatened, no investigation by any governmental or regulatory authority shall have been threatened, against any of the parties or any of their respective principals, officers or directors seeking to restrain, prevent or change the transactions contemplated hereby or questioning the validity or legality of any of such transactions or seeking damages in connections with any of such transactions.

Summary

The purpose of having you read a purchase and sale agreement is not to put you to sleep; rather, it is to expose you to the intense amount of detail that goes into selling a company. Your books and records must be squeaky clean. Taxes must be paid up-to-date. If there is litigation that could attach itself to the buyer, you will have to indemnify the buyer, i.e., agree to pay his costs and damages, if any. The buyer may regard the litigation, or the potential for litigation, as sufficiently serious to escrow a portion of the purchase price for several years until he is comfortable that the litigation is not an issue.

If your company has some loose ends, they will surface when the purchase agreement is drafted, after you have spent megabucks on the deal. This is known as the aim-fire-ready way of doing business. It wastes money. Clean up your messes before posting the *for sale* sign.

13

Avoiding Deal Breakers

◆◆◆◆◆◆◆◆◆

Deal breakers appear primarily in the area of undisclosed liabilities and secondarily in back-end payments; that is, anything that puts either party at risk.

The most common back-end payments are a royalty expressed as a percentage of the company's future sales or earnings paid to the seller over time, a noncompete agreement and a subordinated note. All of these come under the heading of *seller financing*.

In some instances, particularly with companies that are losing money, it is appropriate for the seller to be *at risk* for some portion of the purchase price. In those cases I would recommend that the seller negotiate vigorously for a note, which is a legal obligation to pay, and negotiate vigorously against the percentage of sales or earnings and the noncompete agreement. These latter two back-end payments leave the seller somewhat naked. To assist sellers in their negotiations in this highly critical area without breaking the deal, sellers will want the most facilitative and experienced deal lawyers they can find.

Advice from Your Uncle Harry

Everyone knows an "Uncle Harry" who can buy the best suit in the world for less money than you or I pay, buy the best trip to Europe for the biggest discount and have mail order brain surgery from the best doctor on the planet. When you tell him about the buyer of your company, the price and the terms, he knows with absolute certainty that he can get you a better deal, a better price, more favorable terms, plus a consulting agreement with more money and fewer hours. He makes you feel like a numbskull for agreeing to the deal.

But remember the advice dispensed earlier in this book: Free advice is worth what you pay for it. Nothing.

If you listen to Uncle Harry, you will surely break the deal. Do you want to do that? Probably not.

The Best Deal Lawyers

To avoid deal breakers entirely, owners should hire deal lawyers to handle the sales of their companies. The 25 best deal lawyers, as selected by investment bankers, are listed in Appendix II. These lawyers have been recommended by the nation's most active acquisition funds, which means they have done dozens of acquisitions and are highly knowledgeable. Since you probably will sell a company only once in your life, why not go with the best!

Summary

Your lawyer may be your best friend, may have advised you on commercial matters for more than 20 years. Your lawyer may be one of the finest people on the planet. But that does not qualify him or her to represent you in the sale of your company. Go for an experienced deal lawyer when you are attempting to get the best deal for your company.

Minimizing Taxes

❖❖❖❖❖❖❖❖❖

To understand how to minimize the tax consequences of the sale of your company, you must first understand the difference between *taxable* and *nontaxable acquisitions*.

Structuring the Deal

A seller's goal in structuring a transaction is to maximize after-tax profit, that is, to minimize the government's share. To do this, a seller must structure a transaction to avoid the recognition of gain at more than one taxpaying level—a corporate tax on the sale of assets and a shareholder tax on the liquidation of the corporation. This is one reason why sellers generally prefer to structure a transaction as a stock sale.

The seller must also consider whether to: (1) receive all or substantially all the proceeds at the time of the transaction, or (2) defer the payments, through the installment method, to a year in which it may be more advantageous to recognize such gains. However, recent changes to the provisions of the installment method impose an interest charge on the deferred tax liability for aggregate installment obligations that exceed $5 million.

Generally, a buyer is interested in acquiring a step-up in the tax basis of a seller's assets if the assets have appreciated in value. This allows a buyer to depreciate or amortize the increased value of these assets. Any increase in the asset basis will also reduce subsequent gains to a buyer if unwanted assets are disposed of after the acquisition.

A transaction involving substantially all the seller's business assets can be structured as either an asset acquisition or stock acquisition. The ultimate form of the transaction may be dictated by the overall tax objectives.

Asset Acquisition

Buyers always prefer asset acquisitions. They enable buyers to pick and choose the assets they want, eliminate the ones they do not want, eliminate the trail of potential liabilities that attach to certain contracts of the seller and, subject to tax laws, place the values of the purchase price on assets that are depreciable or amortizable more quickly than those that are not.

Buyer Considerations

To a buyer the most important tax advantage of an asset acquisition is a step-up in the basis of the acquired assets equal to the purchase price. The purchase price includes the amount paid plus any liabilities assumed. A buyer will benefit from a stepped-up basis to the extent the purchase price is allocated to inventory, depreciable or amortizable assets. After acquiring assets a buyer may sell unwanted assets to a third party, with little or no gain, and use the proceeds to help pay part of the purchase price to the seller.

If the assets have not appreciated in value in the hands of the seller, a buyer may not be interested in directly acquiring assets because their basis in the hands of the buyer will be stepped down in value to reflect their cost, thereby reducing future depreciation deductions and increasing taxable income.

When assets of a corporation are acquired, generally, none of the selling corporation's tax attributes, such as earnings and profits and net operating loss carry forwards, survive. A buyer is also not subject to the accounting methods for inventory or depreciation that a seller used and may select any permissible accounting method.

In an asset acquisition, a buyer also has the ability to be selective about which assets to acquire and which liabilities to assume. This can be an advantage to a buyer who is acquiring only a division or certain wanted assets as opposed to all the assets.

For nontax reasons a buyer may not be able to acquire assets. Restrictions in loan agreements, lease agreements or franchise agreements may prevent the transfer of assets, require a renegotiation of such agreements or need the approval of a third party. In those situations it may be necessary for a buyer to acquire stock.

Furthermore, asset sales may be subject to state sales taxes that the seller may insist be borne by the buyer. The sales tax cost could be significant enough to make an asset sale impractical.

Seller Considerations

In an asset acquisition, a seller will recognize a gain or loss equal to the difference between the purchase price received and the tax basis of the assets sold. The character of the gain or loss will be capital or ordinary depending upon the nature of the assets sold. The sale of assets may also result in depreciation and investment tax credit recapture, or even be deemed income under the *tax benefit* rule.

The most significant tax consideration for a corporate seller of assets is the potential double taxation that may result from the repeal of the General Utilities doctrine. This doctrine provided generally for the nonrecognition of income at the corporate level on the appreciated value of assets distributed to shareholders in liquidation. An extension of this principle provided that corporations were not required to recognize income attributable to the sale of most types of property if: (1) the sale was pursuant to a plan of complete liquidation, and (2) the corporation actually liquidated within twelve months of adopting the plan. Therefore, under prior law, a corporation could liquidate or sell its assets with no tax at the corporate level, and only the shareholders would be subject to tax on the difference between their basis in the stock and the proceeds received.

Under current law both the asset sale and the liquidation distribution to the shareholders may be taxable events that significantly reduce the after-tax proceeds to the shareholders.

Stock Acquisition

A seller generally prefers to sell stock because stock sales are often simpler, and they enable a seller to avoid double taxation and thereby maximize after-tax profits. When acquiring stock a buyer steps into the shoes of a seller and, hence, ends up owning stock in a corporation, the assets of which are subject to all of the known, contingent and undisclosed liabilities that existed prior to the sale. As a result a buyer may want to be protected from some of these liabilities (undisclosed and/or contingent) by obtaining from the seller exhaustive representations and warranties concerning the corporation's liabilities and indemnification from any such liabilities. Under certain circumstances a corporate buyer does have the opportunity to elect to treat a purchase of stock as an asset acquisition. Such an election has significant tax consequences.

Buyer Considerations

Since a corporation remains intact in a stock acquisition, it will have no effect on the corporation's tax bases in its assets. A buyer will have a basis in an acquired corporation's stock equal to the price paid to the seller, including debt incurred by the buyer to finance the acquisition.

The principal advantage of a stock acquisition to the buyer is the corporation's retention of its possibly valuable tax attributes. Net operating losses, credit carry forwards and earnings and profits, subject to certain limitations, can still be utilized by the acquired corporation or corporate buyer if the buyer files a consolidated tax return with the acquired corporation.

The future use of the tax attributes by the acquired corporation or buyer's consolidated group may be limited due to Internal Revenue Service Code provisions. Annual limitations are imposed on the use of the acquired corporation's net operating loss carry forwards after more than 50 percent of stock ownership in the acquired corporation changes within a 3-year period. The annual limitation is equal to the federal long-term, tax-exempt rate multiplied by the value of the acquired corporation's stock immediately before the change in ownership. If the acquired corporation's historic business is not continued for 2 years after the ownership change or, alternatively, the acquired corporation's assets are not used in a trade or business during that 2-year period, the acquired corporation's net operating losses are disallowed altogether.

Seller Considerations

The consequences of a stock sale to a seller is a tax measured on the stock's appreciation in value. Gain or loss is measured by the difference between the purchase price received and the seller's tax basis in the stock. The character of the gain or loss generally will be long-term or short-term capital gain, depending on whether the stock was held more than 12 months. This can be important to a seller who has capital loss carry forwards to offset capital gains.

A buyer who is about to make an offer may propose purchasing your company's stock rather than its assets and liabilities. What does this mean for you? What are the differences between a stock acquisition and an asset acquisition? If you are not an accountant by training, some of this discussion of acquisition methods may seem obtuse. I have prepared a summary in Figure 14.1 that amplifies the advantages and disadvantages of the two most common purchase methods.

Nontaxable Acquisitions or Reorganizations

The stock-for-stock, nontaxable reorganization may come into play if the buyer is a public company and uses its stock to make acquisitions. To avoid taxes by either party in an acquisition, you can use the *reorganization*. Under the Internal Revenue Service Code, the target corporation's shareholders may exchange their stock for stock in the acquiring corporation without recognition of gain. To qualify as a nontaxable transaction, the merger or consolidation must be effected under a state merger or consolidation statute, and the target corporation's shareholders must meet one test: the receipt of sufficient stock interest in the acquiring corporation. If the consideration received by the target company's shareholders includes cash in addition to stock, it will result in the transaction being partially taxable.

Stock-for-stock acquisitions are more difficult to effect than mergers or consolidations and, in terms of achieving nontaxability, are the most restrictive of the three basic forms of reorganizations. In such a reorganization, the acquiring corporation tenders stock for the stock of the target company, which becomes a subsidiary of the acquiring corporation. However, stock of the acquiring company is the only

◆ **Figure 14.1** Summary: Pros and Cons of Asset and Stock
Purchases

Assets Purchase

Buyer's Position
Advantages

- ◆ Step-up in basis of assets acquired to purchase price allows higher depreciation and amortization deductions.
- ◆ Recapture tax on presale depreciation and investment tax credit paid by seller.
- ◆ Buyer can pick and choose assets to buy and liabilities to assume.
- ◆ Buyer is generally free of any undisclosed or contingent liabilities.
- ◆ Normally results in termination of labor union collective bargaining contracts.
- ◆ Employee benefit plans may be maintained or terminated.
- ◆ Buyer permitted to change state of incorporation.

Disadvantages

- ◆ No carryover of seller corporation's tax attributes (i.e., tax basis of assets, earnings and profits, operating and capital loss carry forwards, accounting methods, accounting periods and installment reporting on previous sales and employee benefit plan contributions).
- ◆ Nontransferable rights or assets (i.e., licenses, franchises, patents, etc.) cannot be transferred to buyer.
- ◆ Transaction more complex and costly in terms of transferring specific assets/liabilities (i.e., title to each asset transferred, and new title recorded; state sales tax may apply).
- ◆ Lender's consent may be required to assume liabilities.
- ◆ May lose right to use corporation's name.
- ◆ Loss of corporation's liability, unemployment or workers' compensation insurance ratings.

Source: *Buying and Selling a Business*, New York: Price Waterhouse, 1989. Reprinted with permission.

◆ **Figure 14.1**   Summary: Pros and Cons of Asset and Stock
Purchases Disadvantages (Continued)

Seller's Position
Advantages

- ◆ Seller maintains corporate existence.
- ◆ Maintains ownership of nontransferable assets or rights (i.e., licenses, franchises, patents, etc.).
- ◆ Maintains corporate name.

Disadvantages

- ◆ Taxation occurs at the corporate level upon liquidation.
- ◆ Generates various kinds of gain or loss to the seller based on the classification of each asset as capital or ordinary.
- ◆ Transaction may be more complex and costly in terms of transferring specific assets/liabilities (i.e., title to each asset transferred and new title records; sales tax may apply).
- ◆ Lender's consent required to assume liabilities.

Stock Purchase

Buyer's Position
Advantages

- ◆ Tax attributes carry over to buyer (i.e., tax basis of assets, earnings and profits, operating and capital loss carry forwards, accounting methods, accounting periods and installment reporting on previous sales and employee benefit plan contributions). Transaction is less complex (i.e., endorsement of stock certificates).
- ◆ Avoids restrictions imposed on sales of assets in loan agreements and potential sales tax.
- ◆ Preserves the right of the buyer to use corporation's name.
- ◆ No changes in corporation's liability, unemployment or workman's compensation insurance ratings.
- ◆ Nontransferable rights or assets (i.e., licenses, franchises, patents, etc.) can be retained by the buyer.

Source: *Buying and Selling a Business*, New York: Price Waterhouse, 1989. Reprinted with permission.

- No step-up in basis (i.e., seller's basis is carried over to buyer at historical tax basis) unless buyer elects and incurs additional tax cost.
- All assets and obligations (i.e., disclosed, not disclosed, unknown and contingent) are transferred to the buyer.
- Recapture tax on presale depreciation and investment tax credits fall on buyer.
- Normally does not terminate existing labor union collective bargaining contracts.
- Generally results in the continuation of employee benefit plans.
- State of incorporation remains the same.
- Dissenting shareholders' right of appraisal of the value of their shares with the right to be paid appraised value or remain a minority shareholder.

Seller's Position
Advantages

- Avoids taxation at the corporate and shareholder level.
- All obligations (i.e., disclosed, not disclosed, unknown and contingent) and nontransferable rights can be transferred to the buyer.
- Generally provides capital gain or loss so that there is no need to calculate gain or loss by asset type.
- Generally avoids ordinary gain.

Disadvantages

- Seller cannot pick and choose the assets to be retained.
- Ownership of nontransferable rights or assets is lost.
- Requires selling corporation's shareholder approval.

Source: *Buying and Selling a Business*, New York: Price Waterhouse, 1989. Reprinted with permission.

---

consideration that may be received by the target company's shareholders, and no cash or other property may be used by the purchasing corporation to complete the deal.

Stock-for-assets acquisitions generally offer more flexibility than stock-for-stock acquisitions. In such an acquisition, the purchasing corporation needs to acquire substantially all the assets of the target company but does not have to assume all of its liabilities. Also, the acquiring corporation may use a limited amount of cash or property in addition to its stock to effect the acquisition and not jeopardize its generally nontaxable basis.

Legal Requirements for a Nontaxable Reorganization

In addition to meeting the structural requirements of a reorganization, corporate acquisitions must meet certain legal requirements to be nontaxable. First, the acquisition must have a legitimate business purpose, a condition usually satisfied without great difficulty. Second, the shareholders of the acquired corporation must maintain a continuing interest in the acquiring corporation. This means that the shareholders of the target company, as a group, must obtain an equity interest in the acquiring corporation equal to at least 50 percent of the value of the stock that they surrender. Third, the acquiring corporation must continue the historic business of the target company.

The principal benefit of reorganizations is that tax attributes (i.e., net operating losses and profits) of the acquired corporation generally survive the acquisition, and the tax bases of the target company's assets carry over to the acquiring company. The use of such attributes in a nontaxable transaction are typically subject to limitations similar to the limitations applicable to a taxable acquisition of stock of a corporation with net operating losses.

Summary

Once you have agreed to purchase price and payment terms with the buyer, you must also agree on the structure—assets purchase or stock purchase. If your company has had operating losses, more than likely the buyer will want a stock purchase in order to obtain shelter for its income taxes. As the seller, a stock purchase generally reduces your taxes as well.

However, most buyers of privately held companies prefer assets purchases in order to pick assets and liabilities that they want, or to cancel contracts, break leases and leave problems behind. An assets purchase could cause double taxation problems for you, which cuts into the net dollars you take away from the table.

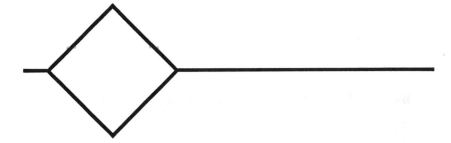

Directory of
Deal Lawyers

Appendix I

Atlanta, GA

King & Spalding
2500 Trust Company Tower
Atlanta, GA 30303
404-572-4600
Fax: 404-572-5100

No. of Attys in Firm: 218
Contact Person(s):
David G. Epstein

Austin, TX

Jenkins & Gilchrist, P.C.
100 Congress, Ste. 1800
Austin, TX 78701
512-499-3800
Fax: 512-404-3520

No. of Attys in Firm: 180
Contact Person(s):
Steven Ray Hake

Boston, MA

Bingham, Dana & Gould
150 Federal St.
Boston, MA 02110
617-951-8211
Fax: 617-951-8736

No. of Attys in Firm: 125
Contact Person(s):
Leslie Shapiro
Dick Harter

Hale & Dorr
60 State St.
Boston, MA 02109
617-742-9100
Fax: 617-526-5000

No. of Attys in Firm: 300
Contact Person(s):
Virginia Kingsley

Hutchins & Wheeler
101 Federal St.
Boston, MA 02110
617-951-6600
Fax: 617-951-1295

No. of Attys in Firm: 93
Contact Person(s):
Mark Berman

Peabody & Brown
One Boston Pl.
Boston, MA 02108
617-345-1000
Fax: 617-345-1300

No. of Attys in Firm: 80
Contact Person(s):
Walter Spiegel

Ropes & Gray
One International Pl.
Boston, MA 02110
617-951-7000
Fax: 617-951-7050

No. of Attys in Firm: 265
Contact Person(s):
William F. McCarthy

Testa, Hurwitz & Thiebault
53 State St.
Boston, MA 02109
617-248-7000
Fax: 617-248-7100

No. of Attys in Firm: 115
Contact Person(s):
William Asher
Edwin Miller

Chicago, IL

Altheimer & Gray
10 S. Wacker Dr.
Chicago, IL 60606
312-715-4955
Fax: 312-715-4800

No. of Attys in Firm: 170
Contact Person(s):
Norman Gold

Hopkins & Sutter
Three First National Plaza
Ste. 4200
Chicago, IL 60602
312-558-6600
Fax: 312-558-6538

No. of Attys in Firm: 285
Contact Person(s):
Michael Solow

Kirkland & Ellis
200 E. Randolph Dr.
Chicago, IL 60601
312-861-2000
Fax: 312-861-2359

No. of Attys in Firm: 400
Contact Person(s):
Ted Swan

Mayer, Brown & Platt
190 S. LaSalle St.
Chicago, IL 60603
312-701-7242
Fax: 312-782-2375

No. of Attys in Firm: 421
Contact Person(s):
David Curry
Harold Kaplan

McBride, Baker & Coles
N.E. Atrium Center
500 W. Madison, 40th Fl.
Chicago, IL 60606
312-853-5700
Fax: 312-993-9350

No. of Attys in Firm: 430
Contact Person(s):
Lawrence Coles

Pederson & Houpt
180 N. LaSalle St., Ste. 3400
Chicago, IL 60601
312-641-6888
Fax: 312-641-6895

No. of Attys in Firm: 227
Contact Person(s):
Head of Commercial Dept.

Winston & Strawn
35 W. Wacker Dr., Ste. 5000
One First National Plaza
Chicago, IL 60601
312-558-5600
Fax: 312-558-5700

No. of Attys in Firm: 450
Contact Person(s):
Gary Fairchild

Cleveland, OH

Baker & Hostetler
National City Center
Cleveland, OH 44114
216-621-0200
Fax: 216-696-0740

No. of Attys in Firm: 450
Contact Person(s):
Richard Turney

Benesch, Friedlander, Coplan, Aronoff
1100 Citizens Bldg.
Cleveland, OH 44114
216-363-4637
Fax: 216-363-4588

No. of Attys in Firm: 167
Contact Person(s):
Richard Margolis
David Ingliss
Ira Kaplan

Calfee, Halter & Griswold
800 Superior Ave., Ste. 1800
Cleveland, OH 44114-2688
216-622-8200
Fax: 216-241-0816

No. of Attys in Firm: 150
Contact Person(s):
Dale LaPort
Lawrence N. Schultz

Kahn, Kleinman, Yanowitz & Aronson
1300 Bond Court Bldg.
Cleveland, OH 44114
216-696-3311
Fax: 216-696-1009

No. of Attys in Firm: 25
Contact Person(s):
Anne L. Meyers

Dallas, TX

Hutcheson & Grundy
6200 NCNB Plaza
901 Main St.
Dallas, TX 75202
214-761-2800
Fax: 214-761-2805

No. of Attys in Firm: 90
Contact Person(s):
Robert Richardson

Jenkins & Gilchrist
1445 Ross Ave., Ste. 3200
Dallas, TX 75202-2711
214-855-4500
Fax: 214-855-4300

No. of Attys in Firm: 180
Contact Person(s):
John Holzgraefe

Denver, CO

Davis, Graham & Stubbs
PO Box 185
370 17th St., Ste. 4700
Denver, CO 80201-0185
303-892-8400
Fax: 303-893-1379

No. of Attys in Firm: 190
Contact Person(s):
Glen Merrick

Grand Rapids, MI

Warner, Norcross & Judd
900 Old Kent Bldg.
111 Lyon St., N.W.
Grand Rapids, MI 49503
616-459-6121
Fax: 616-459-2611

No. of Attys in Firm: 110
Contact Person(s):
Blake Krueger

Greenwich, CT

McGovern & Associates
One Lafayette Pl.
Greenwich, CT 06830
203-622-1101
Fax: 203-622-9192

No. of Attys in Firm: 6
Contact Person(s):
Kevin McGovern

Houston, TX

Hutcheson & Grundy
3300 Citicorp Center
1200 Smith St.
Houston, TX 77002
713-951-2800
Fax: 713-951-2925

No. of Attys in Firm: 90
Contact Person(s):
Jack Carter

Vinson & Elkins
1001 Fannin St.
3300 First City Tower
Houston, TX 77002
713-758-2222
Fax: 713-758-2346

No. of Attys in Firm: 500
Contact Person(s):
Bobbitt D. Noel, Jr.

Jeffersonville, IN

Stites & Harbison
323 E. Court Ave.
Jeffersonville, IN 47130
812-282-7566
Fax: 812-284-5519

No. of Attys in Firm: 102
Contact Person(s):
Robert Lanum

Lexington, KY

Stites & Harbison
2300 Lexington Financial Center
250 W. Main St.
Lexington, KY 40507
606-254-2300
Fax: 606-253-9144

No. of Attys in Firm: 104
Contact Person(s):
Robinson W. Beard

Los Angeles, CA

Graham & James
725 S. Figueroa St., 34th Fl.
Los Angeles, CA 90017
213-642-2500
Fax: 213-642-4581

No. of Attys in Firm: 260
Contact Person(s):
Hillel Cohn

Inglis, Ledbetter & Gower
611 W. Sixth St., Ste. 3200
Los Angeles, CA 90017
213-627-6800
Fax: 213-622-2857

No. of Attys in Firm: 120
Contact Person(s):
Michael Inglis

Latham & Watkins
555 Flower St.
Los Angeles, CA 90071
213-485-1234
Fax: 213-891-8763

No. of Attys in Firm: 430
Contact Person(s):
Thomas Sadler

Morrison & Foerster
555 W. Fifth Ave., Ste. 3500
Los Angeles, CA 90013
213-892-5200
Fax: 213-892-5454

No. of Attys in Firm: 517
Contact Person(s):
Tom Fileti

Sheppard, Mullin, Richter & Hampton
333 S. Hope St., 48th Fl.
Los Angeles, CA 90071
213-620-1780
Fax: 213-620-1398

No. of Attys in Firm: 210
Contact Person(s):
Prentice O'Leary

Louisville, KY

Goldberg & Simpson
2800 First National Tower
Louisville, KY 40202
502-589-4440
Fax: 502-581-1344

No. of Attys in Firm: 25
Contact Person(s):
Cathy Pike

Greenebaum, Doll & McDonald
3300 First National Tower
Louisville, KY 40202
502-589-4200
Fax: 502-587-3695

No. of Attys in Firm: 120
Contact Person(s):
Ed Weinberg

Stites & Harbison
600 W. Main St.
Louisville, KY 40202
502-587-3400
Fax: 502-587-6391

No. of Attys in Firm: 102
Contact Person(s):
Robinson Beard

New York, NY

Battle Fowler
280 Park Ave.
New York, NY 10017
212-856-7000
Fax: 212-986-5135

No. of Attys in Firm: 115
Contact Person(s):
Lawrence Mittman

Davis, Polk & Wardwell
450 Lexington Ave.
New York, NY 11017
212-450-4000
Fax: 212-450-5986

No. of Attys in Firm: 335
Contact Person(s):
Donald S. Bernstein

Debevoise & Plimpton
875 Third Ave.
New York, NY 10022
212-909-6000
Fax: 212-909-6836

No. of Attys in Firm: 350
Contact Person(s):
Meredith Brown

Deckert, Price & Rhoads
477 Madison Ave.
New York, NY 10022
212-326-3500
Fax: 212-308-2041

No. of Attys in Firm: 300
Contact Person(s):
Paul Putney

Dewey, Ballantine, Bushby, Palmer & Wood
140 Broadway
New York, NY 10005
212-259-8000
Fax: 212-259-6333

No. of Attys in Firm: 365
Contact Person(s):
Morton A. Price

Eaton & Van Winkle
600 Third Ave.
New York, NY 10016
212-867-0606
Fax: 212-661-5077

No. of Attys in Firm: 14
Contact Person(s):
Robert Hendrickson

Epstein, Becker & Green
250 Park Ave.
New York, NY 10022
212-351-4500
Fax: 212-661-0989

No. of Attys in Firm: 135
Contact Person(s):
Sidney Todres

Graham & James
885 Third Ave.
New York, NY 10016
212-848-1000
Fax: 212-688-2449

No. of Attys in Firm: 250
Contact Person(s):
Gregory Schwed

Hayth & Curley
237 Park Ave., 20th Fl.
New York, NY 10017
212-880-6000
Fax: 212-682-0200

No. of Attys in Firm: 40
Contact Person(s):
Jay L. Gottleib

Kelley, Drye & Warren
101 Park Ave.
New York, NY 10022
212-808-7800
Fax: 212-808-7897

No. of Attys in Firm: 400
Contact Person(s):
Joseph E. Sarachek

Morrison & Foerster
1290 Avenue of the Americas
New York, NY 10104
212-468-8000
Fax: 212-468-7900

No. of Attys in Firm: 517
Contact Person(s):
Monty Davis

Parker, Chapin, Flattau & Klimpl
1211 Avenue of the Americas
New York, NY 10036
212-704-6264
Fax: 212-704-6288

No. of Attys in Firm: 145
Contact Person(s):
Bill Friedman

Proskauer, Rose, Goetz & Mendelsohn
300 Park Ave.
New York, NY 10022
212-969-3000
Fax: 212-969-2900

No. of Attys in Firm: 300
Contact Person(s):
Sheldon Hirschon

Reid & Price
40 W. 57th St.
New York, NY 10019
212-603-2000
Fax: 212-603-2298

No. of Attys in Firm: 315
Contact Person(s):
Herbert B. Max

Rosenman & Colin
575 Madison Ave.
New York, NY 10112
212-940-8600
Fax: 212-940-7013

No. of Attys in Firm: 225
Contact Person(s):
William W. Golub

Shearman & Sterling
120 E. 57th St.
New York, NY 10021
212-848-4000
Fax: 212-848-7179

No. of Attys in Firm: 503
Contact Person(s):
Peter Lyons

Sherreff, Friedman, Hoffman & Goodman
919 Third Ave.
New York, NY 10022
212-758-9500
Fax: 212-758-9526

No. of Attys in Firm: 50
Contact Person(s):
Charles Weissman

Simpson, Thatcher & Bartlett
425 Lexington Ave.
New York, NY 10017
212-455-2000
Fax: 212-455-2502

No. of Attys in Firm: 600
Contact Person(s):
Richard Beattie

Skadden, Arps, Slate, Meagher & Flom
919 Third Ave.
New York, NY 10022-9931
212-735-3000
Fax: 212-735-2001

No. of Attys in Firm: 900
Contact Person(s):
Earl Yaffa

Weil, Gotshal, & Manges
767 Fifth Ave.
New York, NY 10153
212-310-8000
Fax: 212-310-8007

No. of Attys in Firm: 475
Contact Person(s):
Joseph Allerhand

Palo Alto, CA

Ware & Friedenrich
400 Hamilton Ave.
Palo Alto, CA 94301
415-328-6561
Fax: 415-327-3699

No. of Attys in Firm: 45
Contact Person(s):
Lorraine Elliot

Portland, OR

Perkins, Coie
111 S.W. Fifth Ave.
Portland, OR 97204
503-295-4400
Fax: 503-295-6793

No. of Attys in Firm: 350
Contact Person(s):
Steve Headberg

Schwabe, Williamson, Wyatt & Lenihan
1211 S.W. Fifth Ave.
Stes. 1600-1800
Portland, OR 97207
503-222-9981
Fax: 503-796-2900

No. of Attys in Firm: 138
Contact Person(s):
Jim Larpinger

San Francisco, CA

Graham & James
One Maritime Plaza, 3rd Fl.
San Francisco, CA 94111
415-954-0200
Fax: 415-391-2493

No. of Attys in Firm: 245
Contact Person(s):
Nick Unkovick

Morrison & Foerster
345 California St.
San Francisco, CA 94105
415-677-7584
Fax: 415-677-6405

No. of Attys in Firm: 517
Contact Person(s):
Bruce Mann

Seattle, WA

Perkins, Coie
1201 Third Ave., 40th Fl.
Seattle, WA 98111
206-583-8888
Fax: 206-583-8500

No. of Attys in Firm: 350
Contact Person(s):
Richard H.White

**Schwabe, Williamson,
Ferguson & Burdell**
1415 Fifth Ave., Ste. 900
Seattle, WA 98171-1098
206-621-9168
Fax: 206-292-0460

No. of Attys in Firm: 140
Contact Person(s):
Jim Henkin

Washington, DC

Graham & James
2000 M St., N.W., Ste. 700
Washington, DC 20036
202-463-0800
Fax: 202-463-0823

No. of Attys in Firm: 230
Contact Person(s):
Mike Cavanaugh

Michaels & Wishner
1140 Connecticut Ave., Ste. 900
Washington, DC 20036
202-223-5000
Fax: 202-857-0634

No. of Attys in Firm: 135
Contact Person(s):
Nina Larson

Morrison & Foerster
2000 Pennsylvania Ave., N.W.
Ste. 550
Washington, DC 20006-1518
202-887-1518
Fax: 202-887-0763

No. of Attys in Firm: 517
Contact Person(s):
Stephanie Tsacoumis

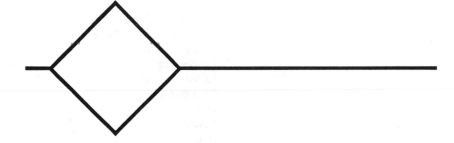

Directory of Equipment Appraisers

Appendix II

AAI Associates
104 Hill St.
PO Box 212
Hartland, WI 53029
414-367-1182
Fax: 414-367-1182

Contact Person(s):
Randy Stewart, ASA
Years in Business: 15
Financial Institution References:
First Wisconsin Banks
M & I Northern
Hanover
Associated Banks
Industries Specialized:
Manufacturing
Processing
Construction
Institutional
Any commercial
Acts as Auction Firm as Well: No
Branch Locations:
Minneapolis/St. Paul, MN
Los Angeles, CA

Accuval Associates, Inc.
10218 N. Port Washington Rd.
Mequon, WI 53092
414-241-1000
Fax: 414-241-1010

Contact Person(s):
David S. (Andy) Gronick, Jr., MAI
Richard E. Schmitt, CPA
Years in Business: 5
Financial Institution References:
Bankers Trust Company
Citicorp North America
Sanwa Business Credit
Industries Specialized:
All industrial
Acts as Auction Firm as Well: Yes
Branch Locations:
None

ACI Associates, Inc.

PO Box 36068
Denver, CO 80236
303-279-3277
Fax: 303-279-4796

Contact Person(s):
Alan C. Iannacito, Pres.
Years in Business: 12
Financial Institution References:
Colorado National Bank of Denver
United Bank of Pueblo
First Interstate Bank, Golden, CO
GATX Commercial Credit, San
    Francisco, CA
Industries Specialized:
Aggregate and asphalt plants
Chemical processing plants
Food processing
High-tech manufacturing
Machine shops and metal fabrication
Plastics/rubber equipment
Textile machinery
Specialized and custom
    manufacturers
Acts as Auction Firm as Well: Yes
Branch Locations:
None

Allied Appraisal Associates, Inc.

3301 Buckeye Rd., Ste. 309
Atlanta, GA
404-451-2246
Fax: 404-451-2717

Contact Person(s):
Joel D. Gonia, ASA
Years in Business: 13
Financial Institution References:
Bank South
Industries Specialized:
Machinery and equipment
All personal property
No real estate
Acts as Auction Firm as Well: No
Branch Locations:
Pensacola, FL

A & M Appraisal Company
59 Old Post Rd.
E. Walpoll, MA 02032
508-668-2258
Fax: 508-668-6311

Contact Person(s):
Merritt Agabian
Years in Business: 23
Financial Institution References:
Baybank, Norwood, MA
U.S. Trust, Norwood, MA
Industries Specialized:
Metalworking
Woodworking
Pulp and paper
Food
Acts as Auction Firm as Well: No
Branch Locations:
None

American Appraisal Associates, Inc.
100 E. Wisconsin Ave., Ste. 2100
Milwaukee, WI 53202
800-228-4888
Fax: 414-225-2014

Contact Person(s):
None in particular
Years in Business: Since 1896
Financial Institution References:
Undisclosed
Industries Specialized:
All
Acts as Auction Firm as Well: No
Branch Locations:
International

Arthur Andersen & Company
711 Louisiana St., Ste. 1300
Houston, TX 77002
713-237-2323
Fax: 713-237-5752

Contact Person(s):
Jeffrey A. Hutton, ASA
John O. Niemann, Jr.
Years in Business: 50+
Financial Institution References:
Upon request
Industries Specialized:
Oil and gas
Petrochemical
Manufacturing
Healthcare
Acts as Auction Firm as Well: No
Branch Locations:
New York, NY
Chicago, IL
Atlanta, GA
San Francisco, CA
Los Angeles, CA

Appraisal & Valuation Service
1 Crosby Circle
Buffalo, NY 14226-3289
800-642-2500
Fax: 716-835-7419

Contact Person(s):
Undisclosed
Years in Business: 33
Financial Institution References:
Undisclosed
Industries Specialized:
Chattels
Industrial
Business
Acts as Auction Firm as Well: Yes
Branch Locations:
None

Appraisal Resource
8219 S.E. 17th Ave., Ste. 3
Portland, OR 97202
503-230-8018
Fax: 503-230-8018

Contact Person(s):
John C. Kruzinski, ASA
Years in Business: 15
Financial Institution References:
U.S. Bank
First Interstate Bank
Key Bank
Industries Specialized:
Industrial plants
Wood products
Food processing
Acts as Auction Firm as Well: No
Branch Locations:
None

Appraisal Sciences, Ltd.
21613 N. 2nd Ave.
Phoenix, AZ 85027
602-248-0005
Fax: 602-248-0282

Contact Person(s):
Richard Biers
Robert Francy
Years in Business: 26
Financial Institution References:
Valley National Bank
First Interstate Bank
Industries Specialized:
Machine tools
Agricultural
Automotive
Food processing
Office equipment
Acts as Auction Firm as Well: N/A
Branch Locations:
4180 S. Sandhill Rd., Ste. 6
Las Vegas, NV 89121
702-434-4944

Appraisal Services, Inc.
PO Box 251
Cedarhurst, NY 11516
516-374-7774
Fax: 516-295-0930

Contact Person(s):
Herbert Friedberg
Years in Business: 16
Financial Institution References:
Undisclosed
Industries Specialized:
All except for
    Aerospace
    Agricultural
    Automotive
    Entertainment
    Machinery and equipment
    Technical valuation
Acts as Auction Firm as Well: No
Branch Locations:
Miami, FL
St. Croix, USVI

Appraisal Technologies/ Asset Resources
1501 W. 9th St., #C
Upland, CA 91786
714-985-9363
Fax: 714-949-6295

Contact Person(s):
Ed Testo, Jr.
Alex Steele
Years in Business: 7
Financial Institution References:
Union Bank
Wells Fargo Bank
Security Pacific Bank
Industries Specialized:
Metal/woodworking
High technology
Food processing
Rolling stock
Medical/biotechnical
Plastics
Inventories
Telecommunications
Acts as Auction Firm as Well: Yes
Branch Locations:
San Francisco, CA
San Diego, CA

Arkay Appraisal Company
Rt. 2, Box 51
Ferris, TX 75125
214-544-2310
Fax: 214-544-2310

Contact Person(s):
Ralph P. Kops, ASA
Years in Business: 14
Financial Institution References:
Nations Bank
FDIC
RTC
Industries Specialized:
Manufacturing
Food processing
Electronics
Acts as Auction Firm as Well: No
Branch Locations:
Dallas, TX 214-855-0410
Ft Worth, TX 817-323-7021
Houston, TX 713-521-0390

Asset Appraisal Corporation
1019F Waterwood Pkwy.
PO Box 687
Edmond, OK 73083-0687
405-348-5256
Fax: 405-348-4132

Contact Person(s):
Larry L. Perdue, ASA
Years in Business: 8
Financial Institution References:
Boatmen's First National Bank
PO Box 25189
Oklahoma City, OK 73125-0189
405-272-4000
Industries Specialized:
Furniture
Property management
Banking institutions
Commercial real estate
Construction
Oil and gas
Medical facilities
Machine shops
Food
Retail
Acts as Auction Firm as Well: Yes
Branch Locations:
N/A

B & R Appraisal
25336 Windsong Ct.
Wind Lake, WI 53185
414-895-7120
Fax: 414-895-7120

Contact Person(s):
J. Brian O'Connell
Years in Business: 9
Financial Institution References:
Barclays Business Credit
M & I Bank
Industries Specialized:
All types manufacturing/equipment
Inventories
Acts as Auction Firm as Well: No
Branch Locations:
None

Best Appraisals, Inc./Best Auctions, Inc.
1660 W. Hill St.
Louisville, KY 40210
502-778-1000
Fax: 502-778-3000

Contact Person(s):
Mike Waltrip
Joe Gribbins
Years in Business: 16
Financial Institution References:
Liberty National Bank
First National Bank
Citizens Fidelity Bank
Industries Specialized:
Woodworking and machine tools
Contractors equipment
Automotive/truck fleets
All commercial and industrial
No aviation or agricultural
Acts as Auction Firm as Well: Yes
Branch Locations:
None

BIA Consulting
PO Box 17307
Washington, DC 20041
703-818-2425
Fax: 703-803-3299

Contact Person(s):
David H. Cole, ASA
Years in Business: 8
Financial Institution References:
Not disclosed
Industries Specialized:
Broadcasting
Mobile communications
Telecommunications
Publishing
Machinery and equipment
Acts as Auction Firm as Well: No
Branch Locations:
None

R.W. Bronstein Corporation
3666 Main St.
Buffalo, NY 14226-3284
800-642-2500
Fax: 716-835-7419

Contact Person(s):
Richard Bronstein
Years in Business: 35
Financial Institution References:
Norstar-Fleet
Manufacturers & Traders Trust
Industries Specialized:
Real estate
Machinery
Equipment
Acts as Auction Firm as Well: Yes
Branch Locations:
4049 Delaware Ave.
Tonawanda, NY 14150
716-873-7000

Business Advisory Services, Inc.
1001 4th Ave., Ste. 3101
Seattle, WA 98154
206-223-5400
Fax: 206-292-8363

Contact Person(s):
Jack B. Sparks
Years in Business: 9
Financial Institution References:
Seafirst Bank
Security Pacific Bank
Industries Specialized:
All
Acts as Auction Firm as Well: No
Branch Locations:
N/A

Business Appraisal Associates
2777 S. Colorado Blvd., Ste. 200
Denver, CO 80222
303-758-8818
Fax: 303-756-6164

Contact Person(s):
Jack Bakken, ASA
George Schaefer, ASA
Years in Business: 18
Financial Institution References:
First Interstate Bank, Golden, CO
Industries Specialized:
All except process industries
Acts as Auction Firm as Well: No
Branch Locations:
None

Campbell & Associates
1795 Peachtree St., Ste. 210
Atlanta, GA 30309
404-876-2976
Fax: 404-897-1053

Contact Person(s):
David Campbell
Peyton Hall
Years in Business: 22
Financial Institution References:
Fioeling National Bank
Nations Bank
Industries Specialized:
All
Acts as Auction Firm as Well: No
Branch Locations:
West Palm Beach, FL
Chattanooga, TN

Charles Cawthra & Associates, Inc.
1036 Alfonso Ave.
Coral Gables, FL 33146
305-666-0669
Fax: 305-665-9371

Contact Person(s):
Charles Cawthra Jr. or Charles III
Years in Business: 20
Financial Institution References:
Barnett Bank of South Florida
Industries Specialized:
Resort hotels
Aircraft
Shipyards
Special purpose properties
Acts as Auction Firm as Well: No
Branch Locations:
N/A

George E. Chase Appraisal Service
19 Norlyon Dr.
Walnut Creek, CA 94590
510-937-9657
Fax: 510-937-9657

Contact Person(s):
George Chase
Years in Business: Since 1947
Financial Institution References:
Undisclosed
Industries Specialized:
All
Acts as Auction Firm as Well: No
Branch Locations:
PO Box 7175
Burbank, CA 91505
818-841-1765

Colgate Engineering, Inc.
PO Box 342
Menomonee Falls, WI 53051
414-255-6373
Fax: 414-255-6370

Contact Person(s):
Terry Duda, Pres.
Years in Business: 15
Financial Institution References:
Bank One, Milwaukee
W. 156 N. 11251 Pilgrim Rd.
Germantown, WI 53022
Industries Specialized:
Metalworking
Woodworking
Plastics
Electronics
Printing
Chemical processing
Packaging
Construction
Food processing
Acts as Auction Firm as Well: No
Branch Locations:
N/A

William F. Comly & Son, Inc.
1825 E. Boston Ave.
Philadelphia, PA 19125
215-634-2500
Fax: 215-634-0496

Contact Person(s):
Andy Comly
Steve Comly
Years in Business: Since 1834
Financial Institution References:
Mellon Bank
Meridian Bank
Fidelity Bank
Provident National
Industries Specialized:
Machinery and equipment
Appraisals and auctions
Acts as Auction Firm as Well: Yes
Branch Locations:
Philadelphia, PA
New Jersey

Consilium, Inc.
5520 S.W. Macadam Ave., Ste 275
Portland, OR 97201-3740
503-220-0078
Fax: 503-228-2032

Contact Person(s):
Larry J. Tapanen, ASA
James K. Elmer & Stephen Olson
Years in Business: 7
Financial Institution References:
U.S. Bank
Security Pacific
Industries Specialized:
Industrial properties
Environmental valuation (loss)
Acts as Auction Firm as Well: Yes
Branch Locations:
Seattle, WA

Continental Appraisal Company, Inc.
PO Box 6415
Mesa, AZ 85216-6415
602-986-7705
Fax: 602-981-7717

Contact Person(s):
Bob Falck
Years in Business: 25
Financial Institution References:
Undisclosed
Industries Specialized:
Heavy construction
Open pit mining equipment
Acts as Auction Firm as Well: No
Branch Locations:
None

Philip H. Cooper, ASA
902 E. Windsor Circle
Fresno, CA 93720
209-434-4513
Fax: 209-434-4513

Contact Person(s):
Phil Cooper
Years in Business: 18
Financial Institution References:
Bank of America
Bank of California
Sunrise Bank
Industries Specialized:
All
Acts as Auction Firm as Well: No
Branch Locations:
N/A

Coopers & Lybrand
203 N. LaSalle St.
Chicago, IL 60601
312-701-5747
Fax: 312-701-6538

Contact Person(s):
Dennis Neilson
Years in Business: 20
Financial Institution References:
Mellon Bank
Bank of America
Sanwa Business Credit
Industries Specialized:
Process industries
Chemicals
Mining
Acts as Auction Firm as Well: No
Branch Locations:
Chicago, IL
Houston, TX

Coopers & Lybrand
1301 Ave. of the Americas
New York, NY 10020
212-259-2753
Fax: 212-259-4999

Contact Person(s):
Phil Clements
Years in Business: 20
Financial Institution References:
Upon request
Industries Specialized:
All
Acts as Auction Firm as Well: No
Branch Locations:
Boston, MA
Chicago, IL
Dallas,TX
Los Angeles, CA
Philadelphia, PA
San Francisco, CA

Daley-Hodkin Corporation
135 Pinelawn Rd.
Melville, NY 11747
516-293-0200
Fax: 516-293-0328

Contact Person(s):
Morris Hodkin
Joe Hodkin
Years in Business: 20
Financial Institution References:
Chase Manhattan
Chemical Bank
Industries Specialized:
All
Acts as Auction Firm as Well: Yes
Branch Locations:
N/A

Harry Davis & Co.
1725 Blvd. Allies
Pittsburgh, PA 15219
412-765-1170
Fax: 412-765-0910

Contact Person(s):
Joel B. Levinson, ASA
Martin I. Davis
Years in Business: 40+
Financial Institution References:
By request
Industries Specialized:
Metalworking
Manufacturing
Dairy
Food processing
Woodworking
Construction
Plastics
Restaurants
Acts as Auction Firm as Well: Yes
Branch Locations:
None

Dean Appraisal Company
690 E. Maple
Birmingham, MI
313-540-0040
Fax: 313-540-8239

Contact Person(s):
Gregory McEachern, ASA
Years in Business: 41
Financial Institution References:
Comerica Bank, Detroit
National Bank of Detroit
Industries Specialized:
Aggregates
Automobiles
Computer related
Electronics
Insurance
Manufacturing
Plastics
Telecommunications
Transportation
Acts as Auction Firm as Well: No
Branch Locations:
None

Edward G. Detwiler, ASA

1255 Sterling Ave.
Palatine, IL 60067
708-359-8802
Fax: 708-359-8802

Contact Person(s):
Ed Detwiler
Years in Business: 10
Financial Institution References:
Chase Manhattan Leasing Company,
  Los Angeles, CA
General Electric Medical Systems,
  Waukesha, WI
IRS, Kansas City, MO
Metlife Capital, Bellevue, WA
Industries Specialized:
Medical equipment
Acts as Auction Firm as Well: No
Branch Locations:
None

Dick's Equipment Appraisal Service

1131 Monica Ln.
San Jose, CA 951128
408-246-5378
Fax: 408-246-5378

Contact Person(s):
Dick Dethlefsen
Years in Business: 11
Financial Institution References:
Bank of America
Industries Specialized:
All types of equipment and aircraft
Acts as Auction Firm as Well: No
Branch Locations:
N/A

The Dobbins Company

Box 20001 Station N.
Atlanta, GA 30325
404-352-2638
Fax: 404-352-9428

Contact Person(s):
Walter B. Dobbins, Pres.
Years in Business: 18
Financial Institution References:
Wachovia Bank
Nations Bank
Trust Company Bank
Industries Specialized:
Building materials
Distribution
Metalworking
Industrial plants
Construction equipment
Mining
Timber, agricultural equipment
Some electronic equipment
Acts as Auction Firm as Well: Yes
Branch Locations:
N/A

Dovetech, Inc.
330 Hatch Dr.
Foster City, CA 94404
415-571-7400
Fax: 415-572-1564

Contact Person(s):
Kevin Otus
Years in Business: 55
Financial Institution References:
Bank of America
Chemical Bank
G.E. Capital
Resolution Trust Corp.
Industries Specialized:
High Technology manufacturing,
    equipment, and inventory
Acts as Auction Firm as Well: Yes
Branch Locations:
Los Angeles, CA
Woburn, MA
St. Louis, MO

Enterprise Appraisal Co.
489 Devon Park Dr.
Wayne, PA 19087
215-687-5855
Fax: 215-971-0760

Contact Person(s):
Kenneth F. Domboski
Years in Business: Undisclosed
Financial Institution References:
Undisclosed
Industries Specialized:
All
Acts as Auction Firm as Well: No
Branch Locations:
None

Donald Freedberg & Associates, Inc.
2734 S. Milwaukee St.
Denver, CO 80210
303-758-1510
Fax: 303-692-0759

Contact Person(s):
Donald Freedberg
Years in Business: 20+
Financial Institution References:
First National Bank S.E. Denver
Norwest Bank, Denver
First National Bank of Aurora
Industries Specialized:
Construction
Mining
Fabricating
Machining
All industrial equipment and
    machines
Aircraft
Acts as Auction Firm as Well: Yes
Branch Locations:
Tampa, FL
Los Angeles, CA

George & Associates, Inc.
2340 Montgomery St.
Silver Spring, MD 20910
301-588-6605
Fax: 301-588-6605

Contact Person(s):
Ralph George
Years in Business: 25
Financial Institution References:
Undisclosed
Industries Specialized:
Construction equipment
Asphalt plants
Concrete plants
Quarries
Acts as Auction Firm as Well: No
Branch Locations:
N/A

Gerlach-Freund, Inc.
510 Hartbrook Dr.
Hartland, WI 53029
414-367-4950
Fax: 414-367-0158

Contact Person(s):
David Gerlach
Years in Business: 57
Financial Institution References:
Bank I, Mr. James Adashek
First Wisconsin Financial
Industries Specialized:
Metalworking
Woodworking
Plastics
Acts as Auction Firm as Well: Yes
Branch Locations:
Freund Real Estate, Inc.
14 Western Ave.
Fond du Lac, WI 54935

Global Industrial Liquidators
8235 Castlebrook Dr.
Indianapolis, IN 46256
317-924-4828
Fax: 317-577-0630

Contact Person(s):
J.L. Heppner, Jr.
Years in Business: 45
Financial Institution References:
Merchants
Bank One (AFNB)
Industries Specialized:
Metalworking
Woodworking
Construction
Acts as Auction Firm as Well: Yes
Branch Locations:
Greenwood, IN
Titusville, FL

Gerald Gray & Associates
7600 Parklawn Ave. S., Ste. 423
Minneapolis, MN 55435
612-835-0606
Fax: 612-835-4598

Contact Person(s):
Gerald Gray
Lynam Steele
Years in Business: 28
Financial Institution References:
First Bank Systems
Norwest Bank
Industries Specialized:
Manufacturing
Food processing
Construction
Acts as Auction Firm as Well: No
Branch Locations:
None

Gray Machinery Co.
PO Box D
Wheeling, IL 60090
708-537-7700
Fax: 708-537-9307

Contact Person(s):
Glenn R. Gray
Years in Business: 26
Financial Institution References:
LaSalle National Bank,
    Larry Richmond, Exec. V.P.
Industries Specialized:
Metalworking and fabrication
Plastics
Woodworking
Printed circuit boards
Acts as Auction Firm as Well: Yes
Branch Locations:
Chicago, IL

Harris & Harris Commercial/Industrial Auctioneers & Appraisers
PO Box 5657
Bellevue, WA 98006
206-451-8922
Fax: 206-451-1570

Contact Person(s):
Keith Harris
Years in Business: 8
Financial Institution References:
Seafirst Bank
Puget Sound Bank
Industries Specialized:
Aggregates
Communications
Computer-related
Construction
Electronics
Manufacturing
Plastics
Telecommunications
Others
Acts as Auction Firm as Well: Yes
Branch Locations:
None

Justin H. Haynes & Co.
2525 16th St., #118
Denver, CO 80211
303-455-1680
Fax: 303-477-2247

Contact Person(s):
Dennis Ingwersen
Years in Business: Since 1923
Financial Institution References:
Central Bank
Jefferson Bank & Trust
Industries Specialized:
All
Acts as Auction Firm as Well: No
Branch Locations:
None

Tom Hennig Company
975 Terra Bella
Mountain View, CA 94043
415-961-6642
Fax: 415-961-4483

Contact Person(s):
Brian Hennig
Years in Business: 30
Financial Institution References:
Bank of California
Security Pacific Bank
ITT Commercial Credit
Industries Specialized:
Construction equipment
Plant and machinery of all types
Acts as Auction Firm as Well: Yes
Branch Locations:
None

Heydon & Associates, Inc.
425 Saddle Horn Circle
Roswell, GA 30076
404-998-6565
Fax: 404-992-4096

Contact Person(s):
Graig I. Heydon
Years in Business: 9
Financial Institution References:
Commercial Federal Mortgage Corp.
Chrysler Financial Corp.
First Boston Corp.
Industries Specialized:
All
Acts as Auction Firm as Well: No
Branch Locations:
None

The Hoefer Associates, Inc.
1250 112th Ave.
Bellevue, WA
206-455-9880
Fax: 206-451-2058

Contact Person(s):
Roland James Hoefer
Years in Business: 18
Financial Institution References:
Seafirst Bank
Beneficial Financial
Washington Mutual
First Interstate Bank
Industries Specialized:
All
Acts as Auction Firm as Well: No
Branch Locations:
None

Hughes & Associates
235 E. Ponce De Leon
Decatur, GA 30030
404-373-8947
Fax: 404-373-1598

Contact Person(s):
James Hughes
Years in Business: 13
Financial Institution References:
Fidelity National Bank
Decatur, GA
Industries Specialized:
Real estate appraising
Residential
Commercial
Industrial
Vacant land
Acts as Auction Firm as Well: No
Branch Locations:
None

Hunyady Appraisal Services

1909 S. Broad St.
Lansdale, PA 19446
215-699-8625
Fax: 215-699-0485

Contact Person(s):
Michael Hunyady
Dan Jewin
Tim Schweb
Years in Business: 3
Financial Institution References:
Undisclosed
Industries Specialized:
Construction equipment
Trucks and trailers
Mining
Powerline and pipeline equipment
Asphalt and concrete equipment
Acts as Auction Firm as Well: Yes
Branch Locations:
Altoona, PA

I & F Equipment, Inc.

PO Box 93887
Atlanta, GA 30377
404-351-3652
Fax: 404-350-5836

Contact Person(s):
Larry Z. Isaacson, ASA
Years in Business: 12
Financial Institution References:
Trust Company Bank , Atlanta, GA
Industries Specialized:
Concrete products
Acts as Auction Firm as Well: No
Branch Locations:
None

Independent Appraisals, Inc.

8021 Knue Rd., #110
Indianapolis, IN 46250
317-849-3500
Fax: 317-576-5739

Contact Person(s):
Daniel Clark
Linda Mead
Years in Business: 23
Financial Institution References:
Indiana National Bank
Industries Specialized:
Municipal manufacturing
Banks
Restaurants
Office equipment
Acts as Auction Firm as Well: No
Branch Locations:
N/A

Independent Equipment Company
633 Battery St., 4th Fl.
San Francisco, CA 94111
415-981-0308
Fax: 415-981-1332

Contact Person(s):
Carl Chrappa
Years in Business: 22
Financial Institution References:
Bank of California
Industries Specialized:
All
Business valuations
Acts as Auction Firm as Well: Yes
Branch Locations:
New York, NY
Tampa Bay, FL
Houston, TX
Chicago, IL

Industrial Appraisal Company
222 Blvd. of the Allies
Pittsburgh, PA 15222
412-471-2566
Fax: 412-471-1758

Contact Person(s):
W.J. Moorhead, VP
Years in Business: 60
Financial Institution References:
Mellon Bank, NA
PNC Bank
Industries Specialized:
All
Acts as Auction Firm as Well: No
Branch Locations:
New York, NY
Chicago, IL
Los Angeles, CA

Industrial Evaluation
PO Box 1032
Creswell, OR 97426
503-895-4909
Fax: 503-895-4909

Contact Person(s):
Donald Gwyther
Years in Business: 8
Financial Institution References:
First Interstate of Oregon
U.S. Bank
Chase Manhattan Bank
Industries Specialized:
Heavy equipment
Wood products and logging
Agricultural
Road building
Certified commercial appraiser
Acts as Auction Firm as Well: No
Branch Locations:
None

International Appraisals, Inc.

3905 Vincennes Rd., Ste 303
Indianapolis, IN 46268
317-638-2222
Fax: 317-471-3508

Contact Person(s):
Ren Savill, ASA
David Strange, ASA
Years in Business: Undisclosed
Financial Institution References:
INB National Bank
Ameritrust Commercial Corp.
Lincoln National Bank
Bank One
Industries Specialized:
Construction
Manufacturing
Plastics
Transportation
Woodworking
Foundry
Agricultural
Acts as Auction Firm as Well: No
Branch Locations:
None

IWA, Inc.

PO Box 2685
Winter Park, FL 32790
407-629-0738
Fax: 407-629-0063

Contact Person(s):
Willard F. Martin
Miriam A. Russell
Years in Business: 35
Financial Institution References:
Undisclosed
Industries Specialized:
Printing
Acts as Auction Firm as Well: No
Branch Locations:
N/A

JK Consulting
82 Sherbon Ln.
Crystal Lake, IL 60014
815-455-6451
Fax: 815-455-6451

Contact Person(s):
John Kott
Years in Business: 10
Financial Institution References:
Undisclosed
Industries Specialized:
Broadcasting
Food processing
Chemical
Metalworking
Acts as Auction Firm as Well: No
Branch Locations:
None

William Kasper & Associates
1829 High Grove Dr.
Escondido, CA 92027
619-746-1927
Fax: 619-746-1927

Contact Person(s):
William Kasper
Gary Cohen
Years in Business: 22
Financial Institution References:
Union Bank
Escondido, CA 92027
Industries Specialized:
All types of machinery and
equipment
Acts as Auction Firm as Well: No
Branch Locations:
None

Kemper National Appraisal Group
1 Kemper Dr., D-7
Long Grove, IL 60049
708-540-2059
Fax: 708-540-4271

Contact Person(s):
Richard C. Lunt
Years in Business: 14
Financial Institution References:
Undisclosed
Industries Specialized:
All
Acts as Auction Firm as Well: No
Branch Locations:
Boston, MA
Atlanta, GA

Kempler Industries, Inc.
2461 Greenleaf Ave.
Elk Grove Village, IL 60007
708-640-8600
Fax: 708-640-0431

Contact Person(s):
Howard Kempler
Years in Business: 30
Financial Institution References:
NBD Bank of Elk Grove
Harris Trust & Savings Bank,
   Chicago, IL 60007
Industries Specialized:
Metalworking machinery
Rubber machinery
Plastic machinery
Processing equipment
Acts as Auction Firm as Well: Yes
Branch Locations:
N/A

Kirk Marketing Group, Inc.
280 W. Canton Ave., Ste. 106
Winter Park, FL 32789-3146
407-628-9737
Fax: 407-644-0921

Contact Person(s):
William Kirk, ASA
Brian Kirk
Years in Business: 16
Financial Institution References:
United American Bank of Central
   Florida
Industries Specialized:
Printing and publishing only
Acts as Auction Firm as Well: No
Branch Locations:
N/A

KPMG Peat Marwick
303 Peachtree St. N.E., Ste. 2000
Atlanta, GA 30308
404-222-3000
Fax: 404-222-3432

Contact Person(s):
David Adams
Tom Rowles
Years in Business: 98
Financial Institution References:
Undisclosed
Industries Specialized:
Manufacturing
High technology
Textiles
Mining
Food processing and others
Acts as Auction Firm as Well: No
Branch Locations:
Most major cities

KPMG Peat Marwick
345 Park Ave.
New York, NY 10154
212-872-3457
Fax: 212-872-3313

Contact Person(s):
Kenneth A. Martin, ASA
Years in Business: 30
Financial Institution References:
Undisclosed
Industries Specialized:
All
Acts as Auction Firm as Well: No
Branch Locations:
N/A

John C. Kruzinski
8219 S.E. 17th Ave., Ste. 3
Portland, OR 97202
503-230-8018
Fax: Undisclosed

Contact Person(s):
John Kruzinski
Years in Business: Since 1977
Financial Institution References:
Arthur Andersen
First City Trust
First Interstate Bank
Mercantile Bancorp
Merrill Lynch Capital Markets
Industries Specialized:
Agricultural
Food products
Forest products
Metal products/manufacturers
Printing/graphics
Hospitals
Acts as Auction Firm as Well: No
Branch Locations:
N/A

Fred B. Ladue & Associates, Inc.

14501 Walsingham Rd., Ste. E
Largo, FL 84644
813-595-0052
Fax: 813-593-0040

Contact Person(s):
Fred Ladue II, ASA
Years in Business: 12
Financial Institution References:
RTC
FDIC
First Union
Barnett Bank, S.B.A.
C&S Bank
Industries Specialized:
Hotels
Metal fabrication
Food processing
Bottling plants
Woodworking
Construction equipment
Medical/hospital equipment
Acts as Auction Firm as Well: No
Branch Locations:
N/A

Sidney Land, Inc.

10 Hackensack Ave.
Weehawken, NJ 07087
201-864-1010
Fax: 201-864-7686

Contact Person(s):
Charles Land
Years in Business: 30
Financial Institution References:
Merchants Bank of New York,
    NYC
The Trust Company of New Jersey
Industries Specialized:
All
Acts as Auction Firm as Well: No
Branch Locations:
N/A

Dave Lang & Associates, Inc.

250 Thompson Hill Rd.
Aliquippa, PA 15001
412-375-2110
Fax: 412-375-7799

Contact Person(s):
David N. Lang, ASA, CEA
Years in Business: 30
Financial Institution References:
Ameritrust Company N.A.
Integra Financial Corporation
S & T Bank
Industries Specialized:
Aluminum
Metalworking
Steel
Acts as Auction Firm as Well: No
Branch Locations:
N/A

Peter J. Lazarus, ASA
37 Farragut Dr.
Shore Acres, NJ 08723-7508
908-920-6527
Fax: Undisclosed

Contact Person(s):
Peter J. Lazarus
Years in Business: 30
Financial Institution References:
Bankers Trust
Citibank
National Westminster Bank
Industries Specialized:
Chemicals, drugs and allied
    products
Durable goods manufacturing
Nondurable goods manufacturing
Service
Acts as Auction Firm as Well: No
Branch Locations:
N/A

Norman Levy Associates, Inc.
21415 Civic Center Dr., Ste. 306
Southfield, MI 48076
313-353-8640
Fax: 313-353-1442

Contact Person(s):
David Levy
Years in Business: 40
Financial Institution References:
National Bank of Detroit, Detroit
CIT Group, New York, NY
Industries Specialized:
Machinery and equipment
Inventories
Acts as Auction Firm as Well: Yes
Branch Locations:
Boston, MA
Chicago, IL
Coventry, England

Lloyd-Thomas/Coats & Burchard Co.

6676 Howard St.
Niles, IL 60714
708-470-1800
Fax: 708-470-9852

Contact Person(s):
Walter J. Kapecki
Carol L. Storz
Years in Business: 98
Financial Institution References:
Uptown National Bank, Chicago, IL,
Richard Ostrum
Industries Specialized:
All
Acts as Auction Firm as Well: Yes
Branch Locations:
Cincinnati, OH
Minneapolis, MN
Milwaukee, WI
New York, NY
Philadelphia, PA
Los Angeles, CA
San Francisco, CA

Management Advisory Services, Inc.

2401 4th Ave., 3rd Fl.
Seattle, WA 98121-1436
206-441-0500
Fax: 206-728-9107

Contact Person(s):
Mark Tibergian
David Duryee
Years in Business: 12
Financial Institution References:
David Gasca
U.S. Bank
502 S. Lucille St.
Seattle, WA 98108
Industries Specialized:
Manufacturing
Service
Retail
Auto dealers
Acts as Auction Firm as Well: No
Branch Locations:
N/A

M & E Appraisers, Inc.
1625 S. Broadway, Ste. 200
Denver, CO 80210
303-722-7177
Fax: 303-722-7191

Contact Person(s):
Harry M. Fleenor
Years in Business: 27
Financial Institution References:
Norwest Bank Bear Valley, N.A.
Colorado National Bank
Industries Specialized:
Printing equipment
Plastic extruders
General equipment
Acts as Auction Firm as Well: No
Branch Locations:
None

M & M Appraisal
37 E. Huntington Dr.
Arcadia, CA 91000
818-440-4668
Fax: 818-440-1218

Contact Person(s):
Frederick Masterman
Years in Business: 25
Financial Institution References:
Bank of America
Security Pacific
Industries Specialized:
Manufacturing
Metalworking
Rubber and plastic
Chemical and oil liquidation
Acts as Auction Firm as Well:
Undisclosed
Branch Locations:
San Diego, CA
San Jose, CA
Arcadia, CA

The Manufacturers Appraisal Company

3201 Arch St.
Philadelphia, PA 19104
215-568-6739
Fax: 215-222-2492

Contact Person(s):
Hugh MacMillian, Pres.
Years in Business: 94
Financial Institution References:
On request
Industries Specialized:
All
Acts as Auction Firm as Well: No
Branch Locations:
New York, NY
Connecticut
Cleveland, OH
Detroit, MI
Cincinnati, OH
Dallas, TX
Los Angeles, CA
San Francisco, CA

Marketing & Consultant Services, Inc.

10222 W. Central
Wichita, KS 67212
316-838-5827
Fax: 316-721-5894

Contact Person(s):
John Harris, ASA
Years in Business: 20
Financial Institution References:
Bank IV, Wichita, KS
First National Bank, Wichita, KS
American National Bank, Wichita, KS
Industries Specialized:
All machinery/equipment
Aircraft
Office equipment
Acts as Auction Firm as Well: No
Branch Locations:
N/A

Marshall & Stevens, Inc.
600 S. Commonwealth Ave.
Los Angeles, CA 90005
213-385-1515
Fax: 213-386-8911

Contact Person(s):
John Chapman, Valuation
   Consultant
15851 Dallas Pkwy., Ste. 308
Dallas, TX 75248
Years in Business: 60
Financial Institution References:
Inquire for extensive list including
   Citicorp
   Bank of America
   Chemical Bank
   Wells Fargo
Industries Specialized:
No limitations
Acts as Auction Firm as Well: No
Branch Locations:
Most major cities

MB Valuation Services, Inc.
1111 Empire Central Pl.
Dallas, TX 75247
800-969-1111
Fax: 214-638-7576

Contact Person(s):
Leslie Miles
Allen Bealmear
Jackie Montalvo
Kai Naranong
Years in Business: 8
Financial Institution References:
Congress Financial Corporation
Nations Bank
Sanwa Business Credit Corporation
Industries Specialized:
Certified appraisal in all disciplines
Acts as Auction Firm as Well: Yes
Branch Locations:
Dallas, TX
Houston, TX
Stamford, CT
New York, NY
Denver, CO
Chicago, IL
Tampa, FL

Gregory McEachern
690 E. Maple
Birmingham, MI
313-540-0040
Fax: 313-540-8239

Contact Person(s):
Greg McEachern
Years in Business: 10+
Financial Institution References:
Comerica Bank
National Bank of Detroit
Industries Specialized:
All
Acts as Auction Firm as Well: No
Branch Locations:
N/A

McKinzie Metro Appraisals
2174 3rd St., Ste. 200
White Bear Lake, MN 55110
612-426-7144
Fax: 612-426-9458

Contact Person(s):
Jerry McKinzie
Years in Business: 22
Financial Institution References:
First Bank, White Bear Lake
Central Bank, White Bear Lake
Lake Area Security Bank, White
  Bear Lake
Industries Specialized:
Restaurant and bar
Heavy construction
Food processing
Manufacturing
Retail
Acts as Auction Firm as Well: No
Branch Locations:
None—but will travel anywhere

Metropolitan Appraisal Co.
5500 Bolsa Ave., Ste. 155
Huntington Beach, CA 92649
714-894-8186
Fax: 714-894-9745

Contact Person(s):
William F. Jacobs
Years in Business: 35
Financial Institution References:
Undisclosed
Industries Specialized:
Medical
Drug
Commercial
Industrial low or high tech
Automobiles/antiques
Acts as Auction Firm as Well: No
Branch Locations:
N/A

Murray, Devine & Co., Inc.
One Logan Square, Ste. 2800
Philadelphia, PA 19103
215-977-8700
Fax: 215-977-8181

Contact Person(s):
Dennis J. Murray
Francis J. Murray
Years in Business: 4
Financial Institution References:
Undisclosed
Industries Specialized:
All
Acts as Auction Firm as Well: No
Branch Locations:
None

National Industrial Appraisal Corp.
5585 Pershing, Ste. 200
St. Louis, MO 63112
800-327-6474
Fax: 314-454-9366

Contact Person(s):
Bruce Schneider
Jim Wells
Years in Business: 12
Financial Institution References:
Mark Twain Bank 314-727-1000
Magna Bank 314-576-7733
Industries Specialized:
Metalworking
Plastics
Foundries
Food processing
Glass manufacturing
Steel processing
Acts as Auction Firm as Well: Yes
Branch Locations:
Joint venture partnership with
    American Appraisal Association
    offices worldwide.

National Valuations, Inc.
152 Deming St.
PO Box 1037
South Windsor, CT 06074
203-644-4793
Fax: 203-644-4859

Contact Person(s):
Steven M. Piletz, ASA
Years in Business: 10
Financial Institution References:
Undisclosed
Industries Specialized:
Metalworking
Textiles
Chemicals
Woodworking
Paper plants
Electronics
Printing
Food processing
Plastics
Contractors equipment
Office furniture
Acts as Auction Firm as Well: No
Branch Locations:
PO Box 1797
Dover, NH 03820

D.G. Neuman Company
PO Box 1057
Wheeling, IL 60090
708-577-8051
Fax: 708-577-0857

Contact Person(s):
Daniel Neuman
Years in Business: 25
Financial Institution References:
First Chicago
Affiliated Banks
Continental Bank
Industries Specialized:
Machinery and equipment
Acts as Auction Firm as Well: No
Branch Locations:
N/A

North American Systems
875-A Airport Rd.
Monterey, CA 95940
408-372-1404
Fax: 408-375-3622

Contact Person(s):
Claude Bennett, ASA
Years in Business: 17
Financial Institution References:
Bank of America, Seaside, CA
Industries Specialized:
All
Acts as Auction Firm as Well: No
Branch Locations:
None

Palmer, Groth & Pieka
50 S.W. Pine St., Ste. 200
Portland, OR 97204
503-226-0983
Fax: 503-273-4273

Contact Person(s):
Ray Springer
Dave Pietka
Years in Business: 20
Financial Institution References:
Valley Bank Leasing, Mark Belac
   602-261-1158
First Interstate Bank, Kathryn
   GearHeard 503-721-5354
Bank Amerilease, Robert Podwalny
   415-953-6415
Industries Specialized:
Food processing
Metalworking
Pulp and paper
Concrete
Retail
Forest products
Specializes in market data research
Acts as Auction Firm as Well: No
Branch Locations:
Portland, OR
Seattle, WA
Bellevue, WA
Tacoma, WA
Vancouver, WA
Sacramento, CA

C.R. Pelton & Associates, Inc.
4661 Hwy. 61, Ste. 201
St. Paul, MN 55110
612-426-1175
Fax: 612-426-1284

Contact Person(s):
Robert Pelton
Years in Business: 30
Financial Institution References:
Norwest Equipment Finance
Norwest Banks
First Bank Systems
Industries Specialized:
All metalworking
Manufacturing
Plastics
Printing
Woodworking
Chemical
Food
Oil
Acts as Auction Firm as Well: No
Branch Locations:
Phoenix, AZ
Houston, TX
Austin, TX
Las Vegas, NV

Nat Quinn Appraisal Company
18 Plitt Ave.
PO Box 368
Farmingdale, NY 11735
516-293-2866
Fax: 516-249-2943

Contact Person(s):
Nathaniel Quinn
Arthur G. Bauer
Years in Business: 20
Financial Institution References:
European-American Bank
Main St.
Farmingdale, NY 11735
Fleet
National Westminster
Industries Specialized:
Machinery and equipment
Industrial real estate
Aircraft
Damage assessment
Acts as Auction Firm as Well: No
Branch Locations:
80 Allen Blvd.
Farmingdale, NY 11735

Ramberg Appraisal Service
10821 Russell Ave. S.
Bloomington, MN 55431
612-888-9166
Fax: Undisclosed

Contact Person(s):
Roger Ramberg
Years in Business: 17
Financial Institution References:
Marquette Bank, Minneapolis, MN
Norwest Bank, Minneapolis, MN
First Bank, Minneapolis, MN
Industries Specialized:
General manufacturing
Metalworking
Plastics
Woodworking
Agri-business
Acts as Auction Firm as Well: No
Branch Locations:
N/A

The Rice Group
1321 N. Orange
La Habra, CA 90631
310-690-1366
Fax: 310-690-1366

Contact Person(s):
Claudia E. Rice
Charles D. Rice
Years in Business: 5
Financial Institution References:
Downey S & L, Mary Holzhaur
3501 Jamboree
Newport Beach, CA

Bank of America, Robert Podwalny
Two Embarcadero, Dept. 5829
San Franciso, CA
Industries Specialized:
Accounting
Aerospace
Appraisal
Banking
Cities and municipalities
Entertainment
Heavy equipment
Hotel and motel
Manufacturing
Municipal water
Acts as Auction Firm as Well: No
Branch Locations:
La Habra, CA
San Francisco, CA
Detroit, MI

Rosen & Company

401 Euclid Ave., Ste. 319
The Arcade
Cleveland, OH 44114
216-621-1860
Fax: 216-621-4544

Contact Person(s):
Stanley H. Rosen
Kenneth B. Miller
Years in Business: 75
Financial Institution References:
Society National Bank
Industries Specialized:
All especially
   Metalworking
   Woodworking
   Trucking
   Earth moving
   Construction
   Electrical/electronics
Acts as Auction Firm as Well: Yes
Branch Locations:
2916 SOM Center Rd.
Willoughby Hills, OH 44094
216-585-1901
Fax-585-4119

Herbert H. Rosen & Sons, Appraisers

11001 York Rd.
Cockeysville, MD 21030
410-771-6800
Fax: 410-771-6815

Contact Person(s):
Steve Rosen
Years in Business: 60
Financial Institution References:
Maryland National Bank
201 International Circle
Hunt Valley, MD 21030
Industries Specialized:
Office furniture and screen systems
Office machines and equipment
Computers, copiers, fax machines
Material handling equipment
Acts as Auction Firm as Well: No
Branch Locations:
N/A

Rosen Systems, Inc.
2520 W. Mockingbird Ln.
Dallas, TX 75235
800-527-5134
Fax: 214-350-2464

Contact Person(s):
Warren H. Fitch
Years in Business: 75
Financial Institution References:
Nations Bank
Bank One
Bank America Business Credit
Industries Specialized:
Manufacturing
Processing
Printing
Plastics
Machine tools
Metal fabrication
Computer
Telecommunications
Industrial/commercial real estate
Acts as Auction Firm as Well: Yes
Branch Locations:
Bellaire, TX
Harrisburg, NC

Frederick J. Rossi & Associates
RR2, PO Box 292
Greentown, PA 18426
717-857-0933
Fax: 717-857-9888

Contact Person(s):
Frederick J. Rossi
Years in Business: 9
Financial Institution References:
Merchants Bank
24W Market St.
Wilkes Barre, PA 18711
Industries Specialized:
All types of industrial plants
    specializing in machinery
    and equipment
Acts as Auction Firm as Well: No
Branch Locations:
None

Sencer Appraisal Associates
2 Wooster St.
New York, NY 10013
212-226-0727
Fax: 212-941-0308

Contact Person(s):
Bernard M. Sencer
Years in Business: 38
Financial Institution References:
RTC
FDIC
FADA
NYC-Corp. Counsel
GSA
TASA
Industries Specialized:
Banking institutions
Communications
Computers
Electronics
Food
Entertainment
Government
Insurance
Restaurants
Others
Acts as Auction Firm as Well: No
Branch Locations:
Trumbull, CT
Silver Spring, MD
Port Washington, NY

St. Claire Appraisal Co.
1216 W. 65th St.
Cleveland, OH 44102
216-651-4422
Fax: 216-651-4422

Contact Person(s):
Richard Sander, ASA
Years in Business: 20
Financial Institution References:
National City Bank
Society Corp.
Industries Specialized:
Manufacturing
Steel fabrication
Plastics
Lumber and woodworking
Stamping
Acts as Auction Firm as Well: No
Branch Locations:
None

Technical Evaluation Consultants
252 Four Seasons Dr.
Drums, PA 18222-1035
717-788-4822
Fax: Undisclosed

Contact Person(s):
Phillip G. Barrho
Years in Business: 9
Financial Institution Referei
Hazelton National Bank
First Eastern Bank
Industries Specialized:
Metal fabrication/processing
Tool and die
Food processing
Animal feeds
Amusement parks
Electrical/electronics
Aggregate processing
Chemical and pharmaceutical
Many others
Acts as Auction Firm as Well
Branch Locations:
SAI Appraisals
633 Azara Ln, Ste. 2
Sunnyvale, CA 94086

Daniel W. Thaxton
PO Box 685
Camarillo, CA 93011
805-482-4693
Fax: 805-987-1937

Contact Person(s):
D.W. Thaxton
Years in Business: 40
Financial Institution Referen
Bank of A. Levy
Camarillo, CA
Industries Specialized:
Equipment appraisals
Acts as Auction Firm as Well
Branch Locations:
Coordinated Equipment Comp
1707 E. Anaheim St.
Wilmington, CA 90744
310-834-8535

Thimons, Inc.
PO Box 872
Ellwood City, PA 16117
800-394-8446
Fax: 412-752-2912

Contact Person(s):
Edward A. Butcher, ASA
Raymond R. Thimons
Years in Business: 29
Financial Institution References:
Integra Bank, Pittsburgh, PA
Ellwood Federal Savings Bank,
    Ellwood City, PA
PNC Financial Corp., Pittsburgh,
    PA
Industries Specialized:
Steel
Metalworking
Foundries
Earth moving and construction
Inventories
Forging
Acts as Auction Firm as Well: No
Branch Locations:
Blawnox, PA
Middletown, OH
Ashland, KY
Kansas City, MO
Pittsburgh, PA
Sydney, Australia
Nova Scotia, Canada

Thomas Industries
74 Forbes Ave.
New Haven, CT 06512
203-469-1713
Fax: 203-469-4928

Contact Person(s):
William Gardner
Years in Business: 45
Financial Institution References:
Undisclosed
Industries Specialized:
Manufacturing
Metalworking
Woodworking
Plastics
Printed circuit boards
Construction
Aerospace
Acts as Auction Firm as Well: Yes
Branch Locations:
Undisclosed

Valpoint, Inc.
380 S.E. Spokane St.
Portland, OR 97202
503-235-2159
Fax: 503-235-3624

Contact Person(s):
Greg Gilbert
Richard Kaufman
Years in Business: 26 as individuals
Financial Institution References:
First Interstate Bank
Wells Fargo Bank
Bank America
Industries Specialized:
All industries, all assets
Acts as Auction Firm as Well: No
Branch Locations:
Seattle, WA
Moorestown, NJ
Dallas, TX
San Francisco, CA

Valuation Associates
2020 Pioneer Ct., Ste. 6
San Mateo, CA 94403
415-572-0361
Fax: Undisclosed

Contact Person(s):
H. Dennis Neumann
Years in Business: 12.5
Financial Institution References:
Borel Bank & Trust Co.
PO Box 5492
San Mateo, CA 94402
Industries Specialized:
Food processing
Agri-business
Forest products
Fabrication
Restaurants
Printing
Acts as Auction Firm as Well: No
Branch Locations:
None

Valuation Counselors Group, Inc.

300 S. Riverside Plaza
Chicago, IL 60606
312-648-0100
Fax: 312-648-5830

Contact Person(s):
David S. Felsenthal
David M. Shade
Years in Business: 22
Financial Institution References:
American National Bank and Trust,
  Chicago, IL
Bankers Trust Company
Citicorp
National Westminster Bank
Sanwa Bank
Industries Specialized:
Hospitals
Nursing homes
Large industrial plants
Banking
Manufacturing
Transportation
Insurance
Construction
Government
Acts as Auction Firm as Well: No
Branch Locations:
340 Interstate N. Pkwy.
Atlanta, GA 30339

3131 Princeton Pike, Building 4A
Laurenceville, NJ 08648

3699 Wilshire Blvd.
Los Angeles, CA 90010

2121 San Jacinto St.
Dallas, TX 75201

Valuation Research Corporation
120 W. 5th St.
Cincinnati, OH 45202
513-579-9100
Fax: 513-579-0141

Contact Person(s):
James C. Farlow
Richard Riddell
Years in Business: 20
Financial Institution References:
Undisclosed
Industries Specialized:
All especially
   Real estate
   Financial
   Machinery and equipment
Acts as Auction Firm as Well: No
Branch Locations:
Milwaukee, WI
Princeton, NJ
Chicago, IL
San Francisco, CA

Valuation Research Corporation
411 E. Wisconsin Ave.
Milwaukee, WI 53202
800-558-1546
Fax: 414-271-3240

Contact Person(s):
Jeffrey N. Trader
James T. Marciniak
Years in Business: 17
Financial Institution References:
Undisclosed
Industries Specialized:
Chemicals
Food processing
Furniture
Manufacturing
Mining
Publishing
Oil and gas extraction
Acts as Auction Firm as Well: No
Branch Locations:
Chicago, IL
Cincinnati, OH
Cleveland, OH
Dallas, TX
Greenwich, CT
Los Angeles, CA
New York, NY
Princeton, NJ
San Francisco, CA

Valuation Specialists
2115 E. Clairemont Ave.
Eau Claire, WI 54702
715-834-8210
Fax: 715-834-5518

Contact Person(s):
Jeff White
Years in Business: 8
Financial Institution References:
Norwest Bank, Eau Claire, WI
First Wisconsin Bank, Eau Claire
Industries Specialized:
Wood products/equipment
Bottling
General manufacturing
Construction
Acts as Auction Firm as Well: No
Branch Locations:
Hodson, WI
Minneapolis, MN

Steven Wall Appraisal Company
17981 S. Shore Ln. W.
Eden Prairie, MN 55346
612-934-5153
Fax: Undisclosed

Contact Person(s):
Steve Wall, ASA
Years in Business: 14
Financial Institution References:
Norwest Banks, MN
First Wisconsin, Milwaukee
Midland Savings Bank
Industries Specialized:
Agri-business
Auto
Building materials
Gouts
Insurance
Manufacturing
Real estate
Restaurants
Wood
Acts as Auction Firm as Well: No
Branch Locations:
None

Wershow-Ash-Lewis, Auctioneers, Appraisers
535 N. Brand Blvd., Ste 838
Glendale, CA 91203
800-356-6830 or 800-547-5551
Fax: 818-247-6342

Contact Person(s):
Dennis R. Ash, VP
Years in Business: 56
Financial Institution References:
First Interstate Bank, Beverly Hills,
    Laurie Blanco 818-992-7149
Industries Specialized:
All
Acts as Auction Firm as Well: Yes
Branch Locations:
16913 S.W. 65th Ave.
Lake Oswego, OR 97035

Williams & Lipton Company
101 Southfield Rd., Ste. 302
Birmingham, MI 48152
313-646-7090
Fax: 313-646-7093

Contact Person(s):
Robert Williams
Gary Lipton
Years in Business: 16
Financial Institution References:
Comerica Bank
National Bank of Detroit
GMAC
Industries Specialized:
Metalworking machine tools
Plastics equipment
Fabrication equipment
Construction equipment
Acts as Auction Firm as Well: Yes
Branch Locations:
None

William Woolford & Associates
12200 E. Iliff Ave. #100
Aurora, CO 80014
303-671-5010
Fax: 303-671-5218

Contact Person(s):
W.A. Woolford
Years in Business: 38
Financial Institution References:
Colorado National Bank
17th Champa St.
Denver, CO 80202
Industries Specialized:
Minerals
Natural resources
Manufacturing
Acts as Auction Firm as Well: No
Branch Locations:
None

Zimmerman-McDonald Machinery, Inc.

1535 N. Broadway
St. Louis, MO 63102
314-231-9360
Fax: 314-231-7018

Contact Person(s):
Stanford L. Zimmerman
Brad Zimmerman
Years in Business: 105
Financial Institution References:
Cass Bank & Trust, St. Louis
Industries Specialized:
Metalworking
Woodworking
Acts as Auction Firm as Well: No
Branch Locations:
None

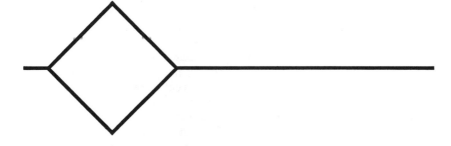

Directory of
Acquisition
Funds

Appendix III

ABS Ventures, L.P.
135 E. Baltimore St.
Baltimore, MD 21202
301-727-1700
Fax: 301-347-2963

Contact(s):
Bruns H. Grayson
Preferred Size Range:
$500,000–$2 million
Industries Specialized:
Technology
Specialty retailing
Do/Not Do Turnarounds: Not
Geographic Preference:
None
Portfolio Companies:
Sensormedics Corporation
Aries Technology
Aetna Shirt Company
Casey & Osh
Branch Office(s):
Arthur H. Reidel, Edward T.
  Anderson
400 Unicorn Park
Woburn, MA 01801

Adler & Shaykin
375 Park Ave.
New York, NY 10152
212-319-2800
Fax: 212-319-2800

Contact(s):
Leonard Shaykin
Preferred Size Range:
$25 million+
Industries Specialized:
All
Do/Not Do Turnarounds: Do
Geographic Preference:
None
Portfolio Companies:
Multiserv International, N.V.
Joy Technologies
The Folger Adam Company
The Sun-Times Company
Best Products, Inc.
Branch Office(s):
None

Advent International Corporation
101 Federal St., 5th Fl.
Boston, MA 02109
617-951-9400
Fax: 617-951-0736

Contact(s):
Steven Gormley
Preferred Size Range:
$1 million–$250 million
Industries Specialized:
Industrial machinery and equipment
Chemicals
Computers
Electronics
Telecommunications
Health care
Do/Not Do Turnarounds: Not
Geographic Preference:
United States
United Kingdom
Canada
Continental Europe
Japan
Australia
Pacific Rim
Portfolio Companies:
Confidential
Branch Office(s):
None

Agatite Ventures, Inc.
913 W. Agatite Ave.
Chicago, IL 60640
312-796-6395
Fax: 312-989-1937

Contact(s):
Michael Wichman
Preferred Size Range:
$1.5 million+
Industries Specialized:
Manufacturing
Services
Distribution
Do/Not Do Turnarounds: Not
Geographic Preference:
United States
Portfolio Companies:
Confidential
Branch Office(s):
None

Ahlberg & Associates
1000 Irvine Blvd.
Tustin, CA 92680
714-730-1000
Fax: 714-730-1752

Contact(s):
Terry Ahlberg
Preferred Size Range:
$2 million+
Industries Specialized:
None
Do/Not Do Turnarounds: Not
Geographic Preference:
Western States
Portfolio Companies:
Undisclosed
Branch Office(s):
None

AIG Global Investors
One World Financial Center
200 Liberty St.
New York, NY 10281
212-226-0400
Fax: 212-945-0418

Contact(s):
David B. Pinkerton
Preferred Size Range:
$5 million–$25 million
Industries Specialized:
Low technology
Do/Not Do Turnarounds: Not
Geographic Preference:
United States
United Kingdom
Continental Europe
Portfolio Companies:
Confidential
Branch Office(s):
None

Alliance Recovery Group, Inc.
7400 York Rd., Ste. 300
Baltimore, MD 21204
410-828-1171
Fax: 410-296-2114

Contact(s):
Michael D. Quinn
Preferred Size Range:
$1.5 million+
Industries Specialized:
Real estate
Financial services
Administrative services
Insurance
Mortgage banking
Do/Not Do Turnarounds: Do
Geographic Preference:
East Coast
Portfolio Companies:
Undisclosed
Branch Office(s):
None

Allied Partners, Ltd.

140 County Rd.
Tenafly, NJ 07670
210-569-6690
Fax: 210-569-0689

Contact(s):
Roger Maggio
Preferred Size Range:
$5 million+
Industries Specialized:
Industrial machinery and equipment
Publishing
Telecommunications
Real estate
Construction
Cable TV
Do/Not Do Turnarounds: Not
Geographic Preference:
United States
United Kingdom
Continental Europe
Portfolio Companies:
Confidential
Branch Office(s):
None

Allsop Venture Partners

2750 First Ave., N.E., Ste. 210
Cedar Rapids, IA 52402
319-363-8971
Fax: 319-363-9519

Contact(s):
Robert W. Allsop
Preferred Size Range:
$25 million+
Industries Specialized:
Computers
Electronics
Consumer services
Industrial machinery
Chemicals
Publishing
Telecommunications
Do/Not Do Turnarounds: Do
Geographic Preference:
Midwest
Portfolio Companies:
Smith & Loveless, Inc.
The Indiana Railroad Co.
Met-Coil Systems, Inc.
Phoenix Venture Acquisitions, Inc.
Branch Office(s):
Larry Maddox, General Partner
740 College Blvd., Ste. 302
Overland Park, KS 66210

Allstate Venture Capital
Allstate Plaza
Northbrook, IL 60062
708-402-5681
Fax: 708-402-0880

Contact(s):
Robert Lestina
Preferred Size Range:
Undisclosed
Industries Specialized:
Communications
Computers
Consumer products
Distribution
Electronics
Alternative energies
Consumer services
Do/Not Do Turnarounds: Do
Geographic Preference:
None
Portfolio Companies:
Federal Express
Mary Kay
Avia Athletic Shoes
Synthetic Blood Corp.
Atlantic American Cablevision
Allscrips
Atlantic Cellular
Argo
Bertuccis
Life Cell Corp.
Branch Office(s):
None

Alton & Company
100 California St.
San Francisco, CA 94111
415-391-1830
Fax: 415-391-1848

Contact(s):
Chris Woodward
Preferred Size Range:
$100 million+
Industries Specialized:
All
Do/Not Do Turnarounds: Not
Geographic Preference:
Western U.S.
Canada
United Kingdom
Europe
Japan
Portfolio Companies:
None
Branch Office(s):
None

American Acquisition Partners

175 South St.
Morristown, NJ 07960
201-267-7800
Fax: 201-267-7695

Contact(s):
Ted Bustany
Judith Mangiero
Preferred Size Range:
$10 million–$200 million
Industries Specialized:
Industrial products
Chemicals
Plastics
Pharmaceuticals
Food
Niche businesses
Do/Not Do Turnarounds: Not
Geographic Preference:
Northeast
Eastern Seaboard
Midwest
Portfolio Companies:
Maynard Manufacturing Co.
Hotel Bar Butter
Kellers
Epic Industries
Estorge Drug Co.
Almo Laboratories
R-Tape Corporation
Branch Office(s):
None

American Equity Partners, Inc.

1301 Ave. of the Americas, 30th Fl.
New York, NY 10019
212-586-0600
Fax: 212-586-0808

Contact(s):
Raymond Wechsler
Preferred Size Range:
$50 million–$200 million
Industries Specialized:
Troubled companies
Do/Not Do Turnarounds: Do
Geographic Preference:
Midwest
Southwest
NYC area
Portfolio Companies:
Undisclosed
Branch Office(s):
Wichita, KS

APA/Fostin

Building 5, Ste. 470
Radnor Corporate Center
Radnor, PA 19087
215-687-3030
Fax: 215-925-8297

Contact(s):
Gregory M. Case
Preferred Size Range:
$5 million–$100 million
Industries Specialized:
Health care
Environmental
Financial services
Computers
Manufacturing
Do/Not Do Turnarounds: Do
Geographic Preference:
East Coast
West to Chicago
Portfolio Companies:
Advacare, Inc.
Business Insurance Company
CLS Corp.
The Metalized Paper Corp. of
    America
Healthfield, Inc.
OSCO, Inc.
Wholesale Depot
Sunglass Hut
Nova Care, Inc.
Synoptic
Branch Office(s):
None

Ardshiel, Inc.
230 Park Ave.
New York, NY 10169
212-697-8570
Fax: 212-972-1809

Contact(s):
Dennis McCormick
Preferred Size Range:
$100 million+
Industries Specialized:
Consumer products
Consumer services
Industrial machinery and equipment
Chemicals
Transportation
Financial services
Oil and gas mining
Do/Not Do Turnarounds: Not
Geographic Preference:
United States
Canada
United Kingdom
Continental Europe
Portfolio Companies:
Confidential
Branch Office(s):
Frank Bryant, Vice Chairman
300 S. Corand Ave.
Los Angeles, CA 90071
213-629-4824

Armory Capital Corp.
325 Greenwich Ave.
Greenwich, CT 06830
203-622-7320
Fax: 203-622-7317

Contact(s):
James J. McCarthy
Preferred Size Range:
$5 million–$50 million
Industries Specialized:
Distribution
Light manufacturing
Do/Not Do Turnarounds: Not
Geographic Preference:
None
Portfolio Companies:
Undisclosed
Branch Office(s):
None

Atlantic Venture Partners
801 N. Fairfax St., Ste. 404
Alexandria, VA 22314
703-548-6026
Fax: 703-683-5348

Contact(s):
Edward C. McCarthy
Preferred Size Range:
$500,000–$5 million
Industries Specialized:
All
Do/Not Do Turnarounds: Not
Geographic Preference:
United States
Portfolio Companies:
Undisclosed
Branch Office(s):
None

B.T. Capital Corporation
280 Park Ave.
New York, NY 10017
212-454-1916
Fax: 212-454-2421

Contact(s):
James G. Helmuth
Preferred Size Range:
$3 million–$7 million
Industries Specialized:
All
Do/Not Do Turnarounds: Not
Geographic Preference:
United States
Portfolio Companies:
Undisclosed
Branch Office(s):
300 S. Grand Ave.
Los Angeles, CA 90071
Attn: Marty Jelenko

Bain Capital/Information Partners

Two Copley Pl.
Boston, MA 02116
617-572-3000
Fax: 617-572-3274

Contact(s):
Geoffrey S. Rehnert
Mark Nunnelly
Preferred Size Range:
$50 million–$1 billion
Industries Specialized:
Consumer products
Manufacturing
Information systems
Retail
Health care
Do/Not Do Turnarounds: Do
Geographic Preference:
United States
Portfolio Companies:
Holson Byrnes Group, Inc.
Brookstone
Gartner Group
AMPAR
Strategic Mapping
Eduserv Technologies
Staples
Branch Office(s):
None

Banc Boston Capital, Inc.

100 Federal St., 31st Fl.
Boston, MA 02110
617-434-2509
Fax: 617-434-1153

Contact(s):
F.M. Fritz
Preferred Size Range:
$15 million–$200 million
Industries Specialized:
Manufacturing
Distribution
Media
Communications
Do/Not Do Turnarounds: Not
Geographic Preference:
United States
Portfolio Companies:
Eagle
EIL Instruments
Kellog Brush Manufacturing
    Company
M. Kamenstein, Inc.
Branch Office(s):
None

Bartizal & Sherby
25010 Jim Bridger Rd.
Calabasas, CA 91302
818-702-9678
Fax: 818-702-9681

Contact(s):
Robert G. Bartizal
Preferred Size Range:
$100 million+
Industries Specialized:
Computers
Electronics
Consumer services
Industrial machinery
Chemicals
Publishing
Telecommunications
Medical
Distribution
Do/Not Do Turnarounds: Not
Geographic Preference:
Southwest
West Coast
Northwest
Western Canada
United Kingdom
Continental Europe
Portfolio Companies:
Confidential
Branch Office(s):
Thomas A. Sherby, General Partner
340 Second St., Ste. 17
Los Altos, CA 94022
415-941-1371

Batterson, Johnson & Wang Venture Partners
303 W. Madison, Ste. 1110
Chicago, IL 60606
312-269-0300
Fax: 312-269-0021

Contact(s):
Leonard Batterson
Preferred Size Range:
$25 million+
Industries Specialized:
Computers
Electronics
Industrial machinery and equipment
Media
Publishing
Telecommunications
Medical
Do/Not Do Turnarounds: Not
Geographic Preference:
United States
Portfolio Companies:
Confidential
Branch Office(s):
None

Battery Ventures
200 Portland St.
Boston, MA 02114
617-367-1011
Fax: 617-367-1070

Contact(s):
Robert G. Barnett
Preferred Size Range:
$1 million–$3 million
Industries Specialized:
Computers
Automation
Communications
Do/Not Do Turnarounds: Do
Geographic Preference:
None
Portfolio Companies:
Undisclosed
Branch Office(s):
None

Baytree Investors, Inc.
9950 W. Lawrence Ave., Ste. 306
Schiller Park, FL 60176-1216
708-928-0600
Fax: 708-928-0637

Contact(s):
Gilbert K. Granet
Preferred Size Range:
$10 million–$100 million
Industries Specialized:
Trucking
Retail
Manufacturing
Printing
Mechanical contracting
Do/Not Do Turnarounds: Do
Geographic Preference:
North America
Portfolio Companies:
Undisclosed
Branch Office(s):
40 United States

BBU Mezzanine Funds
c/o Amsterdam Pacific Corp.
88 Kearny St., Ste. 1850
San Francisco, CA 94108
415-421-3636
Fax: 415-781-1314

Contact(s):
James H. Boettcher
Preferred Size Range:
$5 million–$150 million
Industries Specialized:
Energy
Environmental
Communications
Light manufacturing
Do/Not Do Turnarounds: Do
Geographic Preference:
Western U.S.
Portfolio Companies:
U.S.A. Wastes Services
Evan Rents
Lone Pine Production Associates
U.S. Filter Corp.
Branch Office(s):
None

BCA Enterprises, Inc.
PO Box 5401
Louisville, KY 40205
502-456-2109
Fax: 502-456-6130

Contact(s):
Denis O'Connell
Preferred Size Range:
$1 million–$10 million
Industries Specialized:
Manufacturing
Distribution
Do/Not Do Turnarounds: Not
Geographic Preference:
None
Portfolio Companies:
Confidential
Branch Office(s):
None

Beacon Capital Corp.
150 King St. W., Ste. 1306
PO Box 36
Toronto, Canada M5H1J9
416-593-0090
Fax: 416-593-6045

Contact(s):
Derry R. Thompson
Preferred Size Range:
$50 million–$200 million
Industries Specialized:
Manufacturing
Do/Not Do Turnarounds: Do
Geographic Preference:
United States
Portfolio Companies:
Essex Industries
Eucon Industries
Branch Office(s):
None

Bechtel Investments, Inc.
50 Fremont St., Ste. 3700
San Francisco, CA 94105
415-768-8715
Fax: 415-768-3462

Contact(s):
Kevin Kendrick
Preferred Size Range:
$25 million–$75 million
Industries Specialized:
All
Do/Not Do Turnarounds: Do
Geographic Preference:
Domestic or International
Portfolio Companies:
Crown Pacific, Ltd.
Petro Stopping Centers
CRM Films
Blue Mountain Minerals
Atlantic Cellular
Branch Office(s):
None

The Benefit Capital Companies, Inc.
PO Box 49422
Los Angeles, CA 90049-0422
310-440-2296
Fax: 310-471-4072

Contact(s):
Robert W. Smiley, Jr.
Preferred Size Range:
$10 million–$500 million
Industries Specialized:
Computers
Consumer products
Consumer services
Food
Distribution
Energy
Industrial products
Medical
Agricultural
Do/Not Do Turnarounds: Do
Geographic Preference:
West Coast
Southwest
East Coast
Portfolio Companies:
Confidential
Branch Office(s):
Executive Offices
721 N. Bonhill Rd.
Los Angeles, CA 90049-2303

Berkshire Investment Corporation
150 E. 58th St., Ste. 3400
New York, NY 10155
212-935-5400
Fax: 212-753-0731

Contact(s):
Murray Steinfink
Preferred Size Range:
$10 million–$75 million
Industries Specialized:
All
Do/Not Do Turnarounds: Not
Geographic Preference:
Northeast
Mid-Atlantic
Southeast
Gulf States
Midwest
Portfolio Companies:
Confidential
Branch Office(s):
None

Bessemer Securities Corporation

630 Fifth Ave.
New York, NY 10111
212-708-9300
Fax: 212-265-5826

Contact(s):
John Wechsler
Preferred Size Range:
$25 million–$125 million
Industries Specialized:
All
Do/Not Do Turnarounds: Not
Geographic Preference:
United States
Portfolio Companies:
Prime Computer
ICOT, Inc.
XMX, Inc.
James River Corp.
Midway Airlines
Branch Office(s):
None

Blackstone Capital Partners, L.P.

345 Park Ave.
New York, NY 10154
212-836-9811
Fax: 212-754-8716

Contact(s):
James Mossman
Preferred Size Range:
$50 million+
Industries Specialized:
All
Do/Not Do Turnarounds: Not
Geographic Preference:
None
Portfolio Companies:
Confidential
Branch Office(s):
None

William Blair Venture Partners

135 S. LaSalle St.
Chicago, IL 60603
312-853-8250
Fax: 312-236-1042

Contact(s):
James Crawford
Samuel Guven
Preferred Size Range:
$5 million–$10 million
Industries Specialized:
All
Do/Not Do Turnarounds: Not
Geographic Preference:
United States
Portfolio Companies:
D'Lites of America
Amherst Association
Sanford Corp.
Internet Systems Corp.
Branch Office(s):
None

Bluegrass Capital Corp.

PO Box 35000
Louisville, KY 40232-5000
502-499-1004
Fax: 502-499-8445

Contact(s):
Charles S. Arensberg
Preferred Size Range:
$5 million–$25 million
Industries Specialized:
Manufacturing
Distribution
Medical
Do/Not Do Turnarounds: Do
Geographic Preference:
Midwest
Mid-Atlantic
Portfolio Companies:
Dispensers optical service corp.
Branch Office(s):
1815 Plantside Dr.
Louisville, KY 40299

Boston Capital Ventures

Old City Hall, 45 School St.
Boston, MA 02108
617-227-6550
Fax: 617-227-3847

Contact(s):
A. Dana Callow
Preferred Size Range:
$1 million–$200 million
Industries Specialized:
Health care
Environmental
Biotechnology
Telecommunications
Do/Not Do Turnarounds: Not
Geographic Preference:
Northeast
Midwest
Southeast
Portfolio Companies:
Parexel International
Foster Medical, Inc.
Revelation Technologies, Inc.
Verbex, Inc.
Branch Office(s):
205 N. Michigan Ave., Ste. 3911
Chicago, IL 60601
312-946-1200

Bourgeois Fils & Company, Inc.

Gorham Hall
PO Box 990
Exeter, NH 03833
603-778-1020
Fax: 603-778-7265

Contact(s):
G. Albert Bourgeois
Preferred Size Range:
$2 million–$25 million
Industries Specialized:
Industrial machinery and equipment
Chemicals
Business products
Computers
Telecommunications
Health care
Wholesale
Distribution
Transportation
Construction
Real estate
Do/Not Do Turnarounds: Not
Geographic Preference:
United States
Portfolio Companies:
Confidential
Branch Office(s):
None

Bradford Ventures, Ltd.
1212 Ave. of Americas
New York, NY 10036
212-221-4620
Fax: 212-764-3467

Contact(s):
Robert J. Simon
Preferred Size Range:
$10 million–$100 million
Industries Specialized:
All
Do/Not Do Turnarounds: Not
Geographic Preference:
East of Mississippi
Portfolio Companies:
American Healthcorp, Inc.
Central Sprinkler
Coca Cola Bottling Company of
    Southern Florida
CST Office Products
Denture Care, Inc.
Filtration Sciences
Holopak Technologies
HWC Distribution Corp.
Paramount Cards, Inc.
VSC Corporation
Branch Office(s):
None

Brentwood Associates
11150 Santa Monica Blvd.
Ste. 1200
Los Angeles, CA 90025
310-477-6611
Fax: 310-477-1011

Contact(s):
William M. Barnum
Preferred Size Range:
$5 million–$125 million
Industries Specialized:
Retail
Manufacturing
Distribution
Do/Not Do Turnarounds: Not
Geographic Preference:
United States
Portfolio Companies:
Actel Corporation
Cirrus Logic, Inc.
CPG International
Altus Corporation
Megatape Corporation
Branch Office(s):
3000 Sand Hill Rd.
Bldg. 2, Ste. 210
Menlo Park, CA 94025

Bridge Capital Advisers

Glenpointe Centre West
Teaneck, NJ 07666
201-836-3900
Fax: 201-836-6368

Contact(s):
Donald P. Reney, Managing
  Director
Geoffrey H. Wadsworth, Managing
  Director
Preferred Size Range:
$3 million–$6 million
Industries Specialized:
All
Do/Not Do Turnarounds: Not
Geographic Preference:
United States
Portfolio Companies:
Confidential
Branch Office(s):
Hoyt J. Goodrich
24 Lewis St.
Hartford, CT 06103
203-293-2901

Burr, Egan, Deleage & Company

One Post Office Square
Ste. 3800
Boston, MA 02109
617-482-8020
Fax: 617-482-1944

Contact(s):
Brian W. McNeill
Preferred Size Range:
$5 million–$25 million
Industries Specialized:
Media
Publishing
Computers
Telecommunications
Health care
Do/Not Do Turnarounds: Not
Geographic Preference:
United States
Portfolio Companies:
Codon
Genesys Software
Softsel Computer Products
Chiron Corporation
Telelearning Systems, Inc.
Branch Office(s):
One Embarcadero Center, Ste. 4050
San Francisco, CA 94111
415-362-4022

Butler Capital Corporation
767 Fifth Ave.
New York, NY 10153
212-980-0606
Fax: 212-759-0876

Contact(s):
Peter Lamm
Preferred Size Range:
$25 million–$500 million
Industries Specialized:
Consumer products
Consumer services
Business products
Business services
Media
Distribution
Wholesale
Transportation
Do/Not Do Turnarounds: Not
Geographic Preference:
United States
Portfolio Companies:
Panill Knitting Company
Ithaca Industries, Inc.
Sun Media
Golden State Foods
Branch Office(s):
One First National Plaza
Chicago, IL 60603
312-899-1981

Buyout Partners, Inc.
120 Country Club Dr., Ste. 19
Incline Village, NV 89450
702-832-7771
Fax: 702-832-0173

Contact(s):
Gary M. Acquavello
Preferred Size Range:
No minimum or maximum
Industries Specialized:
All
Do/Not Do Turnarounds: Not
Geographic Preference:
United States
Portfolio Companies:
Confidential
Branch Office(s):
Peter S. Redfield
601 California St., Ste. 1801
San Francisco, CA 94108

Camco & Alliance Recovery
7400 York Rd., Ste. 300
Baltimore, MD 21204-7502
410-828-1171
Fax: 410-296-2114

Contact(s):
Michael D. Quinn
Preferred Size Range:
$2.5 million–$25 million
Industries Specialized:
Consumer products
Consumer services
Industrial machinery and equipment
Business products
Business services
Telecommunications
Transportation
Financial services
Real estate
Construction
Do/Not Do Turnarounds: Not
Geographic Preference:
United States
Portfolio Companies:
Confidential
Branch Office(s):
None

Canita Corp.
PO Box 471028
San Francisco, CA 94123
415-929-1990
Fax: 415-929-1985

Contact(s):
Martin S. Steber
Preferred Size Range:
$5 million–$15 million
Industries Specialized:
Manufacturing
Distribution
Do/Not Do Turnarounds: Not
Geographic Preference:
None
Portfolio Companies:
Undisclosed
Branch Office(s):
1628 Union St., Ste. 1
San Francisco, CA 94123

Capital for Business, Inc.
11 S. Maramec, Ste. 800
St. Louis, MO 63105
314-854-7427
Fax: 314-726-8739

Contact(s):
James F. O'Donnell, Pres.
James J. Webber, Vice Pres.
Preferred Size Range:
$2.5 million–$5 million
Industries Specialized:
Basic technology
Manufacturing
Distribution
Do/Not Do Turnarounds: Not
Geographic Preference:
United States
Portfolio Companies:
Undisclosed
Branch Office(s):
Bart Bergman, Executive VP
1000 Walnut St., 18th Fl.
Kansas City, MO 64106
816-234-2357

Capital Growth Partners
260 Franklin St., Ste. 2260
Boston, MA 02110
617-439-6300
Fax: 617-439-6301

Contact(s):
Robert J. Wickey
Preferred Size Range:
$25 million–$125 million
Industries Specialized:
All
Do/Not Do Turnarounds: Not
Geographic Preference:
International
Portfolio Companies:
Confidential
Branch Office(s):
None

Capital Investment Corp.

351 S. Sherman, #101
Richardson, TX 75081
214-238-1195
Fax: 214-238-1181

Contact(s):
Mitch Wescott
Preferred Size Range:
Up to $1 million
Industries Specialized:
All except for
Real estate
Restaurants
Oil and gas
Do/Not Do Turnarounds: Do
Geographic Preference:
Northern Texas
Portfolio Companies:
Active Control, Inc.
USA Wet, Inc.
Innovation Air Systems, Inc.
Branch Office(s):
None

Capital Partners

One Pickwick Plaza, Ste. 310
Greenwich, CT 06830
203-625-0770
Fax: 203-625-0423

Contact(s):
A. George Gebauer
Preferred Size Range:
$20 million–$200 million
Industries Specialized:
Manufacturing
Do/Not Do Turnarounds: Not
Geographic Preference:
United States
Canada
Portfolio Companies:
Bryant Universal Roofing, Inc.
Alpha Modular Systems
Security Capital Corporation
Flavor House, Inc.
Forenta, Inc.
Branch Office(s):
None

Capital Resource Lenders
175 Portland St., Ste. 300
Boston, MA 02114
617-723-9000
Fax: 617-723-9819

Contact(s):
Fred C. Danforth
Robert Ammerman
Preferred Size Range:
$10 million–$100 million
Industries Specialized:
All
Do/Not Do Turnarounds: Not
Geographic Preference:
United States
Portfolio Companies:
Undisclosed
Branch Office(s):
40 Beach St., Ste. 104
Manchester, MA 01944
508-526-8110
Fax: 508-526-8000

Capital Resources Financial Group, Inc.
4075 El Prado Blvd.
Miami, FL 33133
305-669-9696

Contact(s):
Frank Barra
Preferred Size Range:
$1 million+
Industries Specialized:
Basic industries
Health care
Pharmaceuticals
Broadcasting
Distribution
No start-ups
Do/Not Do Turnarounds: Do
Geographic Preference:
Southeast
East
Portfolio Companies:
Confidential
Branch Office(s):
None

Capital Southwest Corp.
12900 Preston Rd., Ste. 700
Dallas, TX 75230
214-233-8242
Fax: 214-233-7362

Contact(s):
Tim Smith
Scott Collier
Preferred Size Range:
$5 million–$50 million
Industries Specialized:
Chemicals
Technology
Retail
Basic industry
Do/Not Do Turnarounds: Not
Geographic Preference:
United States
Portfolio Companies:
Confidential
Branch Office(s):
None

Castle Harlan, Inc.
150 E. 58th St.
New York, NY 10155
212-644-8600
Fax: 212-607-8042

Contact(s):
John K. Castle
Preferred Size Range:
$50 million+
Industries Specialized:
All
Do/Not Do Turnarounds: Do
Geographic Preference:
United States
Portfolio Companies:
Ethan Allen
Long John Silvers
Delaware Investment Advisors
Sharon Steel
Branch Office(s):
None

Charterhouse Group International, Inc.
535 Madison Ave.
New York, NY 10022
212-421-3125
Fax: 212-750-9704

Contact(s):
Brian E. Kinsman
Preferred Size Range:
$35 million+
Industries Specialized:
All
Do/Not Do Turnarounds: Do
Geographic Preference:
None
Portfolio Companies:
KG Retail Stores, Inc.
CPG International, Inc.
EMI Company, Inc.
AP Parts Manufacturing
Branch Office(s):
None

Chemical Venture Partners
270 Park Ave., 5th Fl.
New York, NY 10017
212-270-2464
Fax: 212-270-2327

Contact(s):
Jeffrey Walker
Preferred Size Range:
$20 million+
Industries Specialized:
All
Do/Not Do Turnarounds: Do
Geographic Preference:
None
Portfolio Companies:
Confidential
Branch Office(s):
Affiliated with Chemical Bank

Clayton & Dubilier, Inc.
126 E. 56th St.
New York, NY 10022
212-355-0740
Fax: 212-752-7629

Contact(s):
Martin H. Dubilier
Preferred Size Range:
$250 million+
Industries Specialized:
All
Do/Not Do Turnarounds: Not
Geographic Preference:
United States
United Kingdom
Continental Europe
Portfolio Companies:
Confidential
Branch Office(s):
None

Code, Hennessey & Simmons

10 S. Wacker Dr., Ste. 3175
Chicago, IL 60606
312-876-1840
Fax: 312-876-3854

Contact(s):
Andrew W. Code
Daniel J. Hennessey
Preferred Size Range:
$5 million–$100 million
Industries Specialized:
All
Do/Not Do Turnarounds: Not
Geographic Preference:
Mid-Atlantic
Midwest
Portfolio Companies:
Confidential
Branch Office(s):
None

Cofin, Inc.

125 E. 56th St.
New York, NY 10022
212-593-6100
Fax: 212-319-6549

Contact(s):
Jerrold Newman, Vice Pres.
Preferred Size Range:
$1 million–$15 million
Industries Specialized:
Consumer products
Consumer services
Retail
Industrial machinery and equipment
Business products
Business services
Distribution
Real estate
Construction
Medical
Education
Childcare
Do/Not Do Turnarounds: Not
Geographic Preference:
Northeast
Mid-Atlantic
Southeast
Portfolio Companies:
Confidential
Branch Office(s):
None

Cogeneration Finance, Inc.
14159 Dickens St., Ste. 306
Sherman Oaks, CA 91423
818-995-6378
Fax: 818-995-6378

Contact(s):
Alan L. Hills
Preferred Size Range:
$5 million+
Industries Specialized:
Utilities
Independent power production
Natural gas exploration
Production and transportation
    pipelines
Do/Not Do Turnarounds: Do
Geographic Preference:
United States
Canada
Portfolio Companies:
Confidential
Branch Office(s):
None

Comann, Howard & Flamen
180 Montgomery St., Ste. 1080
San Francisco, CA 94104
415-249-3737
Fax: 415-393-9493

Contact(s):
Tyler K. Comann
Preferred Size Range:
$10 million+
Industries Specialized:
Manufacturing
Do/Not Do Turnarounds: Do
Geographic Preference:
United States
Portfolio Companies:
20th Century Plastics, Inc.
Burke Industries
M+B Window Fashions
Nazareth/Century Mills
McCalls Patterns
Branch Office(s):
None

Commonwealth Capital Partners

PO Box 984
New Canaan, CT
203-966-9308
Fax: 203-972-0250

Contact(s):
Steven J. Gilbert
Preferred Size Range:
$25 million–$100 million
Industries Specialized:
All
Do/Not Do Turnarounds: Not
Geographic Preference:
United States
United Kingdom
Continental Europe
Japan
Portfolio Companies:
Per request
Branch Office(s):
Elliot Stein
Citicorp Center
153 E. 53rd St., 53rd Fl.
New York, NY 10022-4611
212-326-2000

Concorde Financial Corporation

1500 Three Lincoln Centre
5430 LBJ Freeway
Dallas, TX 75240
214-404-1500
Fax: 214-701-0530

Contact(s):
Dennis Beal
Preferred Size Range:
$1 million–$5 million
Industries Specialized:
Consumer products
Consumer services
Business products
Business services
Distribution
Recreational
Do/Not Do Turnarounds: Not
Geographic Preference:
Mid-Atlantic
South
West Coast–Rocky Mountain Region
Portfolio Companies:
Confidential
Branch Office(s):
None

Conning & Company
City Place II
Hartford, CT 06103
203-527-1131
Fax: 203-520-1240

Contact(s):
John Clinton
Preferred Size Range:
$25 million+
Industries Specialized:
Insurance
Do/Not Do Turnarounds: Do
Geographic Preference:
None
Portfolio Companies:
Mutual Risk
Penn Corp.
Trenwick
Branch Office(s):
None

Consumer Venture Partners
Three Pickwick Plaza
Greenwich, CT 06830
203-629-8800
Fax: 203-629-2019

Contact(s):
Pearson C. Cummin III
Preferred Size Range:
$5 million–$25 million
Industries Specialized:
Consumer products
Consumer services
Do/Not Do Turnarounds: Not
Geographic Preference:
United States
Portfolio Companies:
Confidential
Branch Office(s):
None

Corinthian Capital Corp.
205 N. Michigan Ave., #3911
Chicago, IL 60601
312-946-1204
Fax: 312-946-1103

Contact(s):
William R. Cross
Preferred Size Range:
$5 million–$25 million
Industries Specialized:
Services
Do/Not Do Turnarounds: Not
Geographic Preference:
Midwest
Portfolio Companies:
Confidential
Branch Office(s):
None

Corporate Acquisitions, Inc.

5430 LBJ Fwy., Ste. 1600
Dallas, TX 75240
214-788-5115
Fax: 214-788-5462

Contact(s):
Craig W. Wycoff
Preferred Size Range:
$10 million–$50 million
Industries Specialized:
Manufacturing
Distribution
Do/Not Do Turnarounds: Not
Geographic Preference:
South Central
Southwest
Portfolio Companies:
FM Industries, Inc. (Formerly
  Freightmaster)
Contech
Branch Office(s):
None

Cortec Group, Inc.

200 Park Ave.
New York, NY 10166
212-370-5600
Fax: 212-682-4195

Contact(s):
T. Richard Fishbein
Preferred Size Range:
$20 million–$100 million
Industries Specialized:
Plastics
Electronics
Manufacturing
Do/Not Do Turnarounds: Not
Geographic Preference:
East
Portfolio Companies:
LePages, Inc.
Environmental Analytical Systems
Branch Office(s):
None

Cove Associates, Ltd.
1 Selleck St.
Norwalk, CT 06855
203-855-1006
Fax: 203-855-1718

Contact(s):
Miles Spencer
Preferred Size Range:
$3 million–$30 million
Industries Specialized:
Consumer products
Medical
Light manufacturing
Services
Do/Not Do Turnarounds: Not
Geographic Preference:
Northeast
Portfolio Companies:
Confidential
Branch Office(s):
None

CSS Industries, Inc.
1401 Walnut St.
Philadelphia, PA 19102
215-569-9900
Fax: 215-569-9979

Contact(s):
James Baxter
Preferred Size Range:
$20 million–$80 million
Industries Specialized:
Manufacturing
Paper products
Specialty metal packaging
Do/Not Do Turnarounds: Do
Geographic Preference:
United States
Portfolio Companies:
The Paper Magic Group
Rapidforms, Inc.
Ellisco, Inc.
Branch Office(s):
None

Darien Associates, Inc.

22 Holly Ln.
Darien, CT 06820
203-655-2263
Fax: Undisclosed

Contact(s):
W.S. McAdoo
Preferred Size Range:
$5 million–$25 million
Industries Specialized:
Manufacturing (with product line
and customer base)
Do/Not Do Turnarounds: Do
Geographic Preference:
East
Midwest
Portfolio Companies:
Undisclosed
Branch Office(s):
None

Davis Venture Partners

One Williams Ctr., Ste. 2000
Tulsa, OK 74172
918-584-7272
Fax: 918-582-3403

Contact(s):
Barry M. Davis
Preferred Size Range:
$5 million–$25 million
Industries Specialized:
Consumer services
Chemicals
Media
Health care
Distribution
Transportation
Do/Not Do Turnarounds: Not
Geographic Preference:
United States
Portfolio Companies:
Confidential
Branch Office(s):
Michael A. Stone
2121 San Jacinto St., Ste. 975
Dallas, TX 75201
214-954-1822

Demuth, Folger & Terhune
One Exchange Plaza
New York, NY 10006
212-509-5580
Fax: 212-363-7965

Contact(s):
Donald F. Demuth
Preferred Size Range:
$10 million–$100 million
Industries Specialized:
Medical
Technology
Telecommunications
Do/Not Do Turnarounds: Do
Geographic Preference:
United States
Portfolio Companies:
Compupharm
IEC Electronics
Oriel Corp.
Taylor Medical
Telesciences
Branch Office(s):
None

Dent & Company, Inc.
One Lafayette Pl.
Greenwich, CT 06830
203-629-2900
Fax: 203-629-2473

Contact(s):
John Allen
Preferred Size Range:
$15 million–$150 million
Industries Specialized:
Manufacturing
Do/Not Do Turnarounds: Not
Geographic Preference:
United States
Portfolio Companies:
Rehies, Inc.
Aetna Industries, Inc.
Fibre Glass-Evercoat Company, Inc.
Dominion Automotive Group, Inc.
Seacare Corp.
Marine Division of Lan-O-Sheen, Inc.
Target Tech, Inc.
Branch Office(s):
None

Diehl & Company
1500 Quail, Ste. 550
Newport Beach, CA 92660
714-955-2000
Fax: 714-955-1812

Contact(s):
Michael D. Henton
Preferred Size Range:
$3 million–$100 million
Industries Specialized:
Manufacturing
Distribution
Do/Not Do Turnarounds: Do
Geographic Preference:
West
Portfolio Companies:
Confidential
Branch Office(s):
None

Dillion, Read & Co., Inc.
535 Madison Ave.
New York, NY 10022
212-906-7000
Fax: 212-593-0164

Contact(s):
Bret Russell
Mark Kammert
Preferred Size Range:
$50 million–$400 million
Industries Specialized:
All
Do/Not Do Turnarounds: Not
Geographic Preference:
United States
Canada
Portfolio Companies:
Norfolk Holdings, Inc.
Hi-Lo Automotive, Inc.
Big River Minerals Corporation
Viking Office Products, Inc.
Mustang Fuel Corporation
Formica Corporation
Haas Publishing Companies, Inc.
Atlantic Cellular Company
Cannell Communications, L.P.
Capital Markets Assurance Corp.
Branch Office(s):
None

Dunleavy & Company
477 Madison Ave.
New York, NY 10022
212-888-5700
Fax: 212-888-5719

Contact(s):
Jerome P. Dunleavy
Preferred Size Range:
$50 million–$250 million
Industries Specialized:
Industrial services
Commercial services
Manufacturing (niche markets)
Distribution
Do/Not Do Turnarounds: Not
Geographic Preference:
United States
Portfolio Companies:
Confidential
Branch Office(s):
None

Dyson, Kissner, Moran Corp.
230 Park Ave.
New York, NY 10169
212-661-4600
Fax: 212-599-5105

Contact(s):
John Carleton, Vice Pres.
Preferred Size Range:
$25 million+
Industries Specialized:
All
Do/Not Do Turnarounds: Do
Geographic Preference:
None
Portfolio Companies:
Spectrol
Plaid Enterprises
IMS International
Kearney National
Branch Office(s):
None

Edison Venture Fund
997 Lenox Dr.
Lawrenceville, NJ 08648
609-896-1900
Fax: 609-896-0066

Contact(s):
Gustau H. Kouen
Preferred Size Range:
$10 million–$75 million
Industries Specialized:
Environmental
Health care
Communications
Computers
Chemicals
Food
Financial services
Do/Not Do Turnarounds: Not
Geographic Preference:
Mid-Atlantic
Portfolio Companies:
Summit Environmental
Medifit
ECCS
Consolidated Waste
Branch Office(s):
None

Elders Financial Corporation
200 Park Ave., 26th Fl.
New York, NY 10166
212-909-9900
Fax: 212-909-9990

Contact(s):
Thomas Goossens, Director
Preferred Size Range:
$100 million+
Industries Specialized:
High technology
Computers
Cable TV
Do/Not Do Turnarounds: Not
Geographic Preference:
United States
Canada
Portfolio Companies:
Confidential
Branch Office(s):
None

El Dorado Ventures
800 E. Colorado Blvd., Ste. 530
Pasadena, CA 91101
818-793-1936
Fax: 818-793-2613

Contact(s):
Tom Peterson
Preferred Size Range:
Start up to $5 million
Industries Specialized:
Computers
Electronics
Communications
Health care
Do/Not Do Turnarounds: Not
Geographic Preference:
West
Portfolio Companies:
Access Health
Accom
Cellular Data
Experttest
Gold Disk
Indigo
Optical Specialties
Quorum
Vantage
Voicesort
Branch Office(s):
20300 Stevens Creek Blvd. Ste. 395
Cupertino, CA 95014
408-725-2474
Fax: 408-252-2762

Electra, Inc.
70 E. 55th St., 25th Fl.
New York, NY 10022
212-319-0081
Fax: 212-319-3069

Contact(s):
John Pouschine
Preferred Size Range:
$40 million+
Industries Specialized:
Construction
Environment
Finance
Manufacturing
Medical
Telecommunications
Transportation
Do/Not Do Turnarounds: Do
Geographic Preference:
East of Rocky Mountains
Portfolio Companies:
Act III Cinemas
U.S. Long Distance
Ciro
Danskin
Branch Office(s):
None

Equitable Capital Management Corp.
1285 Ave. of the Americas
New York, NY 10019
212-554-2000
Fax: 212-554-1032

Contact(s):
James R. Wilson
Preferred Size Range:
$50 million+
Industries Specialized:
All
Do/Not Do Turnarounds: Not
Geographic Preference:
United States
Portfolio Companies:
Confidential
Branch Office(s):
Scott D. Rooth, Managing Director
225 W. Washington
Chicago, IL 60606
312-419-7110

Equity Dynamics, Inc.
2116 Financial Ctr.
Des Moines, IA 50309
515-244-5746
Fax: 515-244-2346

Contact(s):
John Pappajohn
Preferred Size Range:
$2 million–$5 million
Industries Specialized:
Medical
High technology
Manufacturing
Distribution
Do/Not Do Turnarounds: Not
Geographic Preference:
Midwest
Portfolio Companies:
Asbestic Industries
Continental Health care Systems, Inc.
Medical Imaging Centers of America
Branch Office(s):
None

Equity Opportunity Associates
210 River Run at the Mill
Greenwich, CT 06831
203-531-4576
Fax: 203-629-2235

Contact(s):
Brewster Kopp
Preferred Size Range:
$50 million–$250 million
Industries Specialized:
Business products
Business services
Consumer services
Industrial machinery and equipment
Chemicals
Publishing
Financial services
Do/Not Do Turnarounds: Not
Geographic Preference:
United States
Canada
Portfolio Companies:
Undisclosed
Branch Office(s):
None

Equity Opportunity Associates

26 Sawyer Ave.
Staten Island, NY 10314
718-447-5581
Fax: 718-273-9576

Contact(s):
Harold Fredheim
Preferred Size Range:
$10 million–$100 million
Industries Specialized:
All
Do/Not Do Turnarounds: Do
Geographic Preference:
None
Portfolio Companies:
Confidential
Branch Office(s):
Riverrun 210, The Mill
Greenwich, CT 06831
718-447-5581

Exeter Capital, L.P.

122 E. 42nd St.
New York, NY 10168
212-984-0778
Fax: 212-984-0668

Contact(s):
Keith Fox
Preferred Size Range:
$10 million+
Industries Specialized:
All except for
   Real estate
Do/Not Do Turnarounds: Not
Geographic Preference:
None
Portfolio Companies:
Flagship Cleaning Services
Jay Packaging
Victor Wire and Cable
Abbott, Inc.
Hanger Orthopedic Group
Flightline Electronics, Inc.
Travcorp
AFCO
Branch Office(s):
None

Fairfield Venture Partners
1275 Summer St.
Stamford, CT 06905
203-358-0255
Fax: 203-348-5815

Contact(s):
Pedro Castillo
Preferred Size Range:
$5 million–$25 million
Industries Specialized:
Diversified companies
High technology
Do/Not Do Turnarounds: Not
Geographic Preference:
United States
Portfolio Companies:
Provided upon request
Branch Office(s):
Randall Lunn
650 Town Center Dr., Ste. 810
Costa Mesa, CA 92626
714-754-5717

FHL Capital Corp.
825 Financial Ctr.
Birmingham, AL 35203
205-328-3098
Fax: 205-328-4010

Contact(s):
Edwin Finch
Preferred Size Range:
$2 million–$25 million
Industries Specialized:
Industrial machinery and equipment
Chemicals
Business products
Business services
Wholesale
Distribution
Do/Not Do Turnarounds: Not
Geographic Preference:
Southeast
Portfolio Companies:
Provided upon request
Branch Office(s):
None

First American Capital Corp.

c/o Smith McDonnell Stone & Co.
450 Park Ave., Ste. 2102
New York, NY 10022
212-750-7780
Fax: 212-754-3362

Contact(s):
Paul Smith
Preferred Size Range:
$20 million–$100 million
Industries Specialized:
Basic manufacturing
Distribution
Do/Not Do Turnarounds: Do
Geographic Preference:
United States
Portfolio Companies:
Matthews & Boucher, Inc.
Branch Office(s):
None

First Atlantic Capital, Ltd.

135 E. 57th St., 29th Fl.
New York, NY 10022
212-750-0300
Fax: 212-750-0954

Contact(s):
Nils Nilsen
Preferred Size Range:
$25 million–$150 million
Industries Specialized:
Manufacturing
Distribution
Specialty retailing
Do/Not Do Turnarounds: Not
Geographic Preference:
United States
Canada
Europe
Portfolio Companies:
Berry Plastics, Inc.
Fort Wayne Plastics, Inc.
Branch Office(s):
None

First Boston Corporation

12 E. 49th St.
New York, NY 10017
212-909-4588
Fax: 212-838-7740

Contact(s):
Jeffrey Parker
Preferred Size Range:
$5 million–$25 million
Industries Specialized:
Business products
Business services
Consumer products
Consumer services
Industrial machinery and equipment
Chemicals
Medical
Do/Not Do Turnarounds: Not
Geographic Preference:
United States
Portfolio Companies:
Confidential
Branch Office(s):
None

First Century Partners

1345 Ave. of the Americas, 47th Fl.
New York, NY 10105
212-698-6688
Fax: 212-698-6363

Contact(s):
David S. Lobel
Preferred Size Range:
$30 million–$200 million
Industries Specialized:
Consumer products
Light manufacturing
Distribution
Do/Not Do Turnarounds: Not
Geographic Preference:
United States
Portfolio Companies:
Hasco International, Inc.
Frame-N-Lens Optical
Office Depot
Rocky Mountain Consumer Bank
Branch Office(s):
None

First Chicago Venture Capital

One First National Plaza, Ste. 1043
Chicago, IL 60670-0501
312-732-2690
Fax: 312-732-1915

Contact(s):
John A. Canning
Allen Dixon
Preferred Size Range:
$25 million–$250 million
Industries Specialized:
All
Do/Not Do Turnarounds: Not
Geographic Preference:
United States
Portfolio Companies:
Western Industries
Univision
Calumet Holdings
Fleet Call, Inc.
Health Management Association
B.C. Holdings
Branch Office(s):
Affiliated with First National Bank
   of Chicago

First New England Capital, L.P.

255 Main St.
Hartford, CT 06106
203-293-3333
Fax: Undisclosed

Contact(s):
Richard Klaffky, Pres.
Preferred Size Range:
$500,000–$1 million
Industries Specialized:
Business products
Business services
Consumer products
Industrial machinery and equipment
Publishing
Distribution
Transportation
Do/Not Do Turnarounds: Not
Geographic Preference:
Northeast
Portfolio Companies:
Confidential
Branch Office(s):
None

First Westinghouse Capital Corp.

One Oxford Centre
Pittsburgh, PA 15219
412-393-3157
Fax: 412-393-3158

Contact(s):
Guy Simmons, Vice Pres.
Dave Heilman, Vice Pres.
Preferred Size Range:
$25 million–$1 billion
Industries Specialized:
All
Do/Not Do Turnarounds: Not
Geographic Preference:
United States
Portfolio Companies:
Confidential
Branch Office(s):
Woburn, MA 617-932-1110
Newport Beach, CA 714-476-3624
Affiliated with Westinghouse
    Credit Corp.

Fleet Mezzanine Capital, Inc.

111 Westminster St.
Providence, RI 02903
401-278-6267
Fax: 401-278-6331

Contact(s):
Colin J. Clapton, Pres.
Preferred Size Range:
$5 million+
Industries Specialized:
Media
Do/Not Do Turnarounds: Do
Geographic Preference:
United States
Portfolio Companies:
Provided upon request
Branch Office(s):
Undisclosed

Florida Capital Partners

101 E. Kennedy Blvd., Ste. 3630
Tampa, FL 33602
813-222-8000
Fax: 813-222-8001

Contact(s):
Glenn Oken
Preferred Size Range:
$5 million–$100 million
Industries Specialized:
Noncyclical
Non-high tech
Noncommodity
Manufacturing
Distribution
Do/Not Do Turnarounds: Not
Geographic Preference:
Texas
East
Portfolio Companies:
Advalite
Niemand Industries, Inc.
Horizon Chemical and Painters
    Supply
Gulf Automotive of Clearwater, Inc.
The Lorvic Corporation
CPP, Inc.
Branch Office(s):
None

Forstman, Little & Company

767 Fifth Ave.
New York, NY 10153
212-355-5656
Fax: 212-759-9059

Contact(s):
Theodore J. Forstman
Preferred Size Range:
$250 million+
Industries Specialized:
All
Do/Not Do Turnarounds: Not
Geographic Preference:
United States
Canada
United Kingdom
Portfolio Companies:
Confidential
Branch Office(s):
None

Founders Court Investors, Inc.

22 Chambers St.
Princeton, NJ 08542-3719
609-921-8700
Fax: 609-921-1986

Contact(s):
N.W. Hare
Preferred Size Range:
$5 million–$50 million
Industries Specialized:
Business products
Business services
Consumer products
Industrial machinery and equipment
Chemicals
Transportation
Health care
Do/Not Do Turnarounds: Not
Geographic Preference:
United States
Portfolio Companies:
Provided upon request
Branch Office(s):
None

Freeman, Spogli & Co.

523 W. 6th St.
Los Angeles, CA 90014
310-444-1822
Fax: 310-444-1870

Contact(s):
Ronald P. Spogli
Preferred Size Range:
$100 million+
Industries Specialized:
All
Do/Not Do Turnarounds: Not
Geographic Preference:
United States
Portfolio Companies:
Confidential
Branch Office(s):
John M. Roth
599 Lexington Ave., 18th Fl.
New York, NY 10022
212-758-2555

Frontenac Venture Capital
208 S. LaSalle St., Ste. 1900
Chicago, IL 60604
312-368-0040
Fax: 312-368-9520

Contact(s):
M. Laird Koldyke
Preferred Size Range:
$50 million–$250 million
Industries Specialized:
Consumer products
Consumer services
Retail
Health care
Manufacturing
Distribution
Do/Not Do Turnarounds: Not
Geographic Preference:
Central
Portfolio Companies:
American Healthcorp, Inc.
Phycor, Inc.
Comlinear Corp.
Platinum Technology, Inc.
Chalk Lime, Inc.
Home Fashions, Inc.
Devry, Inc.
Consolidated Stores
Bradley Printing Company
Prestolite Electric, Inc.
Branch Office(s):
None

Gabelli-Rosenthal & Partners, L.P.
655 Third Ave., 14th Fl.
New York, NY 10017
914-921-5146
Fax: 914-921-5118

Contact(s):
Nicholas E. Stefano
Preferred Size Range:
$5 million–$25 million
Industries Specialized:
All
Do/Not Do Turnarounds: Not
Geographic Preference:
United States
Portfolio Companies:
Confidential
Branch Office(s):
None

J.M. Galef & Company, Inc.
100 Central Park South
New York, NY 10019
212-223-2200
Fax: 212-223-0053

Contact(s):
James M. Galef
Preferred Size Range:
$10 million–$100 million
Industries Specialized:
All
Do/Not Do Turnarounds: Do
Geographic Preference:
United States
Portfolio Companies:
Confidential
Branch Office(s):
None

Gibbons, Green, Van Amerongen & Co.
600 Madison Ave.
New York, NY 10022
212-832-2400
Fax: 212-750-4788

Contact(s):
Edward Gibbons
Preferred Size Range:
$50 million–$500 million
Industries Specialized:
All
Do/Not Do Turnarounds: Not
Geographic Preference:
United States
Canada
Portfolio Companies:
Confidential
Branch Office(s):
None

GKH Investments, L.P.
200 W. Madison
Ste. #3800
Chicago, IL 60606

Contact(s):
William Golberg
Melvyn Klein
Preferred Size Range:
$25million+
Industries Specialized:
Retailing
Oil and gas
Health care
Do/Not Do Turnarounds: Do
Geographic Preference:
None
Portfolio Companies:
American Medical Holdings
Hanover Energy
Savoy Pictures
Santa Fe Energy Resources, Inc.
Branch Office(s):
None

Golder, Thoma & Cressey
120 S. LaSalle, #630
Chicago, IL 60603
312-853-3322
Fax: 312-853-3354

Contact(s):
Carl D. Thoma
Preferred Size Range:
$10 million–$200 million
Industries Specialized:
Health care
Distribution
Communications
Do/Not Do Turnarounds: Not
Geographic Preference:
None
Portfolio Companies:
Paging Network, Inc.
Southern Foods Group, Inc.
Golf Enterprises, Inc.
Heritage Propane Corp.
American Income Holding
Branch Office(s):
None

Goldman, Sachs & Company
85 Broad St.
New York, NY 10004
212-902-0859
Fax: 212-902-4103

Contact(s):
Michael Miele, Analyst
Preferred Size Range:
$50 million–$500 million
Industries Specialized:
All
Do/Not Do Turnarounds: Not
Geographic Preference:
United States
Canada
Continental Europe
Portfolio Companies:
Confidential
Branch Office(s):
None

Grace/Horn Ventures

20300 Stevens Creek Blvd., Ste. 330
Cupertino, CA 95014
408-725-0774
Fax: 408-725-0327

Contact(s):
Christian Horn
Preferred Size Range:
$2 million–$5 million
Industries Specialized:
Biotechnology
Pharmaceuticals
Communications
Computers
Chemicals
Electronics
Automation
Medical
Semiconductors
Do/Not Do Turnarounds: Not
Geographic Preference:
United States
Portfolio Companies:
Undisclosed
Branch Office(s):
None

Green Capital Investors, L.P.

3343 Peachtree Rd., Ste. 1420
Atlanta, GA 30326
404-261-1187
Fax: 404-261-8677

Contact(s):
Holcombe Green
Preferred Size Range:
$25 million–$100 million
Industries Specialized:
All
Do/Not Do Turnarounds: Not
Geographic Preference:
Southeast
Portfolio Companies:
Rhodes, Inc.
Opti World, Inc.
ABC School Supply, Inc.
Branch Office(s):
None

Greenwich Venture Partners

8 Sound Shore Dr., Ste. 100
Greenwich, CT 06830
203-629-4447
Fax: 203-629-4848

Contact(s):
Don Cavicchio
Preferred Size Range:
$1 million–$40 million
Industries Specialized:
Electrical
Electronics
Do/Not Do Turnarounds: Do
Geographic Preference:
United States
Canada
Mexico
Portfolio Companies:
Commonwealth Sprague
Capacitor, Inc
Branch Office(s):
None

GRG Interests, Inc.

120 S. LaSalle St.
Chicago, IL 60603
312-236-8453
Fax: 312-236-8454

Contact(s):
Rudolph Rasin, Pres.
Preferred Size Range:
$2 million+
Industries Specialized:
Consumer products
Retail
Manufacturing
Distribution
Do/Not Do Turnarounds: Not
Geographic Preference:
United States
Canada
Portfolio Companies:
Confidential
Branch Office(s):
None

Gries Investment Company
720 Statler Office Tower
Cleveland, OH 44115
216-861-1146
Fax: 216-861-0106

Contact(s):
Richard Brezic
Preferred Size Range:
$500,000–$5 million
Industries Specialized:
Manufacturing
Distribution
Do/Not Do Turnarounds: Not
Geographic Preference:
United States
Portfolio Companies:
Provided upon request
Branch Office(s):
None

Group One Capital, Inc.
1611 Des Peres, Ste. 395
St. Louis, MO 63131
314-821-5100
Fax: 314-821-6693

Contact(s):
Mark Crawford
Preferred Size Range:
$10 million–$100 million
Industries Specialized:
Distribution
Light manufacturing
Retail
Do/Not Do Turnarounds: Not
Geographic Preference:
United States
Portfolio Companies:
Temple, Inc.
State Supply Warehouse
HomeStar Industries
Sunsations Sunglass, Co.
Branch Office(s):
None

Grubb & Williams, Ltd.
3399 Peachtree Rd., Ste. 1790
Atlanta, GA 30326
404-237-6222
Fax: 404-261-1578

Contact(s):
Steve Grubb
Preferred Size Range:
$2 million–$25 million
Industries Specialized:
All
Do/Not Do Turnarounds: Not
Geographic Preference:
United States
Portfolio Companies:
Provided upon request
Branch Office(s):
None

Gustafson & Company
366 Underhill Ave.
Yorktown Heights, NY 10598
914-962-2200
Fax: 914-962-2204

Contact(s):
Mark Gustafson
Preferred Size Range:
$2 million–$25 million
Industries Specialized:
Industrial machinery and equipment
Chemicals
Business products
Business services
Media
Wholesale
Do/Not Do Turnarounds: Not
Geographic Preference:
United States
Portfolio Companies:
Confidential
Branch Office(s):
None

Hambrecht & Quist, Inc.
One Bush St.
San Francisco, CA 94104
415-576-3300
Fax: 415-576-3624

Contact(s):
Lionel Boissiere
Preferred Size Range:
$2 million–$25 million
Industries Specialized:
Consumer services
Publishing
Retailing
Computers
Electronics
Telecommunications
Medical
Distribution
Do/Not Do Turnarounds: Not
Geographic Preference:
United States
United Kingdom
Portfolio Companies:
Calgene
Read-Rite Corporation
Telequest
Seattle Silicon Technology
Branch Office(s):
Affiliated with Baring Bros.
Hambrecht & Quist, London

Hambro International Venture Fund

17 E. 71st St.
New York, NY 10021
212-223-7400
Fax: 212-223-0195

Contact(s):
Edwin A. Goodman
Preferred Size Range:
$2 million–$125 million
Industries Specialized:
All
Do/Not Do Turnarounds: Not
Geographic Preference:
United States
United Kingdom
Japan
Continental Europe
Portfolio Companies:
Platt Music Corp.
Staples
Founders Communications
Rivendell
Branch Office(s):
Richard A. D'Amore
160 State St.
Boston, MA 02109
617-722-7116

Hamilton, Robinson & Co., Inc.

30 Rockefeller Plaza, Ste. 3318
New York, NY 10112
212-332-1220
Fax: 212-332-1225

Contact(s):
Scott Oakford
Preferred Size Range:
$25 million+
Industries Specialized:
All
Do/Not Do Turnarounds: Not
Geographic Preference:
United States
Canada
Portfolio Companies:
Republic Realty
Maginnis & Associates
ASCO
Branch Office(s):
None

Hampshire Capital Corp.

PO Box 178
New Castle, NH 03854
603-431-1415
Fax: 603-431-7755

Contact(s):
Philip G. Baker
Preferred Size Range:
$1 million–$10 million
Industries Specialized:
Services
Travel
Courier
Art
Do/Not Do Turnarounds: Not
Geographic Preference:
United States
Mexico
Canada
Portfolio Companies:
Topaz Business Development Corp.
Innisquauu Capital Corp.
Branch Office(s):
None

Hancock Venture Partners

One Financial Ctr.
Boston, MA 02111
617-348-3707
Fax: 617-350-0305

Contact(s):
Rob Wadsworth
Preferred Size Range:
$5 million+
Industries Specialized:
Computers
Telecommunications
Industrial products
Industrial services
Health care
Do/Not Do Turnarounds: Not
Geographic Preference:
United States
Portfolio Companies:
Confidential
Branch Office(s):
None

Harbour Group Industries, Inc.
7701 Forsyth, Ste. 550
St. Louis, MO 63105
314-727-5550
Fax: 314-727-9912

Contact(s):
Ralph Lobdell
Preferred Size Range:
$25 million–$125 million
Industries Specialized:
Industrial machinery
Chemicals
Media
Publishing
Medical
Do/Not Do Turnarounds: Not
Geographic Preference:
United States
United Kingdom
Canada
Continental Europe
Portfolio Companies:
Confidential
Branch Office(s):
None

Harvest Ventures, Inc.
767 Third Ave., 7th Fl.
New York, NY 10017
212-838-7776
Fax: 212-593-0734

Contact(s):
Harvey Mallement
Preferred Size Range:
$25 million–$250 million
Industries Specialized:
Manufacturing
Distribution
Health care
Services
Do/Not Do Turnarounds: Do
Geographic Preference:
United States
Western Europe
Portfolio Companies:
Career Horizons, Inc.
Taylor Medical
OK Industries
Industrial Ceramics, Inc.
Branch Office(s):
19200 Stevens Creek Blvd.
Cupertino, CA 95014
408-996-3200
Fax: 408-996-1765

Hawthorne Capital Partners
310 W. Monument Ave., Ste. 400
Dayton, OH 45402-3000
513-461-0091
Fax: 617-542-4209

Contact(s):
William M. Sherk
Preferred Size Range:
$1 million–$5 million
Industries Specialized:
All
Do/Not Do Turnarounds: Do
Geographic Preference:
United States
Portfolio Companies:
Undisclosed
Branch Office(s):
None

Heller Equity Capital Corp.
500 W. Monroe
Chicago, IL 60661
312-441-7200
Fax: 312-441-7378

Contact(s):
John M. Goense
Preferred Size Range:
$15 million–$75 million
Industries Specialized:
Health care
Security
Optical
Manufacturing
Services
Do/Not Do Turnarounds: Not
Geographic Preference:
United States
Portfolio Companies:
Indian Head Industries
The Wilson Center
Vendell Health Care
Preferred Pipe Products
Employers Security Company
DBL Management, Inc.
Expressions, Inc.
Look, S.A.
MERX, Inc.
Branch Office(s):
None

Hickory Venture Group
200 W. Count Square, Ste. 100
Huntsville, AL 35801
205-539-1931
Fax: 205-539-5130

Contact(s):
Monroe B. Lanier
Preferred Size Range:
$5 million–$25 million
Industries Specialized:
Medical
Manufacturing
Food
Do/Not Do Turnarounds: Not
Geographic Preference:
Southeast
Southwest
Midwest
Portfolio Companies:
National Laboratory Center, Inc.
Romanoff International, Inc.
Anquest, Inc.
The Forgotten Woman
Branch Office(s):
None

Hillcrest Group

9 S. 12th St.
Richmond, VA
804-643-7358
Fax: 804-648-3313

Contact(s):
James Farinholt
Preferred Size Range:
$2 million–$25 million
Industries Specialized:
All
Do/Not Do Turnarounds: Not
Geographic Preference:
Mid-Atlantic
Southeast
Portfolio Companies:
Riverton Corporation
Jarvis Corporation
Pearson Yachts
CSVA, Inc.
Do It Yourself, Inc.
Branch Office(s):
None

HMS Capital Partners

170 Middlefield Rd., Ste. 150
Menlo Park, CA 94025
415-324-4672
Fax: 415-324-4684

Contact(s):
Frank R. Atkinson
Preferred Size Range:
$2 million–$7 million
Industries Specialized:
Communications
Do/Not Do Turnarounds: Not
Geographic Preference:
United States
Canada
Portfolio Companies:
Undisclosed
Branch Office(s):
Bank of America Center
555 California St., Ste. 5000
San Francisco, CA 94104

Holding Capital
685 5th Ave., 14th Fl.
New York, NY 10022
212-486-6670
Fax: 212-486-0843

Contact(s):
James W. Donaghy
Preferred Size Range:
$10 million–$100 million
Industries Specialized:
All
Do/Not Do Turnarounds: Do
Geographic Preference:
None
Portfolio Companies:
Confidential
Branch Office(s):
22 Cortland St.
New York, NY 10007
212-732-5670

Horizon Holdings
400 Sansome St., Ste. 204
San Francisco, CA 94111
415-249-3035
Fax: 415-249-3038

Contact(s):
Jim Shorin
Phil Estes
Preferred Size Range:
$5 million–$20 million
Industries Specialized:
Food
Consumer products
Manufacturing
Distribution
Specialty food (retail)
Do/Not Do Turnarounds: Do
Geographic Preference:
West Coast
Portfolio Companies:
Coffee Bean International
Branch Office(s):
None

Indusvest Management, Inc.
405 Park Ave., Ste. 500
New York, NY 10022
212-371-5935
Fax: 212-758-9032

Contact(s):
Antoine Bernheim, Pres.
Preferred Size Range:
$2 million–$25 million
Industries Specialized:
All
Do/Not Do Turnarounds: Not
Geographic Preference:
United States
United Kingdom
Continental Europe
Portfolio Companies:
Confidential
Branch Office(s):
None

Information Partners, L.P.
2 Copley Pl.
Boston, MA 02116
617-572-2100
Fax: 617-572-3274

Contact(s):
Stephen G. Pagliuca
Preferred Size Range:
$10 million–$100 million
Industries Specialized:
Software
Communications
Data processing services
Credit decision services
Data bases
Information publishing
Education and training services
Financial services
Do/Not Do Turnarounds: Not
Geographic Preference:
None
Portfolio Companies:
Confidential
Branch Office(s):
Affiliated with Bain Capital

Ingram Todd, Inc.
34 W. Putnam Ave.
Greenwich, CT 06830
203-869-2500
Fax: 203-869-1666

Contact(s):
Richard Fraser, Pres.
Preferred Size Range:
$1 million–$3 million (profits)
Industries Specialized:
Manufacturing
Distribution (low to medium
    technology)
Do/Not Do Turnarounds: Not
Geographic Preference:
United States
Portfolio Companies:
Undisclosed
Branch Office(s):
None

International Business Consultants
41 Perimeter Center East, #605
Atlanta, GA 30349
404-394-0170
Fax: 404-394-0172

Contact(s):
Carl F. Owen
Preferred Size Range:
$1 million--$75 million
Industries Specialized:
All
Do/Not Do Turnarounds: Do
Geographic Preference:
United States
Europe
Portfolio Companies:
Pratt & Lambert Paints
Rostra Holdings
Banner Industries
Ferguson Enterprises
Harding Group
Campbell Soups
Branch Office(s):
Member M&A International
    11 U.S., 12 European offices
    Primary contact: William E.
    Oliver

Intersouth Partners

PO Box 13546
Research Triangle Park, NC 27709
919-544-6473
Fax: 919-544-6645

Contact(s):
Roy Rodwell
Preferred Size Range:
$2 million–$10 million
Industries Specialized:
Consumer products
Manufacturing
Computers
Medical
Do/Not Do Turnarounds: Not
Geographic Preference:
Southeast
Portfolio Companies:
Confidential
Branch Office(s):
None

Interven Partners

301 Arizona Ave., Ste. 306
Santa Monica, CA 90401
310-587-3550
Fax: 310-587-3440

Contact(s):
David B. Jones
Preferred Size Range:
$5 million–$25 million
Industries Specialized:
Consumer products
Retailing
Industrial machinery
Chemicals
Computers
Distribution
Do/Not Do Turnarounds: Not
Geographic Preference:
Southwest
West Coast
Northwest
West Canada
Rocky Mountain Region
Portfolio Companies:
Gigabit Logic
Sensor Medics Corp.
CR Technology, Inc.
Sunward Technologies
Branch Office(s):
Wayne B. Kingsley, Partner
227 S.W. Pine St., Ste. 4050
Portland, OR 97204
503-223-4334

Interwest Partners
3000 Sand Hill Rd.
Bldg. 3, Ste. 255
Menlo Park, CA 94025

Contact(s):
Wallace R. Hawley
Preferred Size Range:
$5 million–$25 million
Industries Specialized:
Computers
Electronics
Retail
Industrial machinery
Business products
Telecommunications
Medical
Distribution
Business services
Do/Not Do Turnarounds: Not
Geographic Preference:
United States
Portfolio Companies:
HBO & Company
Stamping Technologies Corp.
Bridge Communications
Health Management Association, Inc.
Branch Office(s):
Barry Cash
One Galleria Tower
13355 Noel Rd., #1375/LB 65
Dallas, TX 75240

Johnson, Butler & Company
199 S. Los Robles Ave., Ste. 570
Pasadena, CA 91101
818-499-2222
Fax: 818-449-2237

Contact(s):
John A. Butler
Preferred Size Range:
$5 million–$150 million
Industries Specialized:
Electronics
Apparel
Sports equipment
Construction
Do/Not Do Turnarounds: Not
Geographic Preference:
West
Portfolio Companies:
Confidential
Branch Office(s):
None

Johnson Securities
224 E. 49th St.
New York, NY 10017
212-486-2846
Fax: 212-758-2374

Contact(s):
Walter C. Johnson
Preferred Size Range:
$5 million–$50 million
Industries Specialized:
Medical
Do/Not Do Turnarounds: Do
Geographic Preference:
United States
Portfolio Companies:
Marshall Products, Inc.
Buffalo Medical Specialties, Inc.
Taylor Medical, Inc.
Windsoff, Inc.
ARX, Inc.
Branch Office(s):
None

The Jordan Company
315 Park Ave. South, 20th Fl.
New York, NY 10010
212-460-1915
Fax: 212-477-2461

Contact(s):
John Camp
Adam Max
Preferred Size Range:
$100 million+
Industries Specialized:
All
Do/Not Do Turnarounds: Not
Geographic Preference:
United States
Portfolio Companies:
Coronet Manufacturing
Newflo Industries, Inc.
Carmike Cinemas, Inc.
Eastern Home Products, Inc.
Jordan Industries
Rockwood Industries, Inc.
Hat Brands, Inc.
Branch Office(s):
None

Kelso & Company
350 Park Ave.
New York, NY 10022
212-751-3939
Fax: 212-223-2379

Contact(s):
George E. Matelich
Preferred Size Range:
$100 million+
Industries Specialized:
All
Do/Not Do Turnarounds: Not
Geographic Preference:
United States
Portfolio Companies:
American Standard
Arkansas Best
Club Car
King Broadcasting
Branch Office(s):
None

Keystone Venture Capital Management Company
121 S. Broadstreet, Ste. 310
Philadelphia, PA 19107
215-985-5519
Fax: 215-985-4304

Contact(s):
Kerry Dale
Preferred Size Range:
$1 million–$20 million
Industries Specialized:
Telecommunications
Retail
Computers
Medical
Do/Not Do Turnarounds: Not
Geographic Preference:
Northeast
Mid-Atlantic
Portfolio Companies:
Mothers Work
U.S. Restaurants
Royal Optical
Mayaguez Cable TV
Amcall Communications
American Medical Imaging
Ansoft Corporation
U.S. Vision
Branch Office(s):
None

Kidd, Kamm & Company

Three Pickwick Plaza
Greenwich, CT 06830
203-661-0070
Fax: 203-661-1839

Contact(s):
William J. Kidd
Preferred Size Range:
$50 million–$125 million
Industries Specialized:
Industrial products
Consumer products
Specialty retail products
Services
Distribution
Do/Not Do Turnarounds: Not
Geographic Preference:
United States
Portfolio Companies:
Anchor Continental
Desa International
Heartland Industries
Home X-Ray Services of America
McLaren Environmental
  Engineering
Mitchell Rubber Products
Peerless Chain
Sunglass Hut
Branch Office(s):
Kidd, Kamm & Company
9454 Wilshire Blvd., Ste. 920
Beverly Hills, CA 90212

Kohlberg, Kravis, Roberts & Co.

9 W. 57th St.
New York, NY 10019
212-750-8300
Fax: 212-750-0003

Contact(s):
Henry Kravis
Preferred Size Range:
$100 million–$1 billion
Industries Specialized:
All
Do/Not Do Turnarounds: Not
Geographic Preference:
United States
Portfolio Companies:
Beatrice Foods, Inc.
RJR/Nabisco Corp.
Owens-Illinois, Inc.
SCI Television
Seamans Furniture, Inc.
Branch Office(s):
George Roberts
101 California St.
San Francisco, CA 94111
415-433-6560

Lane Industries, Inc.
1200 Shermer Rd.
Northbrook, IL 60062
708-498-6789
Fax: 708-498-2104

Contact(s):
Forrest M. Schneider
Preferred Size Range:
$10 million–$50 million
Industries Specialized:
Office products
Hotels
Media
Security
Do/Not Do Turnarounds: Do
Geographic Preference:
United States
Portfolio Companies:
General Binding Corporation
Lane Hospitality, Inc.
Broadcast Alchemy, L.P.
Branch Office(s):
None

LaSalle Capital Group, Inc.
70 W. Madison St., Ste. 5710
Chicago, IL 60602
312-236-7014
Fax: 312-236-0720

Contact(s):
Anthony R. Pesavento
Preferred Size Range:
$10 million–$120 million
Industries Specialized:
Manufacturing
Distribution
Do/Not Do Turnarounds: Do
Geographic Preference:
United States
Portfolio Companies:
William E. Wright
Harris & Mallow
Deflecta Shield
SealRite Windows
Copperfield Chimney Supply
Golf Mark
Bearing Belt & Chain
Armstrong Containers
Consolidated Industrial Plastics
Branch Office(s):
None

Lawrence, Tyrell, Ortale & Smith

515 Madison Ave., 29th Fl.
New York, NY 10022
212-826-9080
Fax: 212-759-2561

Contact(s):
Richard W. Smith
Preferred Size Range:
$1 million+
Industries Specialized:
Health care
Computers
Services
Do/Not Do Turnarounds: Not
Geographic Preference:
East of Rocky Mountains
Portfolio Companies:
Confidential
Branch Office(s):
3100 W. End Ave., Ste. 500
Nashville, TN 37203-1304

Lee Capital Holdings

1 International Pl., Ste. 3040
Boston, MA 02110
617-345-0477
Fax: 617-345-0478

Contact(s):
Robert Byrne
Preferred Size Range:
$20 million–$100 million
Industries Specialized:
Housing
Textiles
Metals
Computers
Do/Not Do Turnarounds: Not
Geographic Preference:
United States
Portfolio Companies:
Globe Metallurgical, Inc.
Southern Energy Homes, Inc.
Dartmouth Finishing Corp.
National Computer Distributors
First Security Services
Micromedia of New England
Branch Office(s):
None

Thomas H. Lee Company
75 State St.
Boston, MA 02109
617-227-1050
Fax: 617-227-3514

Contact(s):
Kristina A. Weinberg
Preferred Size Range:
$50 million–$500 million
Industries Specialized:
Light manufacturing
Consumer products
Retail
Banking
Do/Not Do Turnarounds: Not
Geographic Preference:
United States
United Kingdom
Belgium
Germany
Spain
Portfolio Companies:
Provided upon request
Branch Office(s):
None

The Legacy Fund
1400 34th St., N.W.
Washington, DC 20007
202-659-1100
Fax: 202-342-7474

Contact(s):
Ms. Brooke Vosburgh
Preferred Size Range:
Up to $250 million
Industries Specialized:
Distribution
Environmental
Manufacturing
Training
Convention services
Communications
Publishing
Do/Not Do Turnarounds: Not
Geographic Preference:
United States
Portfolio Companies:
Snow Environmental Services
Philadelphia, Inc.
Executours, Inc.
Washington, Inc.
Precision Machine Co.
Production Group International
Branch Office(s):
None

Lehman Brothers Merchant Banking Group

American Express Tower,18th Fl.
World Financial Center
New York, NY 10285
212-298-4836
Fax: 212-619-9716

Contact(s):
James Stern
Preferred Size Range:
$200 million+
Industries Specialized:
No venture capital
No real estate
Do/Not Do Turnarounds: Do
Geographic Preference:
United States
United Kingdom
Portfolio Companies:
R.P. Scherer Corp.
Infinity Broadcasting Corporation
Parisian, Inc.
Lear Seating Corp.
Branch Office(s):
None

Lepercq Capital Management

1675 Broadway
New York, NY 10019
212-698-0795
Fax: 212-262-0144

Contact(s):
Michael J. Connelly
Preferred Size Range:
$50 million and under
Industries Specialized:
Education
Broadcasting
Health care
Advertising
Media
Business services
Do/Not Do Turnarounds: Do
Geographic Preference:
United States
Portfolio Companies:
Children's Discovery Centers of
    America, Inc.
MNI Group, Inc.
The Wescom Broadcasting Group
New Century Education Corp.
Sunrise Preschools, Inc.
Branch Office(s):
None

Levy & Schulte, L.P.
135 E. 57th St., 27th Fl.
New York, NY 10022
212-909-8403
Fax: 212-980-2630

Contact(s):
Peter M. Schulte
Preferred Size Range:
$20 million–$150 million
Industries Specialized:
Mail order
Food
Plastics
Do/Not Do Turnarounds: Do
Geographic Preference:
United States
Portfolio Companies:
Confidential
Branch Office(s):
None

Linsalata Capital Partners
Four Commerce Park Square
Ste. 445
23200 Chagrin Blvd.
Cleveland, OH 44122
216-831-8272
Fax: 216-831-0015

Contact(s):
Eric V. Bacon
Preferred Size Range:
$30 million–$100 million
Industries Specialized:
Manufacturing
Do/Not Do Turnarounds: Do
Geographic Preference:
United States
Portfolio Companies:
Care Free Aluminum Products, Inc.
Somerset Technologies
The Garber Company
Continental Metal Specialties
Branch Office(s):
None

Lubar & Company
3380 First Wisconsin Ctr.
Milwaukee, WI 53702
414-291-9000
Fax: 414-291-9061

Contact(s):
Joe Froehlich
Preferred Size Range:
$10 million–$250 million
Industries Specialized:
Manufacturing
Do/Not Do Turnarounds: Do
Geographic Preference:
Midwest
Portfolio Companies:
Pride Co.
Chicago Gear Works
Gleason Reel
Scoville Press
Branch Office(s):
None

Lummis, Hamilton & Company
712 Main St., Ste. 3000
Houston, TX 77002
713-236-4719
Fax: 713-546-2070

Contact(s):
Frederic C. Hamilton
Preferred Size Range:
$5 million–$100 million
Industries Specialized:
Industrial machinery
Chemicals
Telecommunications
Medical
Distribution
Do/Not Do Turnarounds: Not
Geographic Preference:
United States
United Kingdom
Portfolio Companies:
Confidential
Branch Office(s):
None

Mabon Securities
165 Broadway
New York, NY 10006
212-732-2820
Fax: 212-346-5099

Contact(s):
Peter Bonaparte
Preferred Size Range:
$25 million–$250 million
Industries Specialized:
Media
Telecommunications
Transportation
Real estate
Construction
Oil and gas
Do/Not Do Turnarounds: Not
Geographic Preference:
United States
Canada
United Kingdom
Continental Europe
Portfolio Companies:
Confidential
Branch Office(s):
Boston, MA
London, England
Raleigh, NC

Management Resource Partners
Three Lagoon Dr., Ste. 100
Redwood Shores, CA 94065
415-508-2560
Fax: 415-637-9279

Contact(s):
Robert Jenkins
Preferred Size Range:
$25 million–$150 million
Industries Specialized:
Manufacturing
Distribution
Specialty retailing
Do/Not Do Turnarounds: Do
Geographic Preference:
West Coast
Portfolio Companies:
Bayline Paper Supply
Supreme Castings
Cee Bar Prospect
Branch Office(s):
None

Mancuso & Company
10 E. 53rd St. Ste. 2100
New York, NY 10028
212-308-8611
Fax: 212-308-0183

Contact(s):
Christopher O'Brien
Preferred Size Range:
$40 million–$200 million
Industries Specialized:
Manufacturing
Retailing
Do/Not Do Turnarounds: Not
Geographic Preference:
United States
Portfolio Companies:
Pergament Home Centers, Inc.
Life Fitness
Branch Office(s):
None

M&T Capital Corp.
One M&T Plaza
Buffalo, NY 14240
716-842-5881
Fax: 716-842-4436

Contact(s):
T. William Alexander
Philip A. McNeill
Preferred Size Range:
$2 million–$20 million
Industries Specialized:
All
Do/Not Do Turnarounds: Do
Geographic Preference:
Northeast
Midwest
Portfolio Companies:
Confidential
Branch Office(s):
None

Mapleleaf Capital, Ltd.
55 Waugh Dr., Ste. 710
Houston, TX 77007
713-880-4494
Fax:+33 for fax

Contact(s):
Edward M. Fink
Preferred Size Range:
$2 million–$25 million
Industries Specialized:
All
Do/Not Do Turnarounds: Not
Geographic Preference:
Southwest
Portfolio Companies:
Allied Comprehensive
National Entertainment Corp.
Branch Office(s):
James F. Leary
12221 Merit Dr.
Dallas, TX 75251

Marlborough Capital Advisers, Inc.
399 Boylston St.
Boston, MA 02116
617-578-1722
Fax: 617-421-9631

Contact(s):
Margaret L. Lanoix
Gayle M. Slattery
Preferred Size Range:
$10 million+
Industries Specialized:
All except for
    Real estate
    High-tech
Do/Not Do Turnarounds: Not
Geographic Preference:
United States
Portfolio Companies:
Confidential
Branch Office(s):
Affiliate of New England Mutual
    Life, Boston, MA

Carl Marks & Company, Inc.

135 E. 57th St., 27th Fl.
New York, NY 10022
212-909-8400
Fax: 212-980-2631

Contact(s):
David Gruber, Managing Director
Robert E. Marks, Managing
  Director
Preferred Size Range:
$25 million–$250 million
Industries Specialized:
All
Do/Not Do Turnarounds: Not
Geographic Preference:
United States
United Kingdom
Portfolio Companies:
Instanet
Audio/Video Affiliates, Inc.
Hubco Exploration
Transmagnetics, Inc.
Branch Office(s):
None

Marquette Venture Partners

1751 Lake Cook Rd., Ste. 550
Deerfield, IL 60015
708-940-1700
Fax: 708-940-1724

Contact(s):
James Daverman
Preferred Size Range:
$5 million–$25 million
Industries Specialized:
Consumer products
Retailing
Industrial machinery
Chemicals
Publishing
Computers
Telecommunications
Medical
Distribution
Do/Not Do Turnarounds: Not
Geographic Preference:
United States
Portfolio Companies:
Confidential
Branch Office(s):
None

Massachusetts Capital Resource Company
545 Boylston St.
Boston, MA 02116
617-536-3900
Fax: 617-536-7930

Contact(s):
William Torpey, Pres.
Preferred Size Range:
$2 million–$25 million
Industries Specialized:
All
Do/Not Do Turnarounds: Not
Geographic Preference:
Northeast
Portfolio Companies:
Undisclosed
Branch Office(s):
Affiliated with John Hancock
  Mutual life
Massachusetts Mutual Life

Mayflower Partners, Inc.
393 Commonwealth Ave.
Boston, MA 02115
617-267-9000
Fax: 617-266-6666

Contact(s):
Marshall Sterman
Preferred Size Range:
Undisclosed
Industries Specialized:
All
Do/Not Do Turnarounds: Do
Geographic Preference:
United States
Portfolio Companies:
Rebound!
Branch Office(s):
None

MBW Management, Inc.
365 South St.
Morristown, NJ 07960
201-285-5533
Fax: 201-285-5108

Contact(s):
Philip McCarthy
Preferred Size Range:
$5 million–$25 million
Industries Specialized:
All
Do/Not Do Turnarounds: Not
Geographic Preference:
United States
Portfolio Companies:
Attache Software
Lifescan, Inc.
Innovative Hearing Corp.
Oximetrics
Sequoia Turner Corp.
Branch Office(s):
Ann Arbor, MI 313-747-9701
Los Altos, CA 415-941-2392

McCown De Leeuw & Co.

3000 Sand Hill Rd.
Bldg. 3, Ste. 3290
Menlo Park, CA 94025
415-854-6000
Fax: 415-854-0853

Contact(s):
Steven A. Zuckerman
Preferred Size Range:
$50 million–$300 million
Industries Specialized:
Light manufacturing
Distribution
Do/Not Do Turnarounds: Not
Geographic Preference:
United States
Portfolio Companies:
BMC West
Century Fasteners
Coast Gas
Doktor Pet Centers
Graphic Arts Center
Hawaiian Airlines
National Fiberstock
Papa Gino's
Victorial Mortgage Corp.
Specialty Paperboard
Branch Office(s):
900 Third Ave., 28th Fl.
New York, NY 10022
212-418-6539
Fax: 212-418-6584

Menlo Ventures
3000 Sand Hill Rd.
Bldg. 4, Ste.100
Menlo Park, CA 94025
415-854-8540
Fax: 415-854-7059

Contact(s):
H. Dubose Montgomery
Preferred Size Range:
$2 million–$25 million
Industries Specialized:
Consumer products
Consumer services
Retailing
Industrial machinery
Chemicals
Computers
Telecommunications
Medical
Distribution
Do/Not Do Turnarounds: Not
Geographic Preference:
United States
Portfolio Companies:
Data Electronics, Inc.
Masstor Systems, Corp.
Accountants Microsystems, Inc.
Sensor Medics Corp.
IKOS Systems
Innovative Concepts, Inc.
Branch Office(s):
None

Merrill Lynch Capital Partners
World Financial Center
New York, NY 10281-1201
212-449-1000
Fax: 212-449-7357

Contact(s):
Albert J. Fitzgibbons
Preferred Size Range:
$100 million–$1 billion
Industries Specialized:
All
Do/Not Do Turnarounds: Not
Geographic Preference:
United States
United Kingdom
Europe
Portfolio Companies:
Confidential
Branch Office(s):
None

Mesirow Private Equity Partners
350 N. Clark St.
Chicago, IL 60610
312-670-6099
Fax: 312-670-6211

Contact(s):
Thomas E. Galuhn
Davide P. Howell
Preferred Size Range:
$1 million–$4 million
Industries Specialized:
Manufacturing
Distribution
Services
Do/Not Do Turnarounds: Do
Geographic Preference:
None
Portfolio Companies:
Confidential
Branch Office(s):
None

Metapoint Partners
Three Centennial Dr.
Peabody, MA 01960-7906
508-531-4444
Fax: 508-531-6662

Contact(s):
Keith C. Shaughnessy
Stuart I. Matthews
Preferred Size Range:
$8 million+
Industries Specialized:
Manufacturing
Do/Not Do Turnarounds: Not
Geographic Preference:
United States
Portfolio Companies:
Colonial Mills, Inc.
Gimpel Corporation
Weatherguard Ornamental Iron, Inc.
Fluidrive, Inc.
Branch Office(s):
None

Milley & Company
115 E. Putnam Ave.
Greenwich, CT 06830
203-661-7800
Fax: 203-661-1119

Contact(s):
Brian E. Kinsman
Kevin P. Lynch
Preferred Size Range:
$10 million–$50 million
Industries Specialized:
Manufacturing
Do/Not Do Turnarounds: Not
Geographic Preference:
United States
Portfolio Companies:
Elxi Corporation
Bickfords Restaurants
Contempo Design
Payne Fabrics
Cues, Inc.
Delaware Electro Industries
Branch Office(s):
None

Samuel Montagu, Inc.
560 Lexington Ave.
New York, NY 10022
212-969-7000
Fax: 212-969-7540

Contact(s):
Joel Serebransky
Preferred Size Range:
$25 million–$250 million
Industries Specialized:
Consumer products
Retail
Industrial machinery
Media
Distribution
Transportation
Finance
Insurance
Real estate
Do/Not Do Turnarounds: Not
Geographic Preference:
United States
Canada
United Kingdom
Pacific Rim
Continental Europe
Portfolio Companies:
Confidential
Branch Office(s):
None

Morehouse Industries, Inc.
1600 W. Commonwealth Ave.
Fullerton, CA 92633
714-738-5000
Fax: 714-738-5960

Contact(s):
James R. Swarthout
Preferred Size Range:
$5 million–$20 million
Industries Specialized:
Manufacturing
Do/Not Do Turnarounds: Not
Geographic Preference:
California
Portfolio Companies:
Morehouse-Cowles, Inc.
GST Industries, Inc.
Branch Office(s):
None

Morgan, Lewis, Githens & Ahn
767 Fifth Ave.
New York, NY 10153
212-593-3700
Fax: 212-593-3706

Contact(s):
Thomas F. Githens
Preferred Size Range:
$30 million–$1 billion
Industries Specialized:
All
Do/Not Do Turnarounds: Not
Geographic Preference:
United States
Canada
United Kingdom
Portfolio Companies:
Provided upon request
Branch Office(s):
None

Morganthaler Ventures
700 National City Bank Bldg.
Cleveland, OH 44114
216-621-3070
Fax: 216-621-2817

Contact(s):
John D. Lutsi
Preferred Size Range:
$25 million–$100 million
Industries Specialized:
Manufacturing
Distribution
Health care
Do/Not Do Turnarounds: Do
Geographic Preference:
United States
Portfolio Companies:
Confidential
Branch Office(s):
None

MST Partners
1290 Ave. of the Americas, 29th Fl.
New York, NY 10104
212-704-4300
Fax: 212-704-4305

Contact(s):
J. Andrew McWethy
Barry Solomon
Preferred Size Range:
$1 million–$5 million
Industries Specialized:
All
Do/Not Do Turnarounds: Not
Geographic Preference:
United States
Portfolio Companies:
Confidential
Branch Office(s):
None

Murphy & Fauvere
50 Stanford Dr.
Farmington, CT 06032
203-677-5441
Fax: 203-676-8748

Contact(s):
Jonathan G. Fauver
Preferred Size Range:
$5 million–$25 million
Industries Specialized:
Consumer products
Consumer services
Industrial machinery and equipment
Chemicals
Business products
Business services
Media
Publishing
Health care
Utilities
Do/Not Do Turnarounds: Not
Geographic Preference:
United States
Canada
Portfolio Companies:
Provided upon request
Branch Office(s):
John J. Murphy
599 Lexington Ave., 32nd Fl.
New York, NY 10022
212-326-3641

Narragansett Capital, Inc.
50 Kennedy Plaza, Fleet Center
Providence, RI 02903
401-751-1000
Fax: 401-751-9340

Contact(s):
Gregory P. Barber
Preferred Size Range:
$25 million–$250 million
Industries Specialized:
Media
Publishing
Manufacturing
Do/Not Do Turnarounds: Not
Geographic Preference:
United States
Portfolio Companies:
Bevis Industries
Burro Crane, Inc.
Chicago Transparent Products, Inc.
Photo Systems, Inc.
Century Electric
Selecterm, Inc.
Branch Office(s):
None

National City Capital Corp.
629 Euclid Ave.
Box 73303-N
Cleveland, OH 44114
216-575-2491
Fax: 216-575-3355

Contact(s):
John Naylor
Preferred Size Range:
$1 million–$3 million
Industries Specialized:
All
Do/Not Do Turnarounds: Not
Geographic Preference:
United States
Portfolio Companies:
Confidential
Branch Office(s):
None

National City Venture Corporation
1965 E. Sixth St., Ste. 400
Cleveland, OH 44114
216-575-2491
Fax: 216-575-3355

Contact(s):
Philip L. Rice, VP
Daniel Kellog, VP
Preferred Size Range:
$10 million+
Industries Specialized:
No high-tech
No real estate
Do/Not Do Turnarounds: Do
Geographic Preference:
Midwest
Portfolio Companies:
Tannehill International Industries,
    Inc.
PGI Holding Company
ComfortCare of Michigan
Weisheimer Companies
ZS Mazel, L.P.
Branch Office(s):
None

New England Capital Corp.
One Washington Mall
Boston, MA 02108
617-573-6400
Fax: 617-573-7575

Contact(s):
David Patterson
Michael Gorman
Preferred Size Range:
$2 million–$25 million
Industries Specialized:
Services
Manufacturing
Broadcasting
Computers
Telecommunications
Medical
Distribution
Environmental
Do/Not Do Turnarounds: Not
Geographic Preference:
East of Mississippi
Portfolio Companies:
Confidential
Branch Office(s):
Affiliated with New England
    Commercial Finance Corp.

New Street Capital Corp.
450 Lexington Ave.
New York, NY 10017
212-450-7900
Fax: 212-450-7999

Contact(s):
John F. Sorte, Pres.
Preferred Size Range:
$25 million+
Industries Specialized:
All
Do/Not Do Turnarounds: Do
Geographic Preference:
None
Portfolio Companies:
JPS Textiles
Memorex-Telex
West Point-Pepperell
Gillett Holdings
Branch Office(s):
None

Newtek Ventures
500 Washington St., Ste. 720
San Francisco, CA 94111
415-986-5711
Fax: 415-986-4618

Contact(s):
Peter J. Wardle
Barry M. Weinman
Preferred Size Range:
$2 million–$5 million
Industries Specialized:
Computers
Telecommunications
Medical
Do/Not Do Turnarounds: Not
Geographic Preference:
West of Mississippi
Portfolio Companies:
Phase Two Automation
Cypress Semiconductor Corp.
International Tech. Corp.
Branch Office(s):
None

New West Ventures
4350 Executive Dr., #206
San Diego, CA 92121
619-457-0722
Fax: 619-457-0829

Contact(s):
Tim Haidinger
Preferred Size Range:
$1 million–$25 million
Industries Specialized:
Manufacturing
Chemicals
Business products
Business services
Computers
Telecommunications
Medical
Do/Not Do Turnarounds: Not
Geographic Preference:
West Coast
Portfolio Companies:
Confidential
Branch Office(s):
4600 Campus Dr., #105
Newport Beach, CA 92660
714-756-8940

Noro-Moseley Partners
4200 Northside Pkwy.
Atlanta, GA 30327
404-233-1966
Fax: 404-239-9280

Contact(s):
Charles Moseley
Preferred Size Range:
$5 million–$25 million
Industries Specialized:
All
Do/Not Do Turnarounds: Not
Geographic Preference:
Southeast
Portfolio Companies:
One Price Clothing Stores, Inc.
Branch Office(s):
None

North American Business Development

135 S. LaSalle St., Ste. 4000
Chicago, IL 60603
312-332-4950
Fax: 312-332-1540

Contact(s):
Robert Underwood
Preferred Size Range:
$5 million–$25 million
Industries Specialized:
All except for
    Real estate
Do/Not Do Turnarounds: Not
Geographic Preference:
Midwest
Southeast
Portfolio Companies:
ACR Electronics, Inc.
Gateway Healthcare Corporation
Amtec Precision Products, Inc.
Branch Office(s):
111 E. Las Olas Bousianna
Fort Lauderdale, FL 33301
305-463-0681
Fax: 305-527-0904

North American Fund

135 S. LaSalle St., #4000
Chicago, IL 60603
312-332-4950
Fax: 312-332-1540

Contact(s):
R. David Bergonia
Preferred Size Range:
$5 million–$25 million
Industries Specialized:
All
Do/Not Do Turnarounds: Do
Geographic Preference:
Midwest
Mid-Atlantic
Southeast
Portfolio Companies:
ACR Electronics, Inc.
Minnesota Educational Computing
    Corp.
Gateway Healthcare Corp.
Amtec Precision Products, Inc.
Branch Office(s):
111 E. Las Olas Blvd.
Ft. Lauderdale, FL 33301

North Atlantic Venture Capital Corp.

70 Center St.
Portland, ME 04101
207-772-4470
Fax: 207-772-3257

Contact(s):
David Coit
Preferred Size Range:
$5 million–$25 million
Industries Specialized:
All except for
    Real estate
Do/Not Do Turnarounds: Not
Geographic Preference:
Northeast
New England
Portfolio Companies:
Undisclosed
Branch Office(s):
Manchester, NH 03104
603-644-8110

Burlington, VT 05401
802-658-7364

The Northern Group, Inc.

900 4th Ave., Ste. 3140
Seattle, WA 98164
206-622-0771
Fax: 206-622-3319

Contact(s):
Glenn Kasnasy
Preferred Size Range:
$25 million–$250 million
Industries Specialized:
Food
Retail
Do/Not Do Turnarounds: Not
Geographic Preference:
United States
Portfolio Companies:
Admiral Machine Company
Anthony Manufacturing Company,
    Inc.
Mobile Drilling Company
Mohawk Wire & Cable Corp.
Montrose Products Company
Opti Craft, Inc.
The Torbitt & Castleman Company
Vanguard Electronics Co., Inc.
West Penn Wire Corporation
Branch Office(s):
None

Northwood Ventures
485 Underhill Blvd., Ste. 205
Syosset, NY 11791-3419
516-364-5544
Fax: 516-364-0879

Contact(s):
Peter G. Schiff
Henry T. Wilson
Preferred Size Range:
Start up to $100 million
Industries Specialized:
Manufacturing
Communications
Broadcasting
Do/Not Do Turnarounds: Do
Geographic Preference:
United States
Portfolio Companies:
Office Depot
Mid American Waste
Fleet Call
Branch Office(s):
485 Madison Ave., 20th Fl.
New York, NY 10022
212-935-4595
Fax: 212-826-1093

Norwest Venture Capital
2800 Piper Jaffray Tower
Minneapolis, MN 55402
612-667-1650
Fax: 612-667-1660

Contact(s):
John E. Lindahl
Preferred Size Range:
$5 million–$15 million
Industries Specialized:
Manufacturing
Telemarketing
Technology
Food
Do/Not Do Turnarounds: Not
Geographic Preference:
United States
Portfolio Companies:
Norwest Company, Inc.
Numatics, Inc.
Gelco Payment Systems, Inc.
Automotive Industries
Branch Office(s):
Bellevue, WA
Boston, MA

Norwood Venture Corp.
145 W. 45th St., Ste. 1211
New York, NY 10036
212-869-5075
Fax: 212-869-5331

Contact(s):
Mark Littell, Pres.
Preferred Size Range:
$2 million–$5 million
Industries Specialized:
Consumer products
Consumer services
Business products
Business services
Media
Computers
Electronics
Telecommunications
Health care
Distribution
Transportation
Do/Not Do Turnarounds: Not
Geographic Preference:
United States
Portfolio Companies:
Confidential
Branch Office(s):
None

Odyssey Partners
31 W. 52nd. St.
New York, NY 10019
212-708-0631
Fax: 212-708-0755

Contact(s):
Pat Boroian
Preferred Size Range:
$20 million–$10 billion
Industries Specialized:
Health care
Environmental
Natural gas
Media
High technology
General industry
Apparel
Do/Not Do Turnarounds: Do
Geographic Preference:
United States
South America
Portfolio Companies:
Caldor
Eagle Foods
J.P. Stevens
Air & Water Technologies
Branch Office(s):
None

OTREMBA Capital, Inc.
20 E. 74 St.
New York, NY 10021
212-517-4480
Fax: 212-517-4480

Contact(s):
Toby D. Goldfarb
Preferred Size Range:
$10 million–$50 million
Industries Specialized:
Light manufacturing
Distribution
Niche retailing
Do/Not Do Turnarounds: Do
Geographic Preference:
Northeast
Portfolio Companies:
Confidential
Branch Office(s):
None

The Owosso Group
100 Front St., #1400
W. Conshohocken, PA 19428
215-834-0222
Fax: 215-834-8661

Contact(s):
George B. Lemmons, Jr.
Preferred Size Range:
$5 million–$30 million
Industries Specialized:
Mechanical
Electromechanical
Agricultural
Specialty markets
Industrial controls
Leisure time products
Financial services
Do/Not Do Turnarounds: Not
Geographic Preference:
United States
Portfolio Companies:
The Macton Corporation
Seajay Manufacturing Corp.
Kuker-Parker Industries
Redmond Financial Corp.
Durabond Bearing Company
Branch Office(s):
None

Oxford Partners
1266 Main St.
Stamford, CT 06902
203-964-0592
Fax: 203-964-3192

Contact(s):
Kenneth W. Rind
William R. Lonergan
Preferred Size Range:
$5 million–$25 million
Industries Specialized:
Industrial machinery
Chemicals
Business products
Business services
Computers
Electronics
Telecommunications
Medical
Do/Not Do Turnarounds: Not
Geographic Preference:
Worldwide
Portfolio Companies:
Kurzweil Applied Intelligence
Vitesse Electronics
British Bio-Technologies
Intertherapy
Visual Information Technology
Branch Office(s):
Stevan Birnbaum
223 Wilshire Blvd., Ste. 830
Santa Monica, CA 90401

Pacific Mutual Life
700 Newport Center Dr.
Newport Beach, CA 92660
714-640-3395
Fax: 714-640-3199

Contact(s):
Eric Gritzmacher
Preferred Size Range:
$25 million–$100 million
Industries Specialized:
Consumer products
Consumer services
Industrial machinery and equipment
Business products
Business services
Media
Distribution
Do/Not Do Turnarounds: Not
Geographic Preference:
United States
Portfolio Companies:
Confidential
Branch Office(s):
None

Palmer Partners
300 Unicorn Park Dr.
Woburn, MA 01801
617-933-5445
Fax: 617-933-0698

Contact(s):
William H. Congleton
Michael T. Fitzgerald
Preferred Size Range:
$2 million–$10 million
Industries Specialized:
Medical
Telecommunications
Computers
Distribution
Do/Not Do Turnarounds: Not
Geographic Preference:
United States
Portfolio Companies:
Amnet, Inc.
Advanced Circuit Technology, Inc.
Kaye Instruments, Inc.
Vac Hyde Corp.
Others per request
Branch Office(s):
Harvey L. Dixon
3000 Sand Hill Rd.
Bldg. 4, Ste. 145
Menlo Park, CA 94025

Pathfinder Venture Capital Funds

One Corporation Center
7300 Metro Blvd., Ste. 585
Minneapolis, MN 55435
612-835-1121
Fax: 612-835-8389

Contact(s):
Jack K. Ahrens
Preferred Size Range:
$2 million–$10 million
Industries Specialized:
Medical
Telecommunications
Computers
Distribution
Do/Not Do Turnarounds: Not
Geographic Preference:
United States
Portfolio Companies:
Autographix, Inc.
Central Data Corp.
Cryo2 Corp.
Medinet, Inc.
Raycom Systems
Microdynamics
Others upon request
Branch Office(s):
3000 Sand Hill
Bldg. 3, Ste.255
Menlo Park, CA 94025
415-854-0650

Patricof & Company Ventures

2100 Geng Rd., Ste. 220
Palo Alto, CA 94303
415-494-9944
Fax: 415-494-6751

Contact(s):
W.R. Bottoms
Preferred Size Range:
$3 million–$10 million
Industries Specialized:
All
Do/Not Do Turnarounds: Do
Geographic Preference:
United States
Western Europe
Portfolio Companies:
P1
Chevys
Cygnus
Credence Systems
Branch Office(s):
2100 Geng Rd., Ste. 220
Palo Alto, CA 94303

Peregrine Ventures
1299 Ocean Ave., #306
Santa Monica, CA 90401
310-458-1441
Fax: 310-394-0771

Contact(s):
Gene I. Miller
Preferred Size Range:
Start-up to $30 million
Industries Specialized:
Telecommunications
Health care
Manufacturing
Do/Not Do Turnarounds: Do
Geographic Preference:
West
Portfolio Companies:
Confidential
Branch Office(s):
None

Petrus Partners, Ltd.
730 Fifth Ave.
New York, NY 10019
212-977-3000
Fax: 212-977-5500

Contact(s):
Frank J. Walter
Preferred Size Range:
$25 million+
Industries Specialized:
All
Do/Not Do Turnarounds: Do
Geographic Preference:
United States
Portfolio Companies:
Undisclosed
Branch Office(s):
None

Pexco Holdings, Inc.
7130 S. Lewis, Ste. 920
Tulsa, OK 74136
918-493-7730
Fax: 918-493-7796

Contact(s):
Kurt Kaull
Preferred Size Range:
$25 million+
Industries Specialized:
Leisure
Outdoor products
Sporting goods
Health care
Branded consumer products
Do/Not Do Turnarounds: Not
Geographic Preference:
None
Portfolio Companies:
Crossman Corp.
National Tobacco Company
Branch Office(s):
None

Pfingsten Partners, L.P.
111 Pfingsten Rd., Ste. 312
Deerfield, IL 60015
708-291-9020
Fax: 708-291-9150

Contact(s):
Thomas S. Bagley
Preferred Size Range:
$10 million–$100 million
Industries Specialized:
Manufacturing (low to medium
tech)
Distribution
Services (for business)
Do/Not Do Turnarounds: Not
Geographic Preference:
Midwest
Portfolio Companies:
Undisclosed
Branch Office(s):
None

Philadelphia Industries, Inc.
1401 Walnut St.
Philadelphia, PA 19120
215-569-9900
Fax: 215-569-9979

Contact(s):
Jack Farber
Preferred Size Range:
$5 million–$100 million
Industries Specialized:
Business products
Business services
Distribution
Financial services
Insurance
Do/Not Do Turnarounds: Not
Geographic Preference:
Northeast
United States
Portfolio Companies:
Confidential
Branch Office(s):
None

Phoenix Partners

1000 2nd Ave., Ste. 3600
Seattle, WA 98104
206-624-8968
Fax: 206-624-1907

Contact(s):
Stuart Johnston
Preferred Size Range:
$5 million–$100 million
Industries Specialized:
Computers
Telecommunications
Biotechnology
Do/Not Do Turnarounds: Do
Geographic Preference:
United States
Portfolio Companies:
Confidential
Branch Office(s):
None

J.B. Pointdexter & Company

1100 Louisiana, Ste. 3650
Houston, TX 77025
713-655-9800
Fax: 713-951-9038

Contact(s):
Bruce E. Read
Preferred Size Range:
$25 million+
Industries Specialized:
Technology (mid to low
    distribution)
Do/Not Do Turnarounds: Not
Geographic Preference:
United States
Canada
Portfolio Companies:
Leer
Morgan
EFP
Magnetic Instruments
Loww Group
Branch Office(s):
None

Poly Ventures
199 Middle Neck Rd.
Great Neck, NY 11021
516-829-4625
Fax: 516-466-5561

Contact(s):
Herman Fialkov
Preferred Size Range:
$500,000–$5 million
Industries Specialized:
Technology
Telecommunications
Semiconductors
Do/Not Do Turnarounds: Not
Geographic Preference:
NY Metropolitan Area
Portfolio Companies:
Confidential
Branch Office(s):
None

Premier Venture Capital Corp.
451 Florida St.
Baton Rouge, LA 70801
504-332-4421
Fax: 504-332-4299

Contact(s):
Thomas J. Adamek
Preferred Size Range:
$5 million–$50 million
Industries Specialized:
Diversified
No oil and gas
No real estate
Do/Not Do Turnarounds: Do
Geographic Preference:
Southeast
Southwest
Portfolio Companies:
Confidential
Branch Office(s):
None

Prime Capital Corp.
1177 Summer St.
Stamford, CT 06905
203-964-0642
Fax: 203-964-0862

Contact(s):
Dean Fenton
Preferred Size Range:
$25 million+
Industries Specialized:
Distribution
Electronics
Financial services
Manufacturing
Medical
Technology
Telecommunications
Do/Not Do Turnarounds: Do
Geographic Preference:
Connecticut
New England
Portfolio Companies:
Cobutyx
Discover, RE
National Interstate
Hunter Environmental
Arch Communications
Block Industries
Branch Office(s):
None

Primus Venture Partners
1375 E. Ninth St., Ste. 2140
Cleveland, OH 44114
216-621-2185
Fax: 216-621-4543

Contact(s):
James T. Bartlett
Preferred Size Range:
$5 million–$25 million
Industries Specialized:
All
Do/Not Do Turnarounds: Not
Geographic Preference:
United States
Portfolio Companies:
Action Auto Rental Company
American Steel & Wire Company
Steris Corp
Presto-Lite Electrical
Ohio Business Machines
Branch Office(s):
None

Prism Capital
321 N. Clark St., Ste. 3010
Chicago, IL 60610
312-245-4946
Fax: 312-245-4940

Contact(s):
Bob Finkel
Preferred Size Range:
$5 million–$30 million
Industries Specialized:
Packaging
Labeling
Aerosol
Do/Not Do Turnarounds: Not
Geographic Preference:
United States
Portfolio Companies:
Confidential
Branch Office(s):
None

Private Capital Corp.
2160 Highland Ave.
Birmingham, AL 35205-4015
205-933-4618
Fax: 205-933-4339

Contact(s):
W.W. Featheringill
Preferred Size Range:
$2 million–$5 million
Industries Specialized:
Consumer products
Industrial machinery
Chemicals
Computers
Electronics
Telecommunications
Health care
Distribution
Financial services
Do/Not Do Turnarounds: Not
Geographic Preference:
Southeast
Portfolio Companies:
Seako, Inc.
Industrial Supplies, Inc.
Metretek
Branch Office(s):
W.P. Acker III
Third Fl., Lyric Square, Box 66
Anniston, AL

Prospect Group, Inc.
667 Madison Ave.
New York, NY 10021
212-758-8500
Fax: 212-593-6127

Contact(s):
Wallace McDowell
Preferred Size Range:
$25 million+
Industries Specialized:
Computers
Consumer products
Retail
Industrial machinery
Chemicals
Distribution
Transportation
Utilities
Do/Not Do Turnarounds: Not
Geographic Preference:
United States
Portfolio Companies:
Illinois Central
Sylvan Foods
Branch Office(s):
None

Prudential Equity Investors
717 Fifth Ave., Ste. 1100
New York, NY 10022
212-753-0901
Fax: 212-826-6798

Contact(s):
Paul O. Hirschbiel
Preferred Size Range:
$20 million–$200 million
Industries Specialized:
All except for
    Real estate
    Natural resources
Do/Not Do Turnarounds: Not
Geographic Preference:
United States
Portfolio Companies:
Hospital Management Associates
Auspex Systems, Inc.
Damark International
Keystone Group, Inc.
Branch Office(s):
None

Quincy Partners
PO Box 154
Glen Head, NY 11545
516-759-1752
Fax: 516-759-1754

Contact(s):
Donald Sutherland
Preferred Size Range:
$10 million–$50 million
Industries Specialized:
All
Do/Not Do Turnarounds: Not
Geographic Preference:
United States
Portfolio Companies:
Tectron Tube Corporation
Perfection Forms Corporation
Quincy Spring Company
PCI Group, Inc.
Will & Baumer, Inc.
Branch Office(s):
None

RAF Industries, Inc.
8380 Old York Rd.
Bldg. One, Ste. 200
Elkins Park, PA 19117
215-572-0738
Fax: 215-576-1640

Contact(s):
James Vesey
Preferred Size Range:
$5 million–$50 million
Industries Specialized:
Building products
Manufacturing
Distribution
Proprietary products or technology
    preferred
Do/Not Do Turnarounds: Not
Geographic Preference:
United States
Portfolio Companies:
Grubb Lumber Co.
Porter Industries
Liebco Brush
Bestt Rollr
Hardware Supply Company
Vinyl Building Products
Hanlon & Goodman
Ferchie Millwork
Disston Precision, Inc.
Bar-Plate
Branch Office(s):
None

Rand Capital Corp.
1300 Rand Bldg.
Buffalo, NY 14203
716-853-0802
Fax: 716-854-8480

Contact(s):
George Rand
Preferred Size Range:
$1 million-$3 million
Industries Specialized:
All industries especially
    High technology
    Computers
Do/Not Do Turnarounds: Not
Geographic Preference:
Northeast
Portfolio Companies:
Provided upon request
Branch Office(s):
None

RBG Associates
25010 Jim Bridger Rd.
Calabasas, CA 91302
818-702-9678
Fax: 818-702-9681

Contact(s):
Robert G. Bartizal
Preferred Size Range:
$5 million–$100 million
Industries Specialized:
Technology
Distribution
Electronics
Environmental
Manufacturing
Telecommunications
Do/Not Do Turnarounds: Do
Geographic Preference:
West Coast
Southwest
Portfolio Companies:
Undisclosed
Branch Office(s):
None

Recovery Equity Investors

901 Mariners Island Blvd., Ste. 555
San Mateo, CA 94404
415-578-9752
Fax: 415-578-9842

Contact(s):
Jeffrey Lipkin
Preferred Size Range:
$25 million–$250 million
Industries Specialized:
No real estate
No commodities
No start-ups
Do/Not Do Turnarounds: Do
Geographic Preference:
United States
Portfolio Companies:
Foothill Group
CMI Corporation
Branch Office(s):
None

Red Mountain Venture Corp.

825 Financial Ctr.
Birmingham, AL 35203
205-328-3098
Fax: 205-328-4010

Contact(s):
Ed Finch
Preferred Size Range:
$10 million–$50 million
Industries Specialized:
Companies producing distinguish-
able product
Do/Not Do Turnarounds: Not
Geographic Preference:
Southeast
Portfolio Companies:
FHL Capital Corp.
Dinson Valley Millworks
Transportation Products
WDC Systems
Branch Office(s):
None

Reprise Capital Corp.
400 Post Ave.
Westbury, NY 11590
516-222-2700
Fax: 516-338-2808

Contact(s):
Stanley Tulchin
Preferred Size Range:
$30 million–$150 million
Industries Specialized:
Manufacturing
Distribution
Construction
Do/Not Do Turnarounds: Do
Geographic Preference:
United States
Portfolio Companies:
PCA International
The Simone Group
Matrix Alliance
Branch Office(s):
6345 Balboa Blvd., Ste. 358
Encino, CA 91316

RFE Investment Partners
36 Grove St.
New Canaan, CT 06840
203-966-2800
Fax: 203-966-8639

Contact(s):
Richard K. Whitney
Preferred Size Range:
$15 million+
Industries Specialized:
Basic manufacturing
Distribution
Specialty retail
Health care
Communications
Do/Not Do Turnarounds: Do
Geographic Preference:
Northeast
United States
Portfolio Companies:
Undisclosed
Branch Office(s):
None

Riordan, Lewis & Haden
300 S. Grand Ave., Ste. 2900
Los Angeles, CA 90071
213-229-8500
Fax: 213-229-8550

Contact(s):
J. Christopher Lewis
Preferred Size Range:
$20 million+
Industries Specialized:
Food
Health care
Environmental
Do/Not Do Turnarounds: Do
Geographic Preference:
Southern California
Portfolio Companies:
Adohr Farms, Inc.
Terra Tech, Inc.
Total Pharmaceutical Care
Branch Office(s):
None

River Capital, Inc.
1360 Peachtree St., Ste. 1430
Atlanta, GA 30309
404-873-2166
Fax: 404-873-2158

Contact(s):
Lawrence E. Mock, Jr.
Preferred Size Range:
$5 million–$25 million
Industries Specialized:
All
Do/Not Do Turnarounds: Not
Geographic Preference:
United States
Portfolio Companies:
Confidential
Branch Office(s):
None

Roanoke Capital, Ltd.
1111 Third Ave., Ste. 2220
Seattle, WA 98101
206-628-0606
Fax: 206-628-0479

Contact(s):
Frances M. Conley
Gerald M. Conley
Preferred Size Range:
$1 million–$10 million
Industries Specialized:
Communications
Computers
Consumer products
Electronics
Industrial products
Industrial equipment
Health care
Do/Not Do Turnarounds: Do
Geographic Preference:
Pacific Northwest
Portfolio Companies:
Undisclosed
Branch Office(s):
None

Robertson, Stephens & Company
One Embarcadero Ctr., Ste. 3100
San Francisco, CA 94111
415-781-9700
Fax: 415-781-0278

Contact(s):
Paul H. Stevens
Preferred Size Range:
$25 million–$1 billion
Industries Specialized:
Retail
Computers
Electronics
Telecommunications
Medical
Do/Not Do Turnarounds: Not
Geographic Preference:
United States
Portfolio Companies:
Confidential
Branch Office(s):
Sanford Robertson
450 Park Ave., 15th Fl.
New York, NY 10022

ROI Group
9 Campus Dr.
Parsippany, NJ 07054
201-993-1925
Fax: 201-285-9598

Contact(s):
Sydney M. Leveson
Preferred Size Range:
$5 million–$50 million
Industries Specialized:
Light manufacturing
Distribution
Telecommunications
Do/Not Do Turnarounds: Not
Geographic Preference:
United States
Portfolio Companies:
Confidential
Branch Office(s):
None

The Ropart Group
Two Greenwich Plaza
Greenwich, CT 06830
203-661-1988
Fax: 203-661-1969

Contact(s):
Rick Zellmer
Preferred Size Range:
$50 million–$150 million
Industries Specialized:
Consumer products
Manufacturing
Do/Not Do Turnarounds: Do
Geographic Preference:
United States
Portfolio Companies:
Undisclosed
Branch Office(s):
None

Rosenberg, Druker & Company
380 Foothill Rd.
Bridgewater, NJ 08807
908-231-1000
Fax: 908-231-6894

Contact(s):
Conrad Druker
Preferred Size Range:
$2 million–$5 million
Industries Specialized:
All
Do/Not Do Turnarounds: Not
Geographic Preference:
United States
Canada
United Kingdom
Portfolio Companies:
Confidential
Branch Office(s):
One Greentree Ctr., Ste. 308
Cherry Hill, NJ 08053
609-985-0090

Salomon Brothers, Inc.
One New York Plaza
New York, NY 10004
212-747-7000
Fax: 212-783-3345

Contact(s):
Michael Zimmerman
Preferred Size Range:
$5 million–$2 billion
Industries Specialized:
All
Do/Not Do Turnarounds: Not
Geographic Preference:
United States
Canada
United Kingdom
Continental Europe
Portfolio Companies:
Confidential
Branch Office(s):
None

Saugatuck Capital Company, L.P.
One Canterbury Green
Stamford, CT 06901
203-348-6669
Fax: 203-324-6995

Contact(s):
Frank J. Hawley
Preferred Size Range:
$50 million–$250 million
Industries Specialized:
Medical
Telecommunication
Manufacturing
Consumer products
Environmental
Financial services
Do/Not Do Turnarounds: Do
Geographic Preference:
United States
Portfolio Companies:
Morgan Products, Ltd.
ETG Environmental, Inc.
GDC International
Branch Office(s):
None

Saunders, Garonzik & Karp
667 Madison Ave.
New York, NY 10021
212-303-6600
Fax: 212-755-1624

Contact(s):
John Megrue
Preferred Size Range:
$50 million+
Industries Specialized:
Retail
Health care
Financial services
Basic manufacturing
Do/Not Do Turnarounds: Do
Geographic Preference:
United States
Portfolio Companies:
Undisclosed
Branch Office(s):
None

Scandinavian Corporate Development Group
35 Ostend Ave.
Box 52
Westport, CT 06902
203-227-1682
Fax: 203-222-0530

Contact(s):
C.E. Jacobsson
Preferred Size Range:
$5 million–$100 million
Industries Specialized:
Industrial machinery
Chemicals
Computers
Electronics
Telecommunications
Medical
Distribution
Do/Not Do Turnarounds:
Geographic Preference:
United States
Canada
United Kingdom
Continental Europe
Portfolio Companies:
Confidential
Branch Office(s):
Viktor Rydbergsgatan
15 S-41132 Gothenburg, Sweden
031-162195

Schroder Ventures
787 Seventh Ave., 29th Fl.
New York, NY 10019
212-841-3880
Fax: 212-582-1405

Contact(s):
Timothy F. Howe, ext. 886
Preferred Size Range:
$10 million–$75 million
Industries Specialized:
Biotechnology
Medical
Health care
Developers
Manufacturers
Distributors
Do/Not Do Turnarounds: Do
Geographic Preference:
International
Portfolio Companies:
Neurogen Corp.
Raytel Systems Corporation
Advanced Surgical, Inc.
Envirogen
Imagyn Medical, Inc.
Microprobe Corp.
Anagen
Branch Office(s):
Boston
Seattle
New York
London
Milan
Frankfurt
Tokyo
Paris

Seaport Ventures, Inc.
525 B St., Ste. 630
San Diego, CA 92101
619-232-4069
Fax: 619-231-0636

Contact(s):
Carole Rhoades
Preferred Size Range:
$2 million–$25 million
Industries Specialized:
Consumer products
Retail
Industrial machinery
Chemicals
Media
Computers
Electronics
Telecommunications
Do/Not Do Turnarounds: Not
Geographic Preference:
United States
Portfolio Companies:
Confidential
Branch Office(s):
None

Sears Investment Management Company
Xerox Centre
55 W. Monroe, 32nd Fl.
Chicago, IL 60603
312-875-0416
Fax: 312-875-7529

Contact(s):
Michael Finn
Preferred Size Range:
$2 million–$5 million
Industries Specialized:
All
Do/Not Do Turnarounds: Not
Geographic Preference:
United States
Canada
United Kingdom
Continental Europe
Portfolio Companies:
Confidential
Branch Office(s):
None

SGK Partners

667 Madison Ave.
New York, NY 10022
212-339-7270
Fax: 212-339-7284

Contact(s):
John Megrue
Preferred Size Range:
$50 million+
Industries Specialized:
Retail
Health care
Basic manufacturing
Do/Not Do Turnarounds: Do
Geographic Preference:
None
Portfolio Companies:
New fund with $300 million
 portfolio not established
Branch Office(s):
None

The Shansby Group

250 Montgomery, #1100
San Francisco, CA 94104
415-398-2500
Fax: 415-421-5120

Contact(s):
Michael Sekits
Preferred Size Range:
$10 million–$100 million
Industries Specialized:
Consumer products (branded)
Manufacturing
Food
Retail
Do/Not Do Turnarounds: Do
Geographic Preference:
United States
Portfolio Companies:
Famous Amos Cookies
The Appliance Store
Sybervision
Motherhood Maternity
Diversified Products
Calidad Foods
Branch Office(s):
None

Shaw Acquisition Corp.
425 S. Beverly Dr.
Beverly Hills, CA 90212
310-556-2155
Fax: 310-556-4664

Contact(s):
William A. Shaw
Preferred Size Range:
$500,000–$1 million
Industries Specialized:
Real estate
Do/Not Do Turnarounds: Do
Geographic Preference:
United States
Portfolio Companies:
Controlled Investments
Branch Office(s):
None

Shearson Lehman Brothers
200 Vesey St.
New York, NY 10285-1800
212-298-2000
Fax: 212-619-7165

Contact(s):
James Stern
Preferred Size Range:
$10 million+
Industries Specialized:
All
Do/Not Do Turnarounds: Not
Geographic Preference:
Worldwide
Portfolio Companies:
Prime Computer
K+F Industry
RP Scherer Corp.
Illinois Central Transportation
    Company
Branch Office(s):
None

Sherman, Clay & Co.
851 Traeger Ave., Ste. 200
San Bruno, CA 94066
415-952-2300
Fax: 415-952-6671

Contact(s):
Alan D. Sapp
Preferred Size Range:
$25 million–$500 million
Industries Specialized:
Retail
Chemicals
Distribution
Real estate
Construction
Light manufacturing
Do/Not Do Turnarounds: Not
Geographic Preference:
United States
Portfolio Companies:
Confidential
Branch Office(s):
None

Siegel-Robert, Inc.
8645 S. Broadway
St. Louis, MO 63111
314-638-8300
Fax: 314-544-8475

Contact(s):
David Brown
Preferred Size Range:
$7 million–$35 million
Industries Specialized:
Testing/monitoring equipment
Medical
Environmental
Do/Not Do Turnarounds: Not
Geographic Preference:
East
Rockies
Southeast
Midwest
Portfolio Companies:
Confidential
Branch Office(s):
None

Sierra Industries
1225 W. 190th St., #380
Gardena, CA 90248
310-532-1500
Fax: 310-538-8118

Contact(s):
Ken Bodger
Preferred Size Range:
$1 million+
Industries Specialized:
All except for
  High-tech
  Financial services
Do/Not Do Turnarounds: Yes
Geographic Preference:
West Coast
Portfolio Companies:
Cal Shake
K&K Office Furniture
Sheppard Office Systems
Robert John Industries, Inc.
Branch Office(s):
None

Somerset Holding, Ltd.
365 South St.
Morristown, NJ 07960
201-538-8844
Fax: 201-538-5154

Contact(s):
Dean Porter
Preferred Size Range:
$10 million+
Industries Specialized:
Distribution
Financial services
Manufacturing
Niche retailing
Do/Not Do Turnarounds: Do
Geographic Preference:
Northeast
Midwest
Portfolio Companies:
Undisclosed
Branch Office(s):
None

Soros Capital

888 Seventh Ave., 33rd Fl.
New York, NY 10106
212-262-6300
Fax: 212-315-1221

Contact(s):
Steven J. Gilbert
Preferred Size Range:
$75 million+
Industries Specialized:
All except for
  Real estate
Do/Not Do Turnarounds: Do
Geographic Preference:
International
Portfolio Companies:
Digicon
FRC Industries
Crystal Oil
Mueller Industries
Branch Office(s):
PO Box 984
New Canaan, CT 06840
203-966-6022
Fax: 203-972-0250

South Atlantic Capital Corporation

614 W. Bay St., Ste. 200
Tampa, FL 33606
813-253-2500
Fax: 813-253-2360

Contact(s):
Randall E. Poliner
Preferred Size Range:
$1 million–$50 million
Industries Specialized:
All except for
  Real estate
  Mineral extraction
Do/Not Do Turnarounds: Not
Geographic Preference:
Southeast
Texas
Portfolio Companies:
Alphatronix, Inc.
Banc West BanCorp, Inc.
Coin, Inc.
Digital Transmission Systems
Intercel, Inc.
OK 4U Kiddo
Phoenix Microsystems, Inc.
Branch Office(s):
None

South West Venture Partners

300 Convent, Ste. 1400
San Antonio, TX 78205
512-227-1010
Fax: 512-227-1343

Contact(s):
Michael Bell
Preferred Size Range:
$5 million–$10 million
Industries Specialized:
All with emphasis on
   High technology
   Health care
Do/Not Do Turnarounds: Not
Geographic Preference:
United States
Portfolio Companies:
Confidential
Branch Office(s):
None

Sovran Funding Corporation

Sovran Center, 6th Fl.
Norfolk, VA 23510
804-441-4041
Fax: 804-441-4725

Contact(s):
David King
Preferred Size Range:
$2 million–$10 million
Industries Specialized:
All
Do/Not Do Turnarounds: Not
Geographic Preference:
Southeast
Portfolio Companies:
Confidential
Branch Office(s):
Affiliated with Sovran
Financial Corp.

Sprout Group

140 Broadway
New York, NY 10005
212-504-3600
Fax: 212-504-3444

Contact(s):
Richard Kroon
Preferred Size Range:
$5 million–$25 million
Industries Specialized:
Consumer products
Consumer services
Industrial machinery and equipment
Chemicals
Business products
Business services
Computers
Electronics
Telecommunications
Health care
Do/Not Do Turnarounds: Not
Geographic Preference:
United States
Portfolio Companies:
Rob Roy, Inc.
Fox Meyer Corp.
Illinois Soil Spring Co.
DRG Funding Corp.
SAY Industries, Inc.
Digital Industries
Home Club, Inc.
Branch Office(s):
Menlo Park, CA 415-854-1550
Boston, MA 617-570-8700

Strategic Investments & Holdings, Inc.
Cyclorama Bldg.
369 Franklin St.
Buffalo, NY 14202
716-857-6000
Fax: 716-857-6490

Contact(s):
David Zebro
William Joyce
Preferred Size Range:
$20 million+
Industries Specialized:
Food
Textiles
Light manufacturing
Do/Not Do Turnarounds: Not
Geographic Preference:
None
Portfolio Companies:
Undisclosed
Branch Office(s):
None

Summit Partners
1 Boston Pl.
Boston, MA 02108
617-742-5500
Fax: 617-742-6138

Contact(s):
Paul A. Rubin
Preferred Size Range:
$25 million–$100 million
Industries Specialized:
Medical
Manufacturing (niche)
Technology
Do/Not Do Turnarounds: Not
Geographic Preference:
United States
Canada
Portfolio Companies:
Rosco
Astech
Accurex
Lincare
Branch Office(s):
None

Sunven Capital Corporation
2122 E. Highland Ave., Ste. 425
Phoenix, AZ 85016
602-957-8116
Fax: 602-957-8602

Contact(s):
Scott Eller
Preferred Size Range:
$1 million–$5 million
Industries Specialized:
Retail
Media
Communications
Telecommunications
Financial institutions
Health care
Do/Not Do Turnarounds: Not
Geographic Preference:
United States
Canada
United Kingdom
Continental Europe
Portfolio Companies:
Provided upon request
Branch Office(s):
None

The Sutton Company
126 E. 56th St.
New York, NY 10022
212-697-3700
Fax: 212-421-3046

Contact(s):
David Elenowitz
Preferred Size Range:
$25 million+
Industries Specialized:
Manufacturing
Distribution
Construction
Do/Not Do Turnarounds: Not
Geographic Preference:
None
Portfolio Companies:
Undisclosed
Branch Office(s):
None

TA Associates
45 Milk St.
Boston, MA 02109
617-338-0800
Fax: 617-574-6728

Contact(s):
P. Andrews Mclane
Preferred Size Range:
$10 million–$125 million
Industries Specialized:
All
Do/Not Do Turnarounds: Not
Geographic Preference:
United States
Portfolio Companies:
Guilford Mills, Inc.
AST Research, Inc.
Verilink, Inc.
Insurance Systems, Inc.
Wisconsin Cable Investors
Standex International Corp.
Softsel, Corp.
Others upon request
Branch Office(s):
435 Tosso St., Ste. 200
Palo Alto, CA 94301
415-328-1210

Taconic Capital Corp.
333 W. Wacker Dr., Ste. 700
Chicago, IL 60606
312-444-2062
Fax: 312-750-4520

Contact(s):
Barney Ireland
Preferred Size Range:
$5 million–$30 million
Industries Specialized:
Manufacturing
Distribution
Do/Not Do Turnarounds: Not
Geographic Preference:
Midwest
Portfolio Companies:
Anchor-Harvey Components, Inc.
FPM, L.P.
Branch Office(s):
None

TCW Capital

200 Park Ave., Ste. 2922
New York, NY 10166
212-297-4060
Fax: 212-297-4024

Contact(s):
Charles Sukenik
Preferred Size Range:
$20 million–$150 million
Industries Specialized:
Construction
Distribution
Manufacturing
Medical
Do/Not Do Turnarounds: Not
Geographic Preference:
United States
Portfolio Companies:
Fannie May
Commons Brothers
Belvac
Advance Machine
Act III Broadcasting
Revco Scientific
McCook Gazette
Sun Media
Society Brands
Branch Office(s):
None

Teachers Insurance & Annuity Association

730 Third Ave.
New York, NY 10017
212-490-9000
Fax: 212-986-1525

Contact(s):
Charles Thompson
Preferred Size Range:
$25 million–$500 million
Industries Specialized:
All
Do/Not Do Turnarounds: Not
Geographic Preference:
United States
Portfolio Companies:
Confidential
Branch Office(s):
None

Tessler & Cloherty, Inc.
155 Main St.
Cold Spring, NY 10516
914-265-4244
Fax: 914-265-4158

Contact(s):
Anne Saunders
Daniel Tessler
Preferred Size Range:
$2 million–$25 million
Industries Specialized:
All
Do/Not Do Turnarounds: Not
Geographic Preference:
United States
Portfolio Companies:
Confidential
Branch Office(s):
17 W. 54th St.
New York, NY 10019

Textron Investment Management Company
40 Westminster St.
Providence, RI 02903
401-457-2668
Fax: 401-457-4000

Contact(s):
John Lemery
Rodney Weaver
Preferred Size Range:
$25 million–$100 million
Industries Specialized:
Industrial machinery
Industrial equipment
Do/Not Do Turnarounds: Not
Geographic Preference:
United States
Portfolio Companies:
Provided upon request
Branch Office(s):
None

3I Capital

99 High St., Ste. 1530
Boston, MA 02110
617-542-8560
Fax: 617-542-0394

Contact(s):
William N. Holm
Preferred Size Range:
$2 million–$25 million
Industries Specialized:
Consumer products
Retail
Industrial machinery
Chemicals
Media
Computers
Electronics
Telecommunications
Health care
Do/Not Do Turnarounds: Not
Geographic Preference:
United States
United Kingdom
Australia
Continental Europe
Portfolio Companies:
Confidential
Branch Office(s):
John Ulrich
450 Newport Center Dr., Ste. 250
Newport Beach, CA 92660

The Trump Group

885 Third Ave., #110
New York, NY 10022
212-838-1000
Fax: 212-397-8296

Contact(s):
James Blazen
Preferred Size Range:
$10 million+
Industries Specialized:
Retail
Consumer products
Consumer services
Do/Not Do Turnarounds: Not
Geographic Preference:
United States
Portfolio Companies:
Confidential
Branch Office(s):
None

TLC Group, L.P.
99 Wall St., 16th Fl.
New York, NY 10281
212-269-4544
Fax: 212-269-4546

Contact(s):
Robert Davenport
Preferred Size Range:
$1 million–$100 million
Industries Specialized:
Consumer products
Financial services
Insurance
Do/Not Do Turnarounds: Not
Geographic Preference:
United States
Canada
United Kingdom
Continental Europe
Portfolio Companies:
Beatrice International, Inc.
Branch Office(s):
None

Trivest, Inc.
2665 S. Bayshore Dr., 8th Fl.
Miami, Fl 33133
305-858-2200
Fax: 305-285-0102

Contact(s):
Peter C. Brockway
Preferred Size Range:
$20 million+
Industries Specialized:
Manufacturing
Do/Not Do Turnarounds: Not
Geographic Preference:
United States
Portfolio Companies:
Winston Furniture Company
The Shannon Group
Richielu Group, Inc.
Sun Pharmaceuticals
Lowenstein Furniture
S.P. Industries
Atlantis Group, Inc.
Biscayne Holdings
Branch Office(s):
None

Tullis, Dickerson & Company

One Greenwich Plaza
Greenwich, CT 06830
203-629-8700
Fax: 203-629-9293

Contact(s):
Joan P. Neuschelor
Preferred Size Range:
$5 million+
Industries Specialized:
Health care (only)
Do/Not Do Turnarounds: Not
Geographic Preference:
None
Portfolio Companies:
Physician Sales & Service
Chattanooga Group, Ltd.
Frantz Medical Development
Medx, Inc.
Salvatori Opthalmics, Inc.
Branch Office(s):
None

Tweedy Browne Company, LP

52 Vanderbilt Ave.
New York, NY 10017
212-916-0600
Fax: 212-916-0637

Contact(s):
Mary Joe Sentner
Preferred Size Range:
$5 million–$50 million
Industries Specialized:
Consumer products
Retail
Business products
Business services
Media
Distribution
Apparel
Do/Not Do Turnarounds: Not
Geographic Preference:
United States
Portfolio Companies:
Provided upon request
Branch Office(s):
None

UIS, Inc.
600 Fifth Ave
New York, NY 10020
212-581-7660
Fax: 212-581-7517

Contact(s):
Richard Pasculano
Preferred Size Range:
$10 million+
Industries Specialized:
Auto/truck parts
Millworks
Confectionery
Do/Not Do Turnarounds: Not
Geographic Preference:
None
Portfolio Companies:
Airtex Products
Champion Laboratories, Inc.
Neapco, Inc.
HKM
Wells Manufacturing Corp.
New England Confectionery
Hurd Millwork Company, Inc.
Three States Supply Co., Inc.
Branch Office(s):
None

Union Capital
405 Park Ave., Ste. 1003
New York, NY 10022
212-832-1141
Fax: 212-832-0554

Contact(s):
Greg Garville
Preferred Size Range:
To $175 million
Industries Specialized:
Printing
Corporate travel
Advertising
Business services
Do/Not Do Turnarounds: Do
Geographic Preference:
East Coast
Midwest
Portfolio Companies:
Sandy Alexander, Inc.
Modern Graphic Arts
Partners & Shevack
Bender, Browning, Dolby &
    Sanderson, Inc.
Ventura Associates International
SPV Publishing, Inc.
Branch Office(s):
None

Union Venture Corporation

445 S. Figueroa St.
Los Angeles, CA 90071
213-236-4092
Fax: 213-688-0101

Contact(s):
Jeffrey Watts
Preferred Size Range:
$10 million–$50 million
Industries Specialized:
Communications
Computers
Electronics
Biotechnology
Industrial products
Industrial equipment
Health care
Do/Not Do Turnarounds: Not
Geographic Preference:
United States
Portfolio Companies:
Microbeam, Inc.
Novatech Corp.
Telagene Corp.
Carlyle Systems, Inc.
Branch Office(s):
Affiliated with Union Bank

U.S. Diversified Corp.

26087 Getty Dr.
Laguna Niguel, CA 92677
714-582-2565
Fax: 714-582-7111

Contact(s):
Jeff Shirkani
Preferred Size Range:
$50,000–$2,000,000
Industries Specialized:
All
Do/Not Do Turnarounds: Not
Geographic Preference:
Southern California
Portfolio Companies:
Confidential
Branch Office(s):
None

Van Kasper & Company
50 California St., Ste. 2400
San Francisco, CA 94111
415-391-5600
Fax: 415-397-2744

Contact(s):
Payson Smith
F. Van Kasper
Preferred Size Range:
$2 million–$100 million
Industries Specialized:
Industrial machinery
Computers
Telecommunications
Medical
Distribution
Financial services
Do/Not Do Turnarounds: Not
Geographic Preference:
West
Portfolio Companies:
Provided upon request
Branch Office(s):
3687 Mount Diablo Blvd., Ste. 240
Lafayette, CA 94549

VCI Capital, Inc.
Box 375
Long Lake, MN 55356
612-476-2637
Fax: 612-476-4340

Contact(s):
Robert P. White
Preferred Size Range:
$5 million–$30 million
Industries Specialized:
Consumer products
Manufacturing
Chemicals
Business products
Health care
Do/Not Do Turnarounds: Not
Geographic Preference:
United States
Portfolio Companies:
Steel King Industries
Northwestern Motor Co.
Stratford Homes
Ex-L-Tube
Medallion Kitchens
Branch Office(s):
Box 2509
Carefree, AZ 85377
602-488-2785

Venrock Associates

30 Rockefeller Plaza
New York, NY 10112
212-649-5600
Fax: 212-649-5788

Contact(s):
Peter Crisp
David Hathaway
Preferred Size Range:
$5 million–$25 million
Industries Specialized:
Business products
Business services
Health care
Biotech
Do/Not Do Turnarounds: Not
Geographic Preference:
United States
Portfolio Companies:
Provided upon request
Branch Office(s):
Anthony Sun
Two Palo Alto Square
Palo Alto, CA 94306

Venture Associates

355 Sweetbrier Rd.
Memphis, TN 38120
901-763-1434
Fax: 901-763-1428

Contact(s):
Burton B. Weil
Preferred Size Range:
$15 million–$30 million
Industries Specialized:
Manufacturers
Distribution
Do/Not Do Turnarounds: Do
Geographic Preference:
United States
Portfolio Companies:
Undisclosed
Branch Office(s):
None

Venture Counsel, Inc.
One Oakshore Dr.
Bratenahl, OH 44108
216-681-5248
Fax: 216-861-0106

Contact(s):
Richard F. Brezic
Preferred Size Range:
500,000+
Industries Specialized:
Manufacturing
Distribution
Do/Not Do Turnarounds: Do
Geographic Preference:
Northern Ohio
Portfolio Companies:
Confidential
Branch Office(s):
None

Veritas Capital, Inc.
10 E. 50th St.
New York, NY 10022
212-688-0020
Fax: 212-688-3808

Contact(s):
Robert B. McKeon
Preferred Size Range:
$5 million–$75 million
Industries Specialized:
Consumer products
Auto parts
Aerospace
Do/Not Do Turnarounds: Do
Geographic Preference:
None
Portfolio Companies:
Composite Energy Management
    Systems, Inc.
H. Koch & Sons Company
Branch Office(s):
None

Vista Group
36 Grove St.
New Canaan, CT 06840
203-972-3400
Fax: 203-966-0844

Contact(s):
Robert Cummins
Preferred Size Range:
Start up to $1 million
Industries Specialized:
Agricultural
Chemical
Environmental
Medical
Technology
Telecommunications
Manufacturing
Do/Not Do Turnarounds: Not
Geographic Preference:
None
Portfolio Companies:
Regeneron
Cyberonics
Superior Air Parts
Goal Systems
Others
Branch Office(s):
445 Marine View Ave.
Del Mar, CA

Wachtel & Company, Inc.
1101 14th St., N.W.
Washington, DC 20005-5680
202-898-1144
Fax: 202-898-1016

Contact(s):
Sidney Wachtel
Bonnie Wachtel
Preferred Size Range:
$2 million–$25 million
Industries Specialized:
Retail
Media
Computers
Telecommunications
Financial services
Do/Not Do Turnarounds: Not
Geographic Preference:
Mid-Atlantic
Southeast
Portfolio Companies:
Integral Systems
Branch Office(s):
None

Walnut Capital Corp.
2 N. LaSalle St., Ste 2240
Chicago, IL 60602
312-346-2033
Fax: 312-346-2231

Contact(s):
Michael Faber, Esq.
Preferred Size Range:
No minimum or maximum
Industries Specialized:
All except for
   Real estate
Do/Not Do Turnarounds: Do
Geographic Preference:
United States
Portfolio Companies:
Undisclosed
Branch Office(s):
8300 Boone Blvd., Ste 780
Vienna, VA 22182
703-448-3771

Warburg, Pincus & Company
466 Lexington Ave.
New York, NY 10017
212-878-0600
Fax: 212-878-9361

Contact(s):
Lionel Pincus
Grrol Cook
Preferred Size Range:
$25 million–$500 million
Industries Specialized:
All
Do/Not Do Turnarounds: Not
Geographic Preference:
United States
Canada
United Kingdom
Europe
Portfolio Companies:
Dallas Media Investors
Shaughnessy Holdings
Symbion, Inc.
SFN Companies
Orion Pictures Corp.
Others upon request
Branch Office(s):
London, England 1-629-2484
Los Angeles, CA 213-203-0500

Washington Square Capital
512 Nicollet Mall, #9402
Minneapolis, MN 55440
612-342-3204
Fax: 612-372-5368

Contact(s):
James Tobin
Preferred Size Range:
$25 million–$250 million
Industries Specialized:
All
Do/Not Do Turnarounds: Not
Geographic Preference:
United States
Canada
Portfolio Companies:
Provided upon request
Branch Office(s):
None

Wasserstein, Perella Group, Inc.
31 W. 52nd St.
New York, NY 10019
212-969-2700
Fax: 212-247-4360

Contact(s):
George R. Hornig
Preferred Size Range:
$500 million+
Industries Specialized:
All
Do/Not Do Turnarounds: Not
Geographic Preference:
United States
Canada
United Kingdom
Continental Europe
Portfolio Companies:
Confidential
Branch Office(s):
Chicago, IL 312-263-2020
Los Angeles, CA 213-201-5050
London, England 441-629-9606

Wechsler Management Corp.
PO Box 941
Quogue, NY 11959
516-653-6100
Fax: 516-653-1413

Contact(s):
Raymond H. Wechsler
Preferred Size Range:
$25 million–$100 million
Industries Specialized:
Low capital intensive
No real estate
Do/Not Do Turnarounds: Do
Geographic Preference:
NYC area
California
Portfolio Companies:
Undisclosed
Branch Office(s):
None

Wedbush Capital Partners
1000 Wilshire
Los Angeles, CA 90017-2465
213-688-4545
Fax: 213-688-6642

Contact(s):
Barton I. Gurewitz
Stephen Burge
Preferred Size Range:
$2 million–$15 million
Industries Specialized:
All
Do/Not Do Turnarounds: Not
Geographic Preference:
West Coast
Southern California
Portfolio Companies:
Provided upon request
Branch Office(s):
None

Weeden Capital Management, LP

180 Maiden Ln.
New York, NY 10038
212-797-3877
Fax: 212-797-4738

Contact(s):
Donald Weeden
Preferred Size Range:
$2 million–$5 million
Industries Specialized:
Media
Computers
Electronics
Telecommunications
Do/Not Do Turnarounds: Not
Geographic Preference:
United States
Portfolio Companies:
Confidential
Branch Office(s):
Los Altos Hills, CA
415-948-9580

Weinstein Associates, Ltd.

PO Box 402828
Miami Beach, FL 33140
305-672-7177
Fax: 305-672-7078

Contact(s):
Stanley Weinstein
Preferred Size Range:
$50,000–$50 million
Industries Specialized:
All
Do/Not Do Turnarounds: Do
Geographic Preference:
Wisconsin
NYC area
Florida
Portfolio Companies:
The Ice Factory
John Stuart
U.S. Axminster
Florida Glass
Branch Office(s):
None

Weiss, Peck & Greer
One New York Plaza
New York, NY 10004
212-908-9773
Fax: 212-908-0112

Contact(s):
Matthew M. Meehan
Preferred Size Range:
$20 million+
Industries Specialized:
All except for
   High-tech
   Real estate
Do/Not Do Turnarounds: Do
Geographic Preference:
None
Portfolio Companies:
Durakon Industries
Meridian Aggregates
ADN
Alfalfas
Branch Office(s):
None

Welsh, Carson, Anderson & Stowe
One World Financial Center, Ste. 360
New York, NY 10281
212-945-2000
Fax: 212-945-2000

Contact(s):
Bruce K. Anderson
Preferred Size Range:
$20 million–$100 million
Industries Specialized:
Health care
Information processing
Do/Not Do Turnarounds: Do
Geographic Preference:
United States
Portfolio Companies:
Quorum Health Group
EmCare
BiSys
American Residential
Branch Office(s):
None

Wesmar Partners
3 Gateway Ctr., Ste. 16 South
Pittsburgh, PA 15222
412-392-2350
Fax: 412-392-2361

Contact(s):
Rick Maurer
Preferred Size Range:
$25 million+
Industries Specialized:
Manufacturing
Distribution
Do/Not Do Turnarounds: Do
Geographic Preference:
United States
Portfolio Companies:
S2 Golf
St. Charles Manufacturing
Twelve other varied companies
Branch Office(s):
None

Wesray Capital Corp.
375 Park Ave.
New York, NY 10152
212-752-1900
Fax: 212-752-1974

Contact(s):
Frank E. Richardson
John Howard
Preferred Size Range:
$1 million+
Industries Specialized:
All
Do/Not Do Turnarounds: Not
Geographic Preference:
United States
Canada
United Kingdom
Continental Europe
Portfolio Companies:
Avis Car Rental
Gibson Greeting Cards Co.
Branch Office(s):
Burke Ross
Morristown, NJ
201-540-9020

Westfield Capital Corp.
72 Cummings Point Rd.
Stamford, CT 06902
203-977-1139
Fax: 203-967-2886

Contact(s):
J. Herbert Ogden, Jr.
Preferred Size Range:
Up to $200 million
Industries Specialized:
Distribution
Metal fabrication
Injection molding
Consumer houseware and hardware
Metal bending and stamping
Do/Not Do Turnarounds: Not
Geographic Preference:
East
Midwest
West Coast
Portfolio Companies:
Kolko Paper Company, Inc.
Daily Dryer Corp.
Delaware Valley Products
Benchmark Carpet Mills
Candle Corporation of America
Branch Office(s):
None

White Oak Group
One Northfield Plaza
Northfield, IL 60093
708-441-2692
Fax: 708-441-3293

Contact(s):
Murray Lessinger, Managing
  Partner
Preferred Size Range:
$5 million+
Industries Specialized:
Manufacturing
Consumer products
Distribution
Do/Not Do Turnarounds: Not
Geographic Preference:
None
Portfolio Companies:
Flavor Brands, Inc.
Louis Sherry Candies
Branch Office(s):
None

Whitman, Heffernan, Rhein & Co.
767 Third Ave., 5th Fl.
New York, NY 10017
212-888-5222
Fax: 212-888-6704

Contact(s):
James Heffernan
Kirk Rhein
Preferred Size Range:
$100 million+
Industries Specialized:
All
Do/Not Do Turnarounds: Not
Geographic Preference:
None
Portfolio Companies:
Danielson Holding Corp.
Reading & Bates
Branch Office(s):
None

Wind Point Partners
676 N. Michigan Ave. Ste. 3300
Chicago, IL 60611
312-649-4000
Fax: 312-649-9644

Contact(s):
Art Del Vesco
Preferred Size Range:
$1 million–$5 million
Industries Specialized:
Health care
Telecommunications
Do/Not Do Turnarounds: Not
Geographic Preference:
Midwest
National
Portfolio Companies:
Undisclosed
Branch Office(s):
Wind Point Partners
Main Place
245 Main St.
Racine, WI 53403

Wingate Partners
750 N. St. Paul, Ste. 1200
Dallas, TX 75201
214-720-1313
Fax: 214-720-8799

Contact(s):
Jay Applebaum ("Bud")
Preferred Size Range:
$100 million–$750 million
Industries Specialized:
Manufacturing
Distribution
Do/Not Do Turnarounds: Do
Geographic Preference:
United States
Portfolio Companies:
Redman Homes
Century Products
R&P Holdings
Loomis Armored
Associated Stationers
Branch Office(s):
950 Echo Ln.
Houston, TX 77024

WR Group
950 Third Ave., 9th Fl.
New York, NY 10022
212-826-4370
Fax: 212-826-6819

Contact(s):
John Wechsler
Preferred Size Range:
$10 million–$150 million
Industries Specialized:
Manufacturing (industrial)
Distribution
Do/Not Do Turnarounds: Do
Geographic Preference:
United States
Canada
Portfolio Companies:
Undisclosed
Branch Office(s):
None

ZS Fund L.P.

120 W. 45th St., Ste. 2600
New York, NY 10036
212-398-1800
Fax: 212-398-1808

Contact(s):
Robert Horne
Ned Sherwood
Preferred Size Range:
$20 million–$150 million
Industries Specialized:
Manufacturing low-tech to
   medium-tech
Wholesale distribution
Service companies
Do/Not Do Turnarounds: Do
Geographic Preference:
United States
Portfolio Companies:
Undisclosed
Branch Office(s):
None

Index